As a child, Marilyn Garson was wired to notice power and vulnerability. She studied political science and philosophy, and then set off to apply them. Working with people who support their families at the edge of war, Marilyn has established creative and technology social enterprises.

Marilyn lives in Wellington and Hokianga, with a pen in one hand and a ball of wool in the other.

STILL LIVES

A MEMOIR OF GAZA

Marilyn Garson

MARY EGAN
PUBLISHING

Advance praise for *Still Lives: A Memoir of Gaza* by Marilyn Garson

Marilyn Garson's *Still Lives: A Memoir of Gaza* is an invaluable contribution to the literature on Gaza and the Israeli-Palestinian conflict. Few books achieve what this one does: it allows the reader to see Gazans as they see themselves, as ordinary human beings living – not surviving – under extraordinary, unending conditions, an 'audaciously human society' insisting on a future that is continually denied them... With compelling elegance Garson does not speak for Palestinians but allows them to speak for themselves and the result is as illuminating as it is absorbing. I have read exhaustively on Gaza and on the conflict; Garson's book is one of the most powerful and affecting. It is not to be missed.

Sara Roy, Senior Research Scholar,
Center for Middle Eastern Studies, Harvard University,
author of *The Gaza Strip: The Political Economy of De-Development*

In this moving and stunningly eloquent memoir, Marilyn Garson fulfils her promise 'to tell what she saw' during her four years in Gaza as a Jewish humanitarian worker and social entrepreneur from New Zealand... At the same time, it plots her own journey of discovery of the core of her Jewish identity and the 'thing of beauty' that is the prophetic tradition... Garson was changed forever by her experience in Gaza and by the individuals there who taught her that the true measure of one's life is not what one builds – which bombs can blow away anyway – but what one gives. Anyone who reads her powerful and compassionate narrative cannot fail to be changed in some way as well.

Professor Christopher Marshall,
Diana Unwin Chair in Restorative Justice,
Victoria University of Wellington, New Zealand

Under Hamas rule and Israeli blockade, few Westerners have the opportunity to see Gaza for themselves. In this extraordinary new book, Marilyn Garson takes the reader behind the blockade walls, to the very heart of the Gaza Strip and its extraordinary inhabitants. No one reading her account can be indifferent to the fate of the people of Gaza. A gripping story, *Still Lives* deserves the widest readership, as a book that can make a difference.

Eugene Rogan, Professor of Modern Middle Eastern History, Oxford University, author of *The Arabs: A History*

Intimate, knowing, humane; effortlessly moving from the personal to the political and back; embracing as it interweaves the neoliberal world order and the impoverished Gaza microcosm; written with a novelist's eye for detail, in a prose that is as lush and evocative as it is gripping – in short, to read Marilyn Garson's portrait of Gaza is a transformative experience.

Norman G. Finkelstein, author of *Gaza: An Inquest into Its Martyrdom*

Eloquent, animated and abounding with humanity. This is an absorbing book about many journeys: from Canada and New Zealand to living in Gaza during its darkest hours; from an innocent abroad to becoming a proficient humanitarian professional; and from daughter and sister to finding her own moral voice in lands of tragedy. Marilyn Garson dissolves the stereotypes about Gaza, as human beings march through its pages. Read it, and you will never think about the Israeli–Palestinian conflict in the same way again.

S. Michael Lynk, UN Special Rapporteur for the Situation of Human Rights in the Palestinian Territory Occupied since 1967

Marilyn's website is www.marilyngarson.com

or follow Marilyn on Twitter @skinonbothsides

Published by Mary Egan Publishing
www.maryegan.co.nz

This edition published 2019

Designed, typeset and produced by Mary Egan Publishing
Cover designed by Anna Egan-Reid
Printed in New Zealand

ISBN 978-0-473-48840-6

For my team, of course.

And for my mother
Lily Michele Hirsch Garson
1920–2017
the humanitarian at our dinner table

Life is what you do, about what you notice.

—Beth Goldring

Preface

This is a story about Gaza. Not Israel, just Gaza.

I was invited to work in the Gaza Strip in 2011. Like most people, I thought of Gaza as an object of Israeli security policy. I hadn't given much thought to Gaza *qua* Gaza – Gaza as itself. I thought even less about the consequences of letting supercharged politics draw my eye away from the human beings who live behind blockade walls. That was odd, because I noticed such things elsewhere. I had let the walls hide the Gazans.[1]

I arrived in Gaza as a secular professional. Four years, two wars and one social enterprise later, I left as an activist and a more cognizant Jew.

This is, first, the story of a few recognizable young Gazan adults; parents and aspiring professionals. They – my colleagues – have never fired a rocket. They add adjectives to the limited public portrait of Gaza: educated, ambitious, hopeful, life-loving. They have generously agreed to let me tell our story. They have read and added to it, but the perspective and the errors are mine alone.

As we worked, they and their community overturned things that I thought I knew. This is also the story of my own journey beyond the common wisdom, to a better understanding of Palestine.

The Gaza I knew was forever altered by fifty days of bombardment in July and August of 2014. I volunteered to remain in Gaza as part of the United Nations Relief and Works Agency for Palestine Refugees in the Near East (UNRWA – pronounced *un-rua*) emergency response team. My Gazan colleagues survived

1 A Gazan is a Palestinian who lives in the Gaza Strip. Because this story is set in Gaza, I tend to write 'Gazan'. My usage should not detract from the unity of the Palestinian people.

in minutes, while I confronted the massive scale and nature of Israel's military strategy. UNRWA was prepared to shelter 35,000 displaced civilians in its schools, but 292,959 people walked through the school gates. I notified the Israeli army of the precise location of each flagged, legally protected United Nations shelter-school. Israeli forces struck seven shelters anyway. I was a witness to the utter impossibility of protecting civilians from such an attack behind a wall.

I was a witness as well to UNRWA's emergency role. No one else could have done what UNRWA did. Only UNRWA has the schools and warehouses with standby emergency stocks, the vehicle fleet, the blockade logistics, the communications and most essentially, the experienced people in place, in every neighbourhood of the Gaza Strip. In the words of Robert Turner, who led UNRWA Gaza through those days, 'I would say there is not another non-governmental agency or organization on the planet that can do what UNRWA Gaza did because . . . of [UNRWA's] existing infrastructure. We were vertically integrated in a way no one other than governments are'.

Donald Trump's de-funding of UNRWA is gutting this emergency infrastructure, and jeopardizing Gazan lives in any future emergency.

I worked one further year in post-war Gaza. Neither my team, nor Gaza around us was the same. It has never been the same again. It has gotten much worse.

Yet this story is more than elegy. To step into Gaza is to ask, 'Why Gaza? Why is it allowed here?' To meet and recognize Gazans is to know that solutions are possible. To know the whole of Gaza is to reject the pessimism of endless conflict maintenance. The more we know, the more Gaza demands that we – beyond the walls – wield pressure to bring about justice.

Here is what this book is not.

I have written what I saw. I do not speak for Gaza, nor for my team or anyone else.

This is not an exposé about privileged foreigners, overpaid and sleep-deprived. I have put aside most of the foreigners (and all of the really good gossip) in order to focus narrowly on the work that created the GGateway social enterprise.

I have not juxtaposed Israeli and Palestinian views of these events, because this is a story about Gaza.[2] I have kept the recitations of history to a bare minimum, and added a reading list.

My three sisters leave only a trace of their footprints here. I have not represented their thoughts or motives. When my choices gouge at our pre-existing wounds, they have no voice to respond. I'm sorry not to be able to leave them out entirely, as they might have preferred. However, as any Afghan will tell you, no person chooses alone in this world. While I lived in Gaza, one of my sisters held offices in international Zionist organizations. We brought the same genetic starter packs to our family dinner table. We learned different lessons there, and we enacted them for half a century before we found ourselves on either side of the blockade wall. To that, I say three things in declining order of importance. First, my sister is part of me and I love her. Second, I am proud of her achievements. Third, we disagree.

Memoir is a raw cut at a life in progress. It breathes and squirms and begs to have its messy wrinkles ironed flat. Fortunately, I left Gaza with a quarter-million words of journals to hold my wrinkles in place – even the ones that make me cringe in retrospect. I brought to Gaza a certain understanding of Zionism and Palestine, of aid in the neoliberal era, and of my Jewish identity. My language changes through these pages, as Gaza made me ask, 'What am I going to believe: everything I've ever been told or the world in front of my eyes?'

For the sake of brevity, I have compressed my entry into Gaza and excluded the details of interim housing and office restructuring. I have folded the actions of several colleagues into one composite character, named Hani. Each of Hani's comments and experiences is real. However, because the memoir concentrates on a single work stream, I could not do justice to the whole characters

2 For juxtapositions, see Padraig O'Malley, *The Two-State Delusion: Israel and Palestine – A Tale of Two Narratives* (New York: Penguin Books, 2015) or Nathan Thrall, *The Only Language They Understand: Forcing Compromise in Israel and Palestine* (New York: Metropolitan Books, 2017).

of the many team members who were working on other projects.

I have also simplified the institutional context of the GGateway's pilot phase within UNRWA. Several colleagues' vital contributions fell beyond the story, especially Mike McCluskey and Mustafa Abu Tahoun. The GGateway itself has evolved beyond our original vision.

During the attack of 2014, I have concentrated on a few work tasks – and therefore on a few people – in order to illustrate Israel's military strategy and its civilian implications. However, the critical work of those fifty days was being done elsewhere. Approximately 5500 of UNRWA's Gazan staff left their families each morning. They came through the streets to serve their community in shelters, hospitals, warehouses and trucks. They removed rubbish, delivered water and emergency supplies, and distributed food while the bombs fell around them. Their courage humbles me.[3] Eleven UNRWA colleagues were killed.

My journals record the initial reporting of events. I have noted one instance where my dates became confused, and there may be other inaccuracies. I have written the counts of bombs, rockets, casualties and displacement as I received them from initial reporting, which is not always definitive. In short, I have recorded the lived experience of confusing events.

Israel rejects the word 'occupation'. It has disavowed responsibility for Gaza since it removed its settlers and soldiers from the Gaza Strip in 2005. However, the standard of occupation is effective control, not the physical presence of troops. The International Criminal Court, the UN Human Rights Council, and many international human rights organizations have agreed that Israel effectively controls the Gaza Strip. Gisha, an Israeli NGO, summarized Israel's regime of control as follows.

> [Israel's disengagement] deluded many into thinking that this also marked the end of Israel's relationship with and responsibility for Gaza. Despite the disengagement, Israel has held on to central

3 See the bravery routinely required to deliver water to a shelter-school under fire: http://blogs.channel4.com/miller-on-foreign-affairs/gazas-humanitarian-disaster-trapped-gaza/1148

> elements of control over . . . nearly every detail of their lives, from matters of life-and-death to the very mundane. Israel's decisions impact the ability to maintain family life, conduct trade, pursue professional and educational opportunities, access healthcare, maintain civilian infrastructure, not to mention access cultural and leisure activities . . . Israel controls what goods can exit the territory and to where, and also requires that any goods entering Gaza receive its approval . . . The control Israel wields is so pervasive and encompassing that it is difficult to reconcile it with military needs alone . . . In many cases, it is blatantly clear that no effort is made to strike a reasonable balance between legitimate security concerns and the rights of residents of Gaza, including recognition of Israel's responsibility to maintain normal life in the Strip.[4]

Gaza's legal status is important, because it leads to the application of the international laws of armed conflict, occupation and human rights.[5] The United Nations Special Rapporteur on the Situation of Human Rights in the Palestinian Territory, wrote in 2019:

> The relevant body of international humanitarian law, including the law of occupation, applies *in toto* to the Palestinian territory: the West Bank, including East Jerusalem, and Gaza . . . While acting as the temporary occupant, among Israel's most important legal duties is to respect and preserve the fundamental rights of the protected population under international law.[6]

The UN Security Council, UN General Assembly, International Court of Justice, International Committees of the Red Cross, international legal and human rights NGOs have all affirmed that the law of occupation applies to the Gaza Strip and the West Bank. I have written on this basis.

Although I use it and it prevails in general usage, the word 'occupation' is also of diminishing value to describe a regime that is no longer temporary.

---

4 Read Gisha's summary of the control regime at http://gisha.org/50shades-en/ce

5 For a thorough understanding of international law as it relates to Palestine, see Noura Erakat, *Justice for Some: Law and the Question of Palestine* (Stanford: Stanford University Press, 2019).

6 Report of the Special Rapporteur on the Situation of Human Rights in the Palestinian Territory since 1967, March 15, 2019, p. 9. A/HRC/40/73

Fragments of this story have appeared in Mondoweiss, *Ha'aretz, CounterPunch,* the *Jerusalem Report* (a magazine of the *Jerusalem Post*), *Consequence* (under a pseudonym), and elsewhere. I am grateful to each of the editors, and to the NZ Society of Authors for awarding me a mentorship early in the writing process.

There would be no book without my editor, Adrienne Jansen. When I and my first version were both frozen, she set the real story free and believed in it more consistently than I did. I thank everyone who read and agreed to let me tell our stories, and each of the readers who improved my telling.

I owe the most to my loving friends who did not let go when my life crumbled, especially Karen Brosnan, Shelley Flam, Beth Goldring and Joy Tillman. For their staunch and principled perspectives, I admire and thank Fred Albert and the late, great Jane Schaverien; Judy Reinkin, and Sara Roy.

Thank you, Gaza, for your welcome.

Chapter 1

New Zealand, 2011

After five years of work in Afghanistan, I was ready to relax. Instead, a few days out of Kabul, I slipped on the worn stairs of a Kathmandu guest house. I clutched the banister and stayed upright, but my right arm came off its hinge. Cradling its mystifying new weight, I turned to the friend a few steps behind me and said, 'Something tore. I heard something tear.'

Taking charge of the scene, I directed my friend to sit in the garden while I went out for medical supplies. She rolled her eyes and sipped her beer until I returned, nauseous with the pain of my inflating shoulder, and ready to be led to the nearest hospital.

I started my next job in Cambodia on schedule, designing income-earning programmes for women who had been trafficked. I tilted gradually, protectively to the right during each day. Seven months later, a Bangkok surgeon diagnosed and repaired my torn rotator cuff.

My arm had withered. It lay on its armrest like a rubbery stranger. I placed an experimental egg in my right hand, and watched it slip through my fingers and crack open on the floor. Mortified by my frailty, I went home to exercise.

'Home' was New Zealand's subtropical north. My neighbour had built my cedar cottage, near the end of an unpaved, cliffside lane. The front wall of every room opened onto a steep sweep of native bush. The bush fell away like a skirt, with the village roofs at its hem. Then the changeable Hokianga Harbour, the 300-foot sandhills that sparkled along the harbour's north shore, and the endless Tasman Sea.

Twenty-year-old mamaku treeferns scaled the back walls and

gently swept my roof as I woke up each morning. I slid the kitchen doors open to the soft summer air of the north, and propped a book on my music stand. While the harbour went about its hourly, unfinished work of making the land, I read book after book and curled tiny weights until I could raise my fingers, my wrist, my elbow, and eventually my arm. Afternoons I walked, strode, trotted on the treadmill, letting speed increase the amplitude of my arms' arcs. Then I embroidered beneath the trees, lengthening the threads to extend my arm with every stitch. I cured myself of feebleness.

Fifty weeks after the accident, I lifted both of my hands behind my back, fastened my bra and burst into tears. Victory felt so puny. By then, I was crying at everything. It wasn't like any other homecoming.

I had left my house for years at a time. I was driven to seek out the nub of our humanity; the part of us that knows the very worst, and still teaches ethics to children. I left my keys with a neighbour and went to build social enterprises with communities that were trapped by war. The news fed us fragments of these hidden peoples: the vacancy of an amputated limb, the rifle balanced on a thin shoulder, the burkha. I met them through their ambitions, and we established locally owned social enterprises to create jobs and counter their exclusion.

I had set out to work with people who were recovering in the wake of war. Instead, we were being enveloped by unending wars. War had lapped into Kabul like the tide. My mother heard it vicariously, and she tried to impress it upon me. 'You used to explain how far away the bombs were. You gave me a course in Afghan geography! Now, all you say is "Really? I didn't hear that one." '

Safe at home and deprived of crises to manage, my body dredged up everything that my coping mind had deferred. Five years of Afghanistan's lovelessness and despairing violence welled up in my New Zealand kitchen doorway. I cried for hours, for months. I cried for the woman who had to crouch into the smallest space against a concrete wall, camouflaged in her dirty white burkha, facing the wall to make herself blameless in public. I savoured the moment of solidarity at the remote courtyard gates of Nangahar, where Afghan women first lifted the burkhas from each other's heads, before they turned to anyone else. I bade farewell to the serious young man who had frozen in the bloody aftermath of a suicide bomb in our neighbourhood, staring up at the legs in the tree. Stymied by his helplessness, he went to join the bombers and assume their power. And, too fast even to gasp, I watched my office windows bulge inward and shatter into spiderwebs on October 8. The doors leapt into the room. We survived without a scratch. Temporarily deaf, we survived without hearing the cries of all the people who were dying around the corner. Again and again, because repetition does not dull the memory, I conceded that I could not protect the friend who stood framed by those fractured windows. And then I followed his upcast eyes to the remains of the window behind my own head.

I sobbed whenever I left my house to drive down the hill to the Hokianga Harbour. As much as my arm needed to tug against the resistance of my steering wheel, I needed the exercise of leaving my house more. Village boys leapt so heedlessly from the Omapere pier. Those rights – to play, to take up space – felt crumpled and contingent after Afghanistan.

Fifteen months after I slipped on the stair, my mended shoulder wobbled through its first push-up. I declared myself fit. The sadness of Afghanistan had become part of me. I was willing to wear it, but I would not give it the last word.

A few weeks later, a former colleague from Afghanistan wrote me an email. He was now the Middle East Regional Director of an American aid organization called Mercy Corps. He wrote one terse line: would I consider moving to the Gaza Strip?

I replied that I would consider it, if a Jew could be professionally accepted there.

I had never thought of working in Gaza. I wondered why not.

There is a sound native to the ends of unpaved, no-exit country roads like mine; roads whose loose metal has thinned over the corrugations. The sound begins as a ruffle, and it fills into the juddering *dugga dugga* of a visitor's car. As each car accelerates out of the blind corner below Neil's place, it begins to sound like potential. Gaza began to whisper that way: why not Gaza?

Who lived behind that blockade? The neoliberals knocked down walls as a restraint of trade – except that one. Why did a swirling world hold one community still, behind a wall?

The Arab Spring had found its critical mass in Cairo and was still rolling outward, without a single reference to Gaza. Why not – didn't young Gazans dream?

It grew on me, for secular reasons. Someone had built a wall in the desert, and I worked with people trapped behind errant walls.

I emailed two friends who had worked in Palestine. They both cautioned me that Gaza had disheartened them. Nothing worked behind the blockade.

I grinned at my screen.

The too-hard basket? Catnip.

Duggaduggadugga.

I owned some vestigial share in the walls that surrounded Gaza. Although my religion had felt integral to me as a child, as an adult, I had become an absentee Jew. I had never imagined being anything else, but neither did I expend much imagination on being Jewish. I had never entered a synagogue in New Zealand, and I had last visited Israel in 1988. Then, at the gates to the Old City of Jerusalem, young Palestinian men were confronting Israeli army rifles with the stones of the First Intifada. My politics had compelled me to ask what made those odds worthwhile, and my understanding of my religion offered no reply. Stuck, I turned away from the whole, intractable mess. For a quarter-century, I had tempered my reflexive defence of Israel with a measure of underdog bias for the Palestinians. I said token, liberal things about the occupation.

I still visited exotic synagogues when I travelled, like the whitewashed house of worship that Jews and Muslims shared in Yangon. Ancient, enduring currents always drew me. Islam – distinct from Middle Eastern politics – had coursed through Afghanistan. The chorus of muezzin calls to prayer rang through every neighbourhood, and woke something that had been sleeping in me. I loved the nearness of my Muslim colleagues' faith. We discussed our religions at length.

Why not Gaza?

The Mercy Corps email arrived on June 28, 2011, my eldest sister's birthday. A quarter-century of distance had reduced her to a caricature. She was insider to my outsider, and a lifelong Zionist whose titles I no longer knew. From my writing desk beneath the stairs, I searched Garson + Zionism.

'Fu-u-uck,' I breathed, and I laughed out loud at us. My sister Joan chaired the Arzenu bloc of the World Zionist Organization. She was a committee member of the Jewish Agency, the Israeli institution that promoted Jewish immigration and land use. The list continued.

I glanced over my shoulder as if there might be someone to tell, or someone to conceal it from. Then I leaned closer to the screen and swore once more. All four Garson sisters led with the same obstinate chin. Joan and I shared our father's stormfront hazel eyes. With eight extra years of fine lines, Joan's face was a forecast of my own. Her rounding shoulders made me straighten my posture, and I scrunched at my own curls while I inspected the grey in her hair.

I didn't mind being mistaken for Joan when I visited Toronto. But what if a Palestinian searched Garson + Zionism? Would it discomfit Palestinians who reported to me? What might Hamas make of my resemblance to an officer of the World Zionist Organization? Reluctantly, I decided to withhold my Judaism from my Gazan colleagues. I would have to forego a second course in comparative religion.

I had left Canada in 1986, before the internet began to track us. Eschewing the noise of social media, I appeared online only as a New Zealander, with a single image and an assiduously shallow electronic footprint. If I avoided international social gatherings, where images might be uploaded and tagged, I felt reasonably sure that my chin and I would avoid detection.

I contracted to work for a year, and began to pack up my house. Unlike my friends, who amassed stabilizing things with the years, I halved my possessions each time I drove away. Boiling off the clutter intensified the flavour of unpacking because every box held precious things. While I aired the sheets that would shroud my furniture, I emailed my middle sisters, and asked them how to tell Mother.

Just tell her, they wrote.

I phoned her in Halifax uncertainly. We had never really known what to say to each other.

'So, Mum, remember when I left Afghanistan?' I began brightly, and I cringed. Although no language could make the Gaza Strip palatable to a 91-year-old Jewish mother, I saw too late that light humour was going to make it worse. 'You made me swear that I would never go to Iraq.'

'Or Somalia.'

'Right, or Somalia – and I'm not. And then you said . . .'

Nothing. No help at all.

'You said that if I just got out of Afghanistan, you would never complain about me going anywhere else. Remember?'

'Yes,' in a lower register.

I closed one eye and felt my chin fall until I was looking at the ground. 'I'm moving to the Gaza Strip.'

A sigh, an audible closing of the eyes in forbearance. 'Well. I never thought of that. Gaza? Can you even . . . can a Jew go to Gaza?'

'I don't see why not.'

Another sigh, at the many things I did not see. 'Mm hmm. And you've checked that with Hamas, have you? And they have no objections?'

I told my middle sisters that it had gone as well as these things ever went. Six weeks after the first enquiry, I was ready to store the car and fly.

Pulling my glass door shut, I nodded back through the house at my little compendium of things, airtight, dust-covered and tucked snugly beneath the front window of the studio. Through the front window, the patient sandhills would wait. This was always my final, comforting sight of home; all the pared-back bones in their place.

I left my cats dozing beneath a daisy bush, and I left my key in the door. The neighbour would come for them all soon. I threw my bag in the car and drove away, certain as I had always been that I would find my life intact when I returned to unpack it.

Then I went to Gaza.

Chapter 2

Gaza Strip, Palestine, September 2011

Israel ended at an immense concrete wall. I passed through the cavernous Erez Border Crossing terminal, walked through a 900-metre fenced passage known as the tunnel, and stepped into the locked box of Gaza. What had been a wall in Israel, in Gaza became the horizon. Concrete delineated the earth. The air burnt my lungs.

A Palestinian driver plunged into the ingrown, dog-legged maze of Jabalia, and instantly I was lost. Block after block after block, Gaza's face was unrelieved concrete in all the shades of decay, gouged with a fretwork of holes. A pair of boys darted into a capillary alley, into the path of a donkey cart that was plodding out, laden with garbage. Agile, the boys dodged sideways and flattened themselves against a graffiti wall. Then they sprinted, playing tag between furrows of low-hanging laundry, and threw themselves around a corner. I peered after them.

We were driving through the Jabalia urban refugee camp. Each square kilometre was home to 67,000 people. The population density in my district of New Zealand was four. So I did not enter Gaza; it swallowed me.

Tradesmen did their business in doorways, chatting and sipping tea in the sunlight because the buildings had no electricity. Neighbours domesticated the sidewalk. They visited sidelong between parked and oncoming cars, forcing each driver to sidle past them by the meanest of margins. Drivers craned their necks beyond their steering wheels, ceding every last inch to the children who played along the curbs, without adding to the scrapes already collected on their cars' faded side panels. Children were everywhere, tidy, with combed hair and clothes that had recently been clean. I scanned the street without finding any safer place for them to play, because there was no dedicated space for children or commerce or light industry or anything else. Instead, by consensus, every public-commercial-mine-yours-ours inch of that street was home. Each person belonged exactly where they were. My car was a wheeled inconvenience, cluttering their hallway. And then, signs said that we were no longer in the refugee camp. Gliding through one, indivisible conurbation; one dizzy, jostling profusion of lives; we had left Jabalia and entered Gaza City.

The car stopped at an intersection, although there was no stop sign. '*Ahlan!* – you're welcome!' called a circle of men, sipping coffee in cast-off office chairs, in the empty picture window frame of an apartment building.

The car stopped at a supermarket. '*Ahlan,*' a young couple bade me shyly in the aisle. I felt remiss, slow about thanking them all for something.

The cashier elaborated. '*Ahlan* – welcome to Gaza. You are *welcome* in Gaza.'

'*Ahlan,*' a passer-by called as I pulled my bag out at the apartment building.

Foreigners were scarce enough that Palestinians could spot the newcomers. The NGOs and the United Nations each employed a few dozen resident international staff, and confined us to a handful of apartment buildings in the Rimal district of Gaza City. Others commuted irregularly from their homes in East Jerusalem.

Mercy Corps employed one other resident foreigner, Marjie, an affable American in her thirties. We would share a car, briefly an office, and the gossip endemic to a vexed workplace. I soon rented an apartment on the top, fourteenth floor of her building, Beirut Tower. My flat consisted of one open, airy living and kitchen space, with a bedroom behind. The sea adorned it. Fifteen metres of tall windows invited the ruffled, turquoise Mediterranean to fill two walls of the main room.

In my security briefing, they told me that internationals had not been permitted to walk through Gaza's streets, since the kidnapping and murder of an Italian aid worker four months earlier.

'They killed a man,' I repeated quizzically, gearing down from Kabul. 'Just one?'

Denied the sidewalks, I spent my weekend setting up the apartment, and studying the life of the beach across Al Rasheed Road (known as Beach Road in English). I threw all the windows open and dragged the easy chairs up to the window sills. Reclining with my face in the sunshine, I inhaled the only air not encased in concrete. While I cleaned and unpacked, fully clad beachgoers huddled beneath sun umbrellas or rode horses across the sand. Elongated power boats ran up onto the beach, to take on passengers. Then they zipped back and forth through the surf with Palestinian flags snapping smartly behind them. Families thronged the coast in the late afternoon, to turn away from the city and face expansive nature. Military and industrial ships faintly crossed the horizon.

I lived opposite the Shalehat hall. When the molten heat of the day subsided, the Shalehat became a vortex of celebration. I leaned out of my window as Beach Road came to life beneath me. Beribboned wedding cars paraded up and down Beach Road. Videographers stretched far out of their passenger windows to film the drum bands and dancing troupes who followed them on flatbed trucks. I ate my dinner at the windows, watching the convoys because no one, nowhere else, danced as boldly as these young men on moving vehicles. They climbed onto the trucks' handrails and dented the cab roofs with their heels. They balanced on the window ledges of car doors. Exuberant in motion, oblivious to the billboard martyrs glowering down at them, they stamped and whirled against the hot, velvet stripe of sunset.

Guests, arriving at the Shalehat by the carload and the busload, mistook Beach Road for their driveways. Drivers paused to disgorge their passengers and visit in the street, letting traffic clog behind them. The dancers and musicians jumped down from their idling trucks, and set up alongside the receiving line at the Shalehat's entrance. Their music clashed with the honking car horns, and their performance obstructed the guests who were already obstructing the traffic, until they all backed each other into a closed Escher loop.

The wedding season was underway. Another wedding up the road made the whole horizon havoc. Fireworks soared overhead.

Families strolled beside and between the cars, breathing in the temperate evening and lifting their faces to the starbursts. A vein of joy ran through Gaza, as real as the hardship.

I sponged up first impressions, and scribbled through the opening pages of my journal.

Around 10.00 pm, the beachfront fell into profound, spacious calm. Wedding guests tiptoed away with children wilting in their arms. Banks of fishing boat lights delineated the blockaded fishing zone. Israeli gunboats stalked the perimeter.

Sound travelled in layers by night. The squeak and bounce and cheers of a basketball game floated up to meet the monotone of hovering drones. Across the night sky, I traced the points of light which did not behave like stars. The unblinking drones completed the box of Gaza. Every outlook was finite and mechanized and armed.

The NGO security office recorded three or four exchanges of fire between Gaza's fighters and the Israel Defense Forces (IDF) each day. Two eras of armaments whizzed overhead. Gaza's militants lobbed homemade rockets, too primitive to aim. Some carried a few kilos of explosives. They caused occasional property damage in Israeli towns and in Gaza itself, for the rockets regularly fell short. The fact of metal tubes hurtling out of the sky without warning caused Israelis widespread distress and very few casualties. The IDF deployed F16 fighter jets, drones, tanks and naval ships. They aimed, and they fired vastly larger explosives into Gazan cities. In the first eight months of the year, 80 Gazans had been killed by Israeli forces.[7] Forty-five were reported to have been engaged in hostilities when they were killed; thirty-five were not. No Israelis were reported to have been killed by Gazan forces in those months.

By entering Gaza, I had physically crossed the concrete massif that divided Israel from the territory it occupied. I had never been required to unearth the occupation's foundations or challenge its claims. I had not assumed that Israel was always right. I had, though, placed Israel at the centre and drawn combat around it. Surrounded, Israel fired out at enemy objects. Gaza had always

7 B'Tselem tracks Palestinian and Israeli fatalities at https://www.btselem.org/statistics/fatalities/after-cast-lead/by-date-of-event (accessed April 16, 2019).

been one regrettable object among many. In my apartment, leaning on my window sill and watching the drones surveil me, my geography underwent a Copernican shift. The missiles began to fire *in*. They began to encroach on neighbourhoods. Gaza had no defensive weapons, so the Israelis fired at will.

I took a dismayed sort of ownership. They were 'We' overhead, firing the weapons that distinguished my era of Jewishness from my parents'. I had been raised to be proud of 'Us'.

I went to bed, and when a missile strike jarred me awake a few hours later, I wondered how I would manage the pronouns of Gaza. Who was 'We' behind these walls, and who was 'They'?

Early Sunday morning, while the sky was still rosy and mustering heat, I heard chanting in a universal military rhythm. Leaving my coffee on the curved kitchen bar, I leaned out of the window. Fourteen floors below, several units of Hamas police were jogging south along Beach Road in black sweatsuits. They straggled back half an hour later, winded by their exertion. I dismissed these new recruits as athletes.

When I left for work, ranks of fit, seasoned fighters flowed around our car. They chanted 'Allah, Allah,' in low voices, in time with their steps. The swish of the waves took on an undertow of redemptive violence.

I lived next door to a Hamas training facility. They regarded all of Gaza as their obstacle course.

***

The Hamas movement encompassed Gaza's government, army, police and public administration. It provided public sector services to around one-third of Gaza's population; those who were not registered with the United Nations as Palestine refugees.

Hamas had grown by fusing religious observance and community service with violent resistance to the occupation.[8] During

8 Hamas's agenda and violence are local. Unlike Al Qaeda, ISIS or other transnational groups, Hamas resists one illegal occupation. Tareq Baconi writes, 'Hamas is akin to a religious and armed anticolonial resistance movement'. See Tareq Baconi, *Hamas Contained: The Rise and Pacification of Palestinian Resistance* (Stanford: Stanford University Press, 2018).

the Second Intifada, Hamas notoriously deployed suicide bombers against civilian targets in Israel.[9] In the January 2006 elections for the second Palestinian Legislative Council, Hamas squarely defeated its rival, the governing Fatah faction. Observers considered the vote to have been fair, but they disagreed on its meaning. Some Palestinians voted against Fatah's rampant corruption. Others preferred Hamas's resistance to Fatah's recognition and accommodation of Israel, and still others chose Hamas's Islamist authority over secular Fatah. Some may have voted for more prosaic reasons of policy. Untroubled by the fine points of democracy, the US, Israel and others set about destabilizing the elected government.[10]

A year after their electoral victory, Hamas defeated Fatah in vicious street fighting, and asserted full control over the Gaza Strip. Hamas had ruled Gaza since then as a de facto authority, a diplomatic phantom. Fatah ruled the West Bank. The several Occupied Palestinian Territories – Gaza, the West Bank and East Jerusalem – were held apart by the military force and policies of Israel's occupation, and they were further divided by the rivalry of Palestine's own factions.

Israel constructed the first fence around Gaza in 1995, and it had progressively tightened its restrictions on Palestinians' mobility and rights since then.[11] In response to Hamas's 2007 consolidation of power, Israel imposed the Gaza blockade. It controlled the entrance and exit of persons and goods to Gaza, by land and sea. Calling it 'economic warfare', Israel forcibly severed Gazans from their relatives and markets in the rest of Palestine, and the world beyond. A crossing remained open, then, between Gaza and Egypt.

---

9 Hamas is credited with 40 per cent of the suicide attacks, Fatah and Islamic Jihad 26 per cent each. See https://en.wikipedia.org/wiki/List_of_Palestinian_suicide_attacks (accessed March 31, 2019).

10 Hillary Clinton was recorded calling the election a 'mistake . . . And if we were going to push for an election, then we should have made sure that we did something to determine who was going to win.' https://observer.com/2016/10/2006-audio-emerges-of-hillary-clinton-proposing-rigging-palestine-election/#.WBOP6mO8ojs.twitter

11 For a timeline of Israel's restrictions, see https://www.ochaopt.org/theme/gaza-blockade OCHA is the UN Office for the Coordination of Humanitarian Affairs.

The blockade denied Hamas the sovereign tools to govern or develop the Gaza Strip. Paradoxically, it also shielded Hamas from scrutiny of its domestic violations. Within the walls, Hamas wielded a very free hand. Conforming Gazans invoked their ubiquitous authorities like the bogeyman, saying, 'Someone will tell Hamas.' Others closed the door before we talked politics. They cautioned me, 'Hamas is not Gaza, and Gaza is not Hamas.'

Hamas made no bones about creating a society whose *sine qua non* would be resistance to the occupation, and I could not imagine a more stifling Petri dish in which to sprout that resistance.

Hamas was ascendant in 2011. They had captured one Israeli soldier from his tank, and held him hostage for five years. Shortly after I arrived, Hamas released him in exchange for 1027 mostly Gazan prisoners who had been held in Israeli military detention. All of Gaza celebrated a thousand family reunions. Hamas crowed, and thereafter it delighted in taunting Israel with the threat of future hostages. At almost the same time, the Palestinian Authority (the PA, dominated by Fatah) brought Palestine's bid for statehood to the United Nations, where it was defeated. The United States Congress punished the PA's audacity by suspending $200 million of aid to Palestine. Fatah's diplomatic rejection coincided with Hamas's triumph of violence. Grudgingly, I heard lifelong Fatah supporters concede that Hamas spoke Israel's language, while Fatah tilted at windmills.

Even as they sparred overhead; Hamas, Israel and the donor states agreed to palliate the worst of the blockade's suffering by permitting humanitarian aid to be delivered on the ground. Their primary channel was the UN's dedicated agency for Palestine refugees, UNRWA. Neither Israel nor most of the donor states would speak with – let alone directly aid – Hamas. They communicated through explosions in the night, metal rocket tubes with welded fins, trucks with UN logos, and the steady recruitment of young men who intoned, 'Ah-*lah*, Ah-*lah*,' as they jogged alongside my car.

***

The Hamas fighters turned into their compound at the end of their morning run, and our car drove on.

I lived and worked a kilometre apart on Beach Road. Past the

Hamas training fields, a boisterous sunrise fish market slowed traffic. The car crept for a block that smelled of fish, hay and donkey shit. Melting ice soaked the road, and boys played tag around wooden donkey carts.

One block past the market, our six-storey office building stood within a ring of similar, mixed-use buildings. Its entry lane would have been adequate, but for the parked and pausing cars, and the people threading between them. The T-junction at the end of the lane had been squashed into a veiny Y by mounds of sand, a concrete mixer, and construction paraphernalia. We inched along the right branch of the Y between uniformed schoolchildren, parked and pausing cars, a stack of window frames, and all the curious onlookers who came to welcome a new foreigner.

We drove into a dim parking area beneath the building. Composed like a sphinx in a white plastic chair, an elderly Sudanese parking attendant shifted ever so slightly, allowing our car to reverse into a slender parking space, inches from his knees. I squeezed out of the car and frowned back at his kneecaps before I went upstairs.

Mercy Corps occupied two floors of the building. The offices rambled through a maze that might have begun as apartments. Weeks would pass before I made sense of the outlying suites. We, the economic unit, dominated one suite downstairs, with our own kitchen.

***

Mercy Corps' economic programme had fallen behind the rest of its work, and the economic development team had very little time to redesign and restart. But what would work behind a blockade? By Skype from Jerusalem, I had asked everyone on the team to suspend their doubts for one season. Then we would pause, and assess.

My first weeks were a nonlinear jumble. For two hours each morning, we discussed Gaza's economy around a conference table. Each team member had a graduate degree, and spoke at least two languages. Senior team members specialized in one industry or sector. Lacking time for a more considered approach, I asked them to show me whatever they thought I needed to see, and they handed me from industry to industry through the afternoons. The group dissolved into individuals as I met each person for an introductory hour in my office.

I often arrived rubbing my eyes, as I adjusted to the sleep disturbance of missile strikes in the night. My team presented the strongest of each morning's Turkish coffee to the weary parent who lived nearest the previous night's air strikes. Thereafter, they brought chocolate. On the slightest pretext, boxes of chocolate traipsed from desk to desk.

One morning in my first week, I arrived as Hani[12] was setting a coffee cup on Ibrahim's desk with a flourish. Hani always seemed to make the morning coffee.

'*Ya basha,*' Randa said beside him, cocking her head and tossing her hair. 'Did you get any sleep at all?'

Ibrahim gamely matched her grin. 'Not really. Suleiman wouldn't settle down . . .'

'And your windows, hmm?' Hani asked. 'Do you have any windows this morning?'

'A few.'

Others went straight to Ibrahim's desk as they arrived. After a few minutes of brisk humour, each colleague bid him, '*Allah yatik el afiah*' before they slipped away to work and wait for the next thing to explode.[13]

Ibrahim, a softly spoken man who declined the centre of any stage, turned a wan pink from the attention. Then he came to sit with me for his hour of introductions. Boyishly round in repose, Ibrahim straightened each time he spoke. He would hesitate a moment to check his beard, deliberate alone and then share only a few words of his conclusion.

'What do you *want* to do, or to be?'

'I blog,' he declared. 'Long before I got this job. Arabpreneurialism, do you know about it? We promote young Arab enterprise.

12 Hani is a composite character, combining the real thoughts and experiences of several colleagues.

13 This blessing asks for health, vitality, energy, strength. Although a search reveals a range of transliterations and translations, I understood it to mean, 'May Allah give you the strength you need'.

That's what I want to do, business and computers and start-ups.'

'So,' I drew him on, 'this isn't just a job for you. You work from conviction – belief, yes? Why Arabpreneurialism, why is that your place?'

'We can make jobs, not just look for jobs.'

'I agree with that. I mean, there are no jobs to look for. Are you the entrepreneur in that process, or the marketing guy?'

He shook his head and thought. 'Maybe, in the future, I might be the entrepreneur.'

I pictured him in the group, sitting against the wall, stroking his Guy Fawkes beard, listening and nodding. 'For now, are you the strategist? The coach?'

Ibrahim nodded: closer.

'Then, you need strategies.'

'Yes,' he said firmly.

'I understand. Let's find you some strategies.'

I frowned at the team's titles after he left. Ibrahim's vision outranked his junior position. I wrote a few notes, and went to the conference room.

A dozen expectant Palestinians took their seats. Most were parents, aged from their mid-twenties to their early thirties. They were more fortunate and more liberal than Gaza's average. Some were refugees and others were not, but they were all deeply rooted and decidedly Gazan. Those who had studied overseas had chosen to return, to juggle babysitters, viruses and homework drills without predictable supplies of water or electricity.

They, like Gaza itself, were best induced from their details. Not the buildings but the lively interstices between them. Not the matching blond furniture of the conference room, but the blockaded metal rods that made replacements unobtainable. Not the computers but the donor's chain of custody regulations, so onerous that the procurement department would be unable to find me one donor-compliant mouse. Not the monolithic image of Gaza, but this cosmopolitan team.

Around the team's table, I noticed not the women's headscarves, but their brightly patterned fabrics. My team was half female, and all but one of them wore a vivid flowered or plaid hijab, pinned tightly along the sides of their faces and necks.

They wore strong, matching eye shadows and tight jeans. Their colours lifted the room, and none of them deferred to their male colleagues.

We were talking our way through Gaza's industries: construction, manufacturing, hospitality, tailoring, food processing, information technology (IT). Randa, a senior woman who wore her hair loose, spoke that morning about Gaza's elected industry associations, its entrepreneurial families and skilled workforce. In the 1980s, an American scholar named Sara Roy had written about Gaza's 'de-development', the harnessing of its economy to Israel's benefit rather than its own.[14] Randa's story picked up from that process. She detailed the restrictions that had choked off manufacturing, the uninsured war losses, and the careers that had dwindled to a few occasional hours of informal work.

'What do you think?' she concluded. 'What will we do?'

'What have other donors done – what has worked?' I asked in response.

My voluble team balked, each hoping that someone else knew the answer.

'Okaaay,' I said slowly. 'Tell me a little about the context, the political economy.'

Blank.

'Political economy, yes? There is no economy without political economy. Every economy is shaped by choices . . . by interests . . .'

Eyes gave way to bright flowers as the patterned hijabs looked down or glanced sideways.

'Hmm. Have you ever seen a lava lamp? L-a-v-a, lava.'

Everyone reached for a phone. 'I've got it,' Wasim announced. 'That is so cool!' They handed Wasim's video around the table, while I talked about the fluid shifting of interests in the political economy around us.

Less than ten minutes later, I met another circle of fixed smiles. 'Neoliberal?' I repeated.

Someone tried Google Translate, but no one recognized the Arabic word, either. I amended my first impression: they were bilingual and they *looked* cosmopolitan, and I was aiming poorly because

14 Sara Roy, *The Gaza Strip: The Political Economy of De-Development*, expanded third edition (Washington, DC: Institute for Palestine Studies, 2016).

of it. We ended the conversation in a patient, mutual confusion.

As they filed out, several turned to Rasha. She always wrote copious notes, and she photographed everything I wrote on the whiteboard.

'Rasha, will you—'

'Yes, of course!' she replied. 'I will send you everything.'

I associated their names with their roles in the group as they each passed me. What they lacked in theory, they made up for with a village tolerance; the wisdom of people who will live together for a long time. My team cohered without becoming alike. Hani, a few years older and cautious, preferred summary to speculation. So, as each discussion wound down, they waited while he secured himself to the preponderance of their opinions. Ibrahim rarely spoke up, so they turned to him and asked for his thoughts. Although she was new to the team, Rasha's notes were already their communal resource.

Rasha's perfectly oval face materialized in my office doorway like the cure for all of Gaza's concrete. The turquoise, yellow and pink flowers of her hijab matched her uncreased eye shadow, and the pink slippers that had snuck up so silently. Childishly thin in her mid-twenties, Rasha seemed more doll than adult.

'It was hard for me to decide what to study,' she said. 'I had to choose between computers and poetry, like the two sides of me. I thought that computers were the most important for employment, for Gaza's future, so I got my degree in computer science. I have one in business analysis, too. But I will always write.'

'So do I – we have something in common. Tell me, I see that lots of Gazan women study computer science and engineering. At home, some women avoid studying sciences – not here?'

'Why would they do that? Women are very organized, we have organized minds. So we don't have that problem in Gaza. We have many others, but not that one. Families encourage the smartest women to follow the best opportunities in the best universities – we have seven universities, did you know? We see the opportunity in computers. We know that computers will be very important to our future, and we women do very well in the sciences.'

Her inflection seemed pointed, so I coaxed her. What did 'very well' mean? She had placed first in her university, although – she smiled sweetly without dropping her level gaze – 'Only they call it first-female, so that the male can be first. But that's all right.'

'Is it?'

Rasha covered a little laugh with one hand. Her hand rose first, and the laugh waited until the hand was in place. 'Yes, of course. We must not study only to be recognized – and besides, everybody knows. And besides that, it's good to accept what we need to accept. That is strength. Do you agree?'

She had the slight, steely composure of a ballerina, and I began to think of her less florally. 'Yes, it can be. Tell me something else. I see that you write detailed notes in the team discussions, but I don't think that everyone else understands my technical language very well. Is that a good guess?'

'Yes. Yes, it's very good that you see. The first discussions were very difficult for me because there were many new words. Just I wrote them down because I thought, what's this? I'm a business analyst, I speak English, why don't I know this? After the discussion, I googled all the new words and I saw that every one of them was an idea. You were giving us strategies! I know that I am young and I still have so much to learn, and I want to learn all of these things, for Gaza. Then I brought my notes back and I showed them to everyone and we agreed that these words are important for us to know. So you shouldn't stop. We need all of these words. And more. We need more.'

'Wonderful. Then I won't stop, but I will slow down if you tell me when I use new words.'

'Yes, please. *Tammam* – perfect. You will learn some Arabic?'

I nodded. I had found the team's influencer. Soon, I learned to recognize her punctuation-free edits in other people's work, and then I began to rely on her as my walking file retrieval app.

I didn't dumb my language down. The team levered themselves up. They'd been bored silly. When it worked at all, economic development happened through contagion and local adaptation. Ideas moved, while Gazans like my team stagnated behind a wall. The few who got jobs were held in place by slightly older PhDs who, themselves, had nowhere to rise and nothing to do but play defence.

They could learn some things together, but a dozen pent-up minds needed to find distinct directions and methodologies. Lacking the luxury of time, I rained ideas over them. Self-knowledge, I told them, was the basis of professional development. I challenged them to recognize what they needed when they heard it. Many of my early ideas landed with a clunk, like the theory of neoliberalism. Others were just right.

One day, I mentioned distributed leadership. The moment I said, 'orchestra with no conductor,' Ibrahim's body inclined toward me and his hand began to prime his beard. His eyes darted, seeing a start-up strategy, or a configuration that would allow an underrated contributor to unfold in a fast-talking team. One by one, we began to know each other through such moments. In the absence of any ready-made theory of blockaded livelihoods, we seeded a culture of learning and experimentation.

Across our shared office, Marjie retreated to her headphones to escape the hours of individual learning plans and confessions of concealed ambition. After one session she warned, 'You're spoiling them. They're going to expect way too much from their next boss.'

'Oh, I hope so!' I enthused. 'They have decades to give to Gaza. I have only this year, and I want to ruin them for disinterested management forever – theirs or anyone else's.'

Randa later told me that they referred to me as a brain with feet. I didn't hear it. I heard them begin to call me – as they called each other – dear.

Chapter 3

A strip of land no longer than a marathon housed 1.7 million Gazans. What was the space they shared – was it a walled city or a nano-state? Israel called it a stateless 'hostile entity'. Journalists called it an enclave. On a survey, we asked Gazans what 'local' meant, and they overwhelmingly called the Strip half of a single locality, Palestine.

Most of the countries in the world agreed. In 2014, Sweden would become the 135th member state of the United Nations to recognize the State of Palestine; comprised of the West Bank, Gaza and East Jerusalem. International institutions affirmed that Palestine was one state. Yet the donor states, voting members of those same institutions, defrayed the cost of keeping Palestine's parts separate.

Unable to categorize the space, my team named Gaza's actual, generational economies around our conference table. Old Gaza encompassed the pre-blockade industrial employers. They were marking time, waiting for circumstances to improve. Gaza 2.0 was graduating, digital, and demanding a new knowledge economy right now.

We had only weeks to define projects in half a dozen industries. Our mandate was income, not jobs. Real, sustainable jobs would require political change, for which our work was no substitute. That was important: we did not work to render the blockade normal or acceptable. Rather, we looked for ways to improve the incomes that Gazans already earned for their work, and we hunted for pockets of potential income for unemployed people.

We found several. We ran short vocational courses for some of Gaza's informal construction day-labourers. The courses qualified them to carry out specific tasks. They would not be electricians, for example, but they might become qualified to install basic wiring from a diagram. Once qualified, they earned steady, skilled wages for doing superior and safer work. IT graduates could learn to work remotely. Creative artists could adapt arts-business models, in order to earn money for their work. Start-up businesses could be hot-housed as they were elsewhere.

None of these projects changed the structure of Gaza's poverty or challenged its political cause. They eased some household budgets and encouraged good ideas.

We had very little to offer the idle factories which had been sizeable employers. The blockade cut manufacturers off from their materials and markets. In those first weeks, I went from roundtable to factory to business association with Randa. Her flowing hair – auburn that month – was a beacon to every obedient, longing and disapproving eye. Randa drank in their notice and wore it as performance art.

In Khan Younis, we scuffed along the cobwebby aisles of a toy factory, sending dust motes up through slanting stripes of sunlight. A corner of some factories still operated to supply the local market. Often they worked at night, when there was more electricity and less need of air conditioning. Not this one. Away from the open doors, this interior was dim and echoing.

'It's all from Israel,' Randa explained, extending one arm to take in the machinery generally. 'Like the others. He learned his work in Israel, and then he opened his business here.'

Blocks of colour broke the shadows around us, mounds of tricycles and wagons and rocking horses that didn't stack neatly. They winked and waited in every corner. The best, I knew by then, would be stamped 'Made in Israel', to earn a premium price.

The owner, a balding man around my age, wrung his hands over the rocking horses. Randa listened and nodded, inspected a horse, and stroked its painted mane. 'The last of his money is in this inventory. He made it cheaply for the local market, but it isn't selling well. See the paint? The colours aren't bright, and I wonder if it is safe for children.'

I nodded: the reds were ochre and the yellow was more of a sickly puce.

'He wants you to know that he normally works to a higher standard, but he can't get his good inventory out through the blockade. So he tried this, with Egyptian paint. Now he's really in trouble.'

He made us tea from a thermos in his shadowy office. Piles of catalogues gathered fine sand on the chairs. Swiping dust from binders full of documents, he translated their headings from the Hebrew: contracts, partnership agreements, travel documentation. Proof of his years of work and attempted work. Randa dutifully translated a story we both knew by then.

'They stay in touch. His Israeli partners still call. They check on his family and they send their respect to his workers. What can we do for him?' She frowned, drawing in the dust on his desk with one finger. 'Why can't the donors get things out through the blockade?'

'I ask myself the same question. Does he really want to trade with Israel, even after everything that's happened?'

They talked for a bit. 'Yes, he does – he says they all would. He says he associates Israel with better times. But he is explaining that his sons are too young to remember those times. They only connect Israel with war. He says that if you talk to people in Israel, you should tell them. If they want peace, they should make peace while he's still alive.'

As Randa spoke, the manufacturer shrugged, apologizing for the limits of his influence. I often found myself apologizing for the limits of mine, too.

Over and over I wrote in the margins of my notes, *Where are the donors?* I kept hearing that no development worked in Gaza. As far as I could see, very little was tried. Donors left a heavy, credit-seeking footprint elsewhere. In Gaza, they left an anomalous, work-shaped hole.

I had written my master's thesis in Afghanistan, on the changing nature of humanitarian assistance. I watched neoliberal donors tell Afghans that their hardship was an atrophying disease. Rather than receiving help because they needed it, Afghans were increasingly told to work for their relief food. Cash for work. Work for blankets. Work for less than the prevailing daily wage.

While Afghans worked for their food; Gaza's eager, qualified workers were being given passive food aid and told to wait. My team's job was to make incremental improvements to the work and the financial coping that went on while they waited. Our work would always be hemmed in by moral ambiguity, as we sought financial improvements without political acquiescence.

Gaza contained three of the world's fifty largest active rubbish tips. The blockade obstructed the modernization of the solid waste management industry, but we found one worthy point of entry. An officer of the plastic manufacturers' business association mentioned that local factories bought recycled plastic. They made household goods from a mixture of recycled plastics and commercial plastic pellets. Because they sold their housewares locally, these factories were busier than others.

'Value chain. Look it up,' I told Randa happily in the car. 'Or ask Rasha to look it up.'

We mapped the local supply chain of solid and recyclable waste. Instead of factory owners, Randa began to introduce me to women in rural, northern Beit Lahiya. They lived with the grinding poverty that made for endless hours of work and worry, nutritional compromise and short-term, exigent debt. Their homes were made from hollow concrete blocks. The unlined buildings would be blistering in summer, clammy and cold in winter. In the yards, grass sprouted through hoards of salvaged, sharp-edged construction materials.

One family had a sturdy chicken coop. The woman explained that the coop had been part of a chicken-raising project years ago. I looked around for any sign of chickens.

The woman elaborated, and Randa translated. 'The . . . cube?'

'Coop.'

'Coob. The coob is warmer than the house. They don't keep chickens, so that they can sleep in the coob for the winter.'

The value chain showed that Beit Lahiyan women could sell plastic to the housewares factories for some income. It would not be enough to live on, but it would be a useful cash supplement to a household budget. However, they weren't selling plastic now, and that suggested that we were overlooking something. Back we went. By asking different questions, we learned that children sometimes sold plastic to buy snacks. Regardless of the composition of a child's armload of roadside plastic, the plastic traders would give her one Israeli shekel, worth around twenty-five cents. Recycling was thus an untrustworthy, exploitative children's activity. To redeem it, Randa calculated the actual value of each variety and colour of plastic, and the cost of scales. She made templates of records to make the sales transparent.

I shook my head and pushed the umpteenth graphic back across my desk. 'Sorry, it's not there yet. I mean, it's in there somewhere, but I don't see it from the women's perspective.'

'It's right there,' Randa protested, pointing at the numbers.

'No, something's missing. This shows that they *could* sell plastic for income. We understand some of the reasons why they don't, but this doesn't yet show us why they should.'

Randa's voice grew gentle, as it did when I asked her to conjugate the same Arabic verb for the third or fifth time. 'Well, dear? They *should*, because they *can*.'

I clucked my tongue and smothered a giggle. 'And yet they don't, because we're missing something. Or they would.'

We went back to Beit Lahiya again and again. One autumnal day, we followed the smell of bread from a house to its round, adobe outdoor oven. A shy young woman was baking na'an flatbread, the staple of poor diets. She gave us each a piece to nibble, while she described her daily routines. Bundles of paper, plastic and twigs were scattered around the oven. Absently, I nudged a spreading pile with one foot.

'Fuel,' Randa nodded, as if we were agreeing.

'Huh?' I pointed my toe at the plastic.

'Yes, they burn it for fuel to bake the bread. That's why they keep telling about cancer.'

My jaw sagged, belatedly understanding. I let it hang while I formulated.

'There,' I said at length, pointing at the oven and its plume of poisoned smoke. 'Right there, this is the missing piece. We haven't been explaining it right. It isn't about recycling, not for this woman. Recycling is what you do with rubbish, but her plastic isn't rubbish. It's fuel! She needs a profitable substitute fuel. Get it? If you're going to recycle your rubbish, you compare recycling income with no income at all. That makes any income look good, and that's been our baseline. But before you agreed to recycle your fuel, you would want to compare recycling income with the cost of a different fuel. All the costs: money, time, health, and so on. Women will only recycle when they judge that they can earn more by changing to a healthier fuel. We haven't met that burden of proof, so they haven't done it.'

Randa's brown eyes widened. Na'an cooling in one hand, she joined imaginary dots in the air with the other. 'How did you do that?'

'Listening to you.'

Randa turned back to ask the family's baker about her fuel costs.

Randa loved music, and Randa shared what she loved. Most mornings, she sang to the team from the hallway. I could not replicate the quarter-tones of an Arabic melody, any more than Randa could distinguish between a B and a P when she first heard a new English word, but I could listen. We all did. When she finished singing, Randa set off to prove, in dozens of Beit Lahiya homes, that plastic was far too valuable to burn.

***

A four-foot wave sloshed around the car. Striped school tunics, blue jeans and white scrunchie hair ties surged through the narrow street. Half a million voices screamed over every other scream. Children sprang like striped locusts onto car fenders for a free ride – but every vehicle in Gaza had already turned off its engine to wait.

Children and teenagers made up half of Gaza's population. Neither Hamas nor UNRWA (the United Nations agency responsible for refugee children's education) had enough space or money to build schools for 850,000 students. Most schools taught in morning and afternoon shifts, leaving 400,000 children underfoot at any given time. When the school gates loosed the other 400,000, the torrent of pent-up energy and swinging book bags swamped all adult motion.

In the children's wake, a vacuum of sound. One shoe lay on its side in the dust. We tooted the dawdlers and the daydreamers gently aside, and carried on, late.

A visitor had invited me along to see some of the smuggling tunnels that linked Gaza's southernmost Rafah neighbourhoods with Egypt. The November morning was overcast, and the gusty wind disordered the waves and tossed specks of sand at our windscreen. Once we had passed through Gaza City and Zeitoun, the urban density suddenly petered out. Coastal grasses swayed in peace. For a moment, I wondered why no one was enjoying this vacant stretch of beach.

Then, smelling the cause, I turned back from the sea. Gaza's faltering sewage treatment fields made the area uninhabitable. Gaza had plenty of engineers who knew how to treat sewage, if they had been permitted to import the requisite machinery and replacement parts. Instead, the blockade forced skilled technicians to dump 90 million litres of untreated waste into the Mediterranean Sea each day.[15]

'I'm not worried,' the head of the construction contractors' association had growled. He looked like Al Pacino, in one of his insomniac film roles, and he sounded like the sweepings of a gravel pit. Hani translated. 'One day, Israelis are going to notice that they live on the same coast as us. Our sewage is their problem. They'll sue their own government to fix it. We can wait.'

Beyond the reeking sewage ponds, the cities returned to the seashore.

We crossed Gaza's miniature world in forty minutes, and stopped at a chain-link fence. Our driver turned down the volume of ABBA's greatest hits, and pointed ahead at the rest of the world. 'Egypt.'

We turned inland, and drove into the dusty commercial centre of Rafah City. The streets grew bleaker and more muscular as we approached the border. We drove past block after block of

15 See https://www.ochaopt.org/content/study-warns-water-sanitation-crisis-gaza-may-cause-disease-outbreak-and-possible-epidemic for current information on water and sanitation. As of September 2018, 108 million litres of wastewater were being dumped into the sea each day, and 97 per cent of Gaza's tap water was unfit for humans to drink.

scratchy, undifferentiated concrete. Dark windows stared down on us, waiting for electricity.

'I belieeeeve in angels,' ABBA insisted.

Here and there, the mouths of tunnels began to bubble up from the ground. The entrances were draped in white plastic, and I made a note to ask Randa who recycled the plastic sheets.

We parked at the end of a narrow street, nose into a weedy courtyard. Three tunnels rose and yawned, hard against the battle-scarred walls of apartment buildings. The tunnels gave Gaza employment and consumer goods, and they took cover from whoever lived on the other side of those walls. I shuddered at the symbiosis, for tunnels were frequent targets of IDF missiles.

The tunnels comprised another of Gaza's actual, existing economies, and tunnel taxes were thought to provide 40 per cent of Hamas's income. Perhaps as many as a thousand tunnels undermined the blockade. Each tunnel was a privately owned, for-profit business, and tunnel owners had become Gaza's unloved nouveau riche. They employed thousands of Palestinians, often in perilous conditions, and they supplied Gaza with cigarettes and school supplies, candy and electronics, cement and construction materials, foods, livestock, industrial materials like the paint for a rocking horse, a million litres of fuel each day, and weapons. People walked through the tunnels and, briefly, they could order soggy Kentucky Fried Chicken to be delivered from Egypt.

Tunnel imports normalized consumer life for those Gazans who could afford to shop. The electronics industry was one that thrived. I held in my hand the latest tunnel-import Samsung smartphone. Buses or taxis required Israeli permission to enter Gaza by road. Gazans hitch-hiked in droves while they waited.

Sullen watchmen with hard-set jaws leaned against their motorcycles in the courtyard. When they decided we had lingered long enough, they fixed all of their eyes on our driver. He reversed out of the courtyard and drove back inland, parallel to the Israeli fences.

Concrete crammed Gaza's skyline on our left. Then I turned and, as with an unexpected movement, I looked hard without knowing what had drawn my eye. Green had already become the colour of longing, and one sweep of green fields fell away on my right. That was the oddity: one. By some trick of the elevation, the fences were not visible, and I saw one beguiling, verdant, shared land. Then the fence reasserted itself. The mirage broke into a scrubby near stripe of Gaza, a fence, and a far view of irrigated Israeli farmland, dotted with electricity pylons. The fence said that electricity happened somewhere else. To an Israeli, it would have segregated Gaza's suffering as an event that took place *over there*.

Israel had militarized the land extending 300–500 metres into Gaza from these fences. They called it a security buffer. Israeli military vehicles routinely entered the buffer zone to destroy anything that obstructed their vision, including crops. These were called 'incursions', although I assumed that the same armoured vehicles, driving and shooting into Israel, would have been less daintily described as an invasion. Israel supplemented its physical patrols with its remote Sentry weapons system. A team of female soldiers operated Sentry from a distant command centre. The women used joysticks to fire on Gazans approaching the border.[16]

The security buffer constituted one-third of Gaza's farmland. Farming and fishing – obtaining food at the edges of blockaded space – had become two of Gaza's most deadly occupations.

Storage warehouses, rusting auto bodies: we were re-entering Gaza City. Heroic martyrs' billboards dominated the intersections of poorer neighbourhoods, as surely as cheap carbohydrates filled their supermarkets. In the wealthier areas, the martyrs were sandwiched incongruously between billboards for appliances and language schools.

At a large intersection, waiting our turn in the absence of traffic lights, I tried to guess the age of one painted martyr. He wore glasses and a sadder expression than most, and he looked boyish in his halo of cartoon-bright flames. I thought back to my first day out with Randa. Our car had braked sharply when we came upon a unit of Hamas, doing jumping jacks and push-ups in a side street. Their flustered faces were the age of the wedding dancers – and of this bookish martyr. They had probably all gone to school together. If Gaza offered them choices, I wondered how

16 https://www.thenational.ae/world/mena/israel-paves-the-way-for-killing-by-remote-control-1.554627

many of them would have chosen to do burpees in the side streets, grinding pebbles into the palms of their hands.

Randa found the factory that recycled the tunnels' used conveyor belts into plastic garden hoses and pipes.

***

My economic development team was an oddity, as donors sent mostly humanitarian aid to Gaza. Humanitarian relief provided essential commodities to the people in greatest need. Our work was propelled by uneven, self-selecting ambition. Every community needed both, a safety net and encouragement for individual aspirations. However, the two rationales did not always co-exist uneventfully beneath a single roof. As we began to advertise for goods and services for our projects, we often scraped against procurement regulations that had been designed for more standardized operations. The economic team would grow by more than half, and as we began to recruit for new positions, I confronted a polite but firm mismatch of HR policy and style.

'There has to be a right and a wrong,' the HR manager, Adham, objected before we conducted our first interview together. Tall and squared by his suit, Adham's nervous bursts of speech suggested the strain of imposing such binary order upon Gaza. 'It's not fair unless there is a right and a wrong. So, which is it?'

He placed his iPhone precisely beside my Samsung, used his pencil to square their edges, and thrust his chin at me.

I read the offending interview question aloud and grinned at Adham. '"Which smartphone will dominate the market in five years – and why?" Aw, how would I know which smartphone? I mean, each candidate is going to pick whichever phone they use, and we're not scoring anyone's choice of a phone. But their phone was a big purchase. It's a statement. These candidates have MBAs, or computer degrees. They will have thought about smartphones, and we're scoring them on the quality of the thought behind their big purchase. " – and why?" That's the real interview question.'

Adham dotted the desk with the lead of his pencil, showing me his pointillist precision.

I shook my head, apologetic but unmoving.

In Afghanistan or Cambodia, I worked with teams whose

education and entry-level work years had been stolen by war. I interviewed to find individuals who could step into senior work challenges with no junior experience, and then I tried to create the learning environments they needed to succeed. In Gaza, the super-saturated labour market allowed employers to demand a narrow, theoretical overqualification. Before I could short-list CVs, the HR team removed any that lacked a graduate degree. It didn't matter how boldly I underlined 'or equivalent experience'. English interviews then verified each candidate's bilingual proficiency. That kind of screening gave an advantage to applicants whose families could afford to let them stay in school. It excluded everyone who was doing business rather than studying it, and everyone who might have excelled in an Arabic-language interview. I couldn't rewrite the policy, but I insisted on interviews that favoured a smart, informed, speculative cast of mind.

Adham proved his good nature a year later, when one man concluded his interview by pointing at me. 'If I get this job, can I work with you?'

Adham laughed after the fellow left the room. 'You guys, you recognize each other,' he despaired.

Chapter 4

When I saw my team's burden of paperwork, I offered to write everyone's documentation. Liberated from their desks, the team threw themselves at our best ideas. My office door stood open until the heat became too precious to lose, and team members trailed in and out at will with questions. I tried to get to the office early in the mornings, to read the news until the voice of Barbara Streisand or Celine Dion or Marwan Khouri wafted down the hall.

One morning, early on, I followed the violins to the kitchen. I found Hani humming along; toothy, prematurely balding and wearing a cabled sweater of soft burnt orange. What was an expansive man to do under occupation? From the morning coffee to the conference table, Hani hosted us. He filled slightly more of the hallway, his speech took a little more time than the others. He seemed to be decelerating, and his resentments had begun to show. No one minded. If anything, Hani's inability to conceal his feelings made him trustworthy.

He tipped his head to invite me into the kitchen, and explained his musical taste unselfconsciously. 'You hear enough things explode around here. I don't need banging drums, too.'

The morning music became my cue to close the news websites and join Hani. Randa often arrived early, and sometimes Laila from down the hall. We visited around the stove, wearing our sweaters and then our coats as temperate autumn gave way to the startling cold of winter. Hani always made the coffee, smoothing his spoon across the saucepan to make waves, never funnels.

Gaza's police donned their winter uniforms in late November. I announced myself in the kitchen doorway that morning, 'Do you know what Hamas's winter uniform is called in English? Those short jackets? Pockets, knitted collars?' I jammed my hands into imaginary pockets and turned up my collar. 'Those are bomber jackets!'

We laughed, Randa with her open-mouthed bray. Laila lifted one hand and tittered behind it. She hid a temper and a wicked sense of humour behind her soft-focus face. Uncovered like Randa, from whom she was inseparable, Laila wore her hair in 1940s glamour waves.

We fell into yet another discussion of the absent donors. I reframed my usual question. 'What, exactly, *do* the donors do about unemployment?'

'That's easy,' said Hani, addressing the mugs as he spooned out the coffee. 'They send food. And more food. And food is very good, hmm? Everyone is very much appreciating knowing that the poorest people in Gaza—'

'Poorest refugees,' Laila interjected.

'—yes, the poorest-refugees-because-they-have-UNRWA, they get food. But I tell you, food is not enough. You know what happens when they just send food? More and more people start to need food, because they have nothing else.'

He handed me my mug with a white-lipped smile that was first cousin to a sneer.

'Thank you,' I said, wrapping my hands around the mug. The thin china was warm already. 'So, on what conditions do Gazans receive donor food?'

'Ha,' Hani said quickly, 'on condition of being Gazan. That's enough.'

We laughed, mollifying Hani.

'Seriously, though, food relief is a temporary—'

'So is the blockade,' he parried smoothly. 'Isn't it?'

'But . . . in other places, donors have a thing about dependency. Or, forget the donors,' I swept them away with one hand. 'Food aid doesn't change anything. It doesn't solve problems.'

'Here in Gaza, we are welcome to be dependent.'

Randa nodded. 'It's like we're trained now. I need a babysitter for my boys, just one hour after their school, until I get home. But the young girls are afraid to lose their food coupons by being employed for such a short time.'

'How much food do they get? Is it enough to live on?'

'No,' Randa shook her head vigorously, 'No, no. It's just supplies, some cooking oil and flour, like that. But people are afraid of losing their coupons, and having even less.'

We heard the fire doors open as Hani was preparing to speak. We all turned guiltily toward the sound. Hani lowered his voice. 'Do you believe that this is the plan for us? To make every business impossible, and leave Gaza only to relief? To make us completely dependent?' He spoke casually, as if he had nothing of particular value at stake. 'Hmm?'

We lost our eye contact as we moved toward the kitchen door. I brushed my hand along the table, which we heaped high for our Thursday team breakfasts. People took turns cooking and shopping. The younger women sat two to a chair. Randa disdained chairs altogether and rocked from foot to foot while she ate. When others put their empty plates in the sink, Randa retrieved them, refilled them and handed them back, exhorting everyone, 'Eat, eat!'

I wasn't nearly ready to consign this group to futility. 'Impossible? No, I'm not there yet.'

Hani bowed, conceding for the moment. We walked to our offices.

***

On a map of the Middle East, the Sinai Desert resembles a hand grenade. The Gaza Strip is the pin in the grenade, pointing straight up the coast at Tel Aviv. For 4000 years, waves of conquerors have fought for, depopulated and repopulated Gaza's crossroads: Canaanites, Egyptians, Philistines, Israelites, Assyrians, the Macedonian Greeks of Alexander the Great, Bedouins, Seleucid Syrians, Ptolemaic Egyptians, Hasmoneans and Romans. Gaza converted to Christianity and then to Islam. There followed Fatimids, Crusaders, Saladin, Mamluk and the Ottoman Turks. The British captured Gaza in World War I, joining its history to that of the British Mandate of Palestine, and then to modern-day Israel and Palestine.

Mohammad, the taciturn logistics manager of our office, kept the present in perspective. 'To be an optimist in Gaza, you need to take the long view. I only evaluate things every ten years, to allow for the up and the down.'

He ran one long, bony finger around the edge of his car window to frame the city that slid past us. We were driving past the covered produce market. Awnings and women's hijabs flapped in a mild December breeze, while I sounded out the family names stencilled in Arabic on the shopfront windows. Down one alley, I had just bought a cross-trainer to strengthen my shoulder, and I had promised the shop owner that I'd be back for the treadmill. Envying the market-goers, I had shown Mohammad my most ingratiating smile, but he was not inclined to bend the security rules for a stroll that day.

Our car crept, for urban Gazans recognized each other with small-town frequency. Their greetings made the teeming roads more sociable than anonymous Western streets. A simple hierarchy prevailed: people overwhelmed and disregarded the cars. Our driver kept up a patter as he waved and tapped his horn, his brake, his horn, his brake. 'My neighbour's brother-in-law . . . My cousin's wife . . . My son went to school with . . .'

I loved the gossipy village vitality of the streets – or, perhaps, I was able to love it because I went home alone each afternoon to the soothing accompaniment of the waves. Gazans went home to an average of three people per room.

Shortly after Mohammad and I returned to the office, an Israeli drone fired into a car on the edge of that extroverted commercial district. The explosion killed two militants, and injured four civilian passers-by. Mohammad brought a city map to my office. He traced our route, and pointed to the spot where the car had been blown up.

I cocked my head, moving him to the corner of my vision, and said, 'But it was a crowded street,' as if to correct him. As if he must be mistaken.

'They don't care.'

'But it's a shopping district, in the middle of the day.'

He pecked at the map with the tip of his finger, his nail sounding fastidious. 'They don't care.'

'But they must.'

'But they don't.'

I stroked my chin as if I might find Ibrahim's whiskers there. *But They are We,* I thought. *I am Them.*

Mistaking my concern, Hani leaned into my doorway. 'Don't worry. The Israelis, they never miss.'

I closed one eye and raised the other sceptical eyebrow, but said nothing more. Gazans and Israelis, each for their own reasons, placed boundless faith in Israel's aim.

At home with the computer framed by the setting sun, I scrolled through images. By the standards of Kabul's wide-radius blood-baths, this explosion had been confined. In a remote, sealed process, two Palestinians had been sentenced to die. Neither the identity of the Israeli decision-makers, nor the accuracy of their information would ever be disclosed. The Palestinians had been executed without warning or due process in a civilian street, as far from a battlefield as the blockade walls allowed them to be. A drone could, by implication, carry out an extra-judicial execution at any moment, on any street or in any room around me. We lived on a pinball deck.

Such executions were invisible to Israelis. They kept the war at a comfortable distance. In Gaza, the missile constituted an explosive attack in a public, civilian place. I felt the same revulsion that I felt at the bombing of soft, civilian targets anywhere. A Gazan housewife – like any other – had the right to know that she would not be fired upon while she held her family's vegetables in one hand, and waved at familiar cars with the other.

Just before full dark, the NGO security office reported the launch of the first Gazan rocket, fired in response.

At 6.50, Israel fired two tank shells into Gaza in response.

At 11.35, militants fired two rockets from Beit Lahiya in response.

Two Israeli F16 fighter jets fired four missiles into Gaza in response, killing the third Gazan of the day.

Then I lost track of all the responses that ping-ponged overhead through the night and the following day. Things began to explode at random.

We drank Turkish coffee and yawned and waited through the morning. Randa and I postponed a visit to Beit Lahiya after the

IDF struck there. Faces crowded into my doorway each time my phone beeped, to see whether it would report metal rockets out or explosive missiles in.

The rockets expressed a legal right to armed resistance, although it was not legal to fire rockets (or anything else) indiscriminately. The rockets denied Israelis a normal life while Gazan life remained blockaded. I understood that, yet I had run headlong into the limits of my intellectual tolerance when my niece had immigrated to Israel, shortly after I arrived. She resembled my eldest sister in time-travelling detail. I adored her, and the contrapuntal music of hope that I heard in the voices of my Israeli niece and my Gazan team.

The first time Islamic Jihad had fired a rocket within fifty kilometres of my niece, I'd snatched up my car keys like Auntie Retribution. I knew perfectly well that the rockets caused exceedingly few casualties, but no threat to her felt nominal to me. Gripped by irrational, loving fear for her, I was ready to find the launch site and rip the next rocket apart with my fingernails.

In the corridor beyond my computer screen, my team was coping with the rational risks posed by explosives of a different order of magnitude. They clutched their phones in case news caught them between one room and the next. Until then, until I had skin on both sides, I had not fully grasped the application of international human rights law: human rights were either everyone's rights, or they were nothing. The law treated my Israeli niece and my Palestinian colleagues as equal human beings, and then it went on to acknowledge that they faced grossly unequal dangers. Against that single human standard, the law could evaluate the actual risks and harms of rockets deployed in resistance, and the urban bombing which enforced an illegal blockade. On the morning after the drone's assassination, I made that my language. Equal humans faced wildly different dangers.

Journalists labelled that autumn's level of violence the 'relative calm'. It fell well short of war, although no one would mistake it for peace. I disliked the term. Perhaps Israel was calm, but Gazans lived with a protean anxiety that flew in circles and hovered just out of reach. They watched each other every bit as closely as they were watched by the IDF and the drones and the keystroke monitoring programmes of Israeli intelligence and Hamas. Was there a target in the next car? A tunnel underfoot?

The relative calm made everything contingent, because it would end. Every Gazan breathed in the pause between wars, and went to bed knowing that the next war had crept one day closer. To be Gazan was to be counting down – but how fast?

I under-reacted in the absence of concrete, bad news, while my hypervigilant team scrutinized me for imagined clues. Had something changed? Had my phone warned me – was it soon?

Near mid-morning, Rasha picked at the hem of her sweater in my doorway, and I raised my eyebrows enquiringly. 'Are you all right?' she asked.

'Yes, thank you, why?'

'Well. You . . . your email was very short. No greeting at all, and that's not like you. Are you well?'

'Yes, I'm fine. And you?'

'*Tammam*, perfect, thank you.'

Then it was Randa. 'I notice you're playing with your hair this morning, and you haven't done that before. Did you sleep well?'

'As well as anyone else,' I conceded. 'It was a bit loud. But I'm fine. And you?'

'Good, good.'

Laila's arrival was interrupted by a flurry, as an ashen colleague swept into the suite. A huddle, a conference.

Laila leaned in and translated. 'They fired a rocket from her street. They don't ask before they fire. Sometimes – not very often – an older man can convince them to go away, but they just fire from some other street. Her children are in school, and she has to find someone to care for them after. They can't go home because the street might be a target now.'

I sucked in a breath. 'How long?'

Laila shrugged and made a sour face. 'They don't tell. These guys don't ask, those guys don't tell. Maybe it will be on a list for the next war, or maybe it's on a list for tonight. No one knows. She and her husband, they just decide to go home eventually.'

'Fu-u-u-uck,' I exhaled. First the militants fired from a civilian street.[17] When the IDF retaliated, they would claim to have hit 'terrorist infrastructure'.

The waves of Laila's hair swayed as she nodded. 'Exactly. I'm going out later. Is there anything you need?'

'A little peace, a little justice.'

'Me, too.'

With coffee and chocolates, the escalation passed after a few days.

***

Rasha's silver sweater shimmered in my doorway.

'Come, come,' I beckoned. 'Please – and close the door.'

We had begun to shiver in the draughty hallways, and to overheat our offices. Rasha dispensed flu remedies from the pharmacy drawer of her desk. On the coldest days, she wore a voluminous parka with faux-fur lining her hood. She wore it all day, seeming even thinner within it.

I nudged a chocolate across my desk with little wags of my forefinger, and walked my fingers back. Rasha did not pick it up, so my fingers strode forward and flicked the chocolate into her lap. We all fed her compulsively. She accepted everything with a smile, and recycled most of it through her desk drawer, handing it out with the aspirins and other people's annotated documentation.

Rasha picked up her chocolate obediently. 'I've got them, 240 computer science graduates. All of the screening is done and the curricula and the materials and the trainers and the tests and the rooms—' breath '—and the equipment, we've checked every computer.'

'I'm sure you have.'

'We have. And the coffee. And – you know, everything is done.'

Rasha and Ibrahim were starting the first two of many postgraduate computer courses, seeking to bridge the gulf between university graduation and employment, or at least some hours of paid work. We called them our income-outcome courses, because

17 To understand customary international humanitarian law on the co-location of weapons and civilians, see https://ihl-databases.icrc.org/customary-ihl/eng/docs/v1_rul_rule97

we evaluated them according to the income that graduates earned afterward.

'But . . .' Rasha's eyebrows came together. She searched my office and frowned, 'now that I've got them?'

'*Yalla*,' I encouraged: let's go.

She leaned forward. 'Now that I've got them, what do I do with them?'

'Excuse me?'

'I mean, I know what *we're* doing with them.' She rattled off a precis of the course contents in case she had sounded incompetent, and patted her hijab as I would check my hair after a gust of wind. 'But what do *I* do? You said that I only succeed when they succeed, so what is the task of my management for their success?'

I clapped both hands over my heart. 'Yes – well done! That's exactly the right way to ask exactly the right question. Mm, let me ask you this. In our time together, what feels most transformative for you?'

'That's easy. You truly believe in us, so we believe that we can do new things.'

'I do, and you can, and because that works for you, that can be your organizing principle. The trainer gives them a course, while you give them that transformative knowledge of being believed in. It's statistical madness to believe that you can succeed in Gaza, don't you think? It's much more logical to give up – but they haven't. Your job is to understand the professional they each want to be. Then, ask yourself what that potential, successful professional needs from you. How can you work with the person they dream of being?'

'So that's how you do it,' Rasha said. She, who engineered herself with steely discipline, twirled the chocolate wrapper for some time.

'Watch Ibrahim,' I advised. 'He's a coach by nature. He'll get this.'

He did. Ibrahim memorized 240 names and IT projects, and used his daily monitoring visits to single graduates out by name. Each time a graduate was flattered to be known in such a large group, Ibrahim affirmed that they were worth knowing by name.

Then he sat beside them and showed that their ideas were worth knowing, too.

Ibrahim didn't tell me about his feat then. I overheard him a year later, urging incoming team members to find their own enactments of the power of being believed in. By then, Ibrahim had mapped Gaza in emergent ideas, and all the ways that he could believe them into being. I had promoted him, and several of us had staked out the challenge that would dominate our four years of work together.

I would read well over a thousand CVs of recent university graduates, but our task made itself apparent with the very first set of applications for the income-outcome courses. Every CV showed a university degree. A few candidates had found an internship or a bit of voluntary work after they graduated. Most of the CVs left poignant, blank space on the rest of the page. Young adults were living, unrecorded, in those white spaces. I walked my office chair in circles like a rotisserie chicken before my weak heater, flipped pages and waited for someone to step off the paper and tell me how they were spending their white years. How had they not given up? Where did they find the courage to keep sending out CVs which (they must know) looked just like a thousand others?

Ibrahim and Rasha were in their mid-twenties. They were only slightly older than the graduates in their income-outcome courses, yet they seemed as generationally distinct as the factory owners were from their children. The members of my team enjoyed the privileges of family and education. No less important, the particular years of their head start had been pivotal, life-changing years for the Gaza Strip. Ibrahim and Rasha remembered better times as children. Their families had Israeli or European professional acquaintances. Their peers had studied outside of Gaza. Before the blockade disrupted and deprived them, their adult outlooks had already been anchored by interacting with the world beyond the wall.

Just behind them, Gaza's first blockade cohort was graduating from university. They would have been called millennials anywhere else. In Gaza, they were the Children of Oslo, named for the agreements that had raised some hopes and then dashed all hope. Early in their childhoods, they watched the First Intifada. Palestinian youth stood up, eclipsed the old authorities and led from the front lines. The Children of Oslo watched their big brothers throw rocks. With their first breath, they inhaled a potent mix of political futility and empowering resistance.

Then they watched the first fence encircle Gaza.

The Second Intifada erupted more violently at the turn of the century. The Children of Oslo saw their adolescent prospects dwindle when Israel cancelled safe passage for Palestinians between Gaza and the West Bank, and then forbade Gazans to commute to work in Israel. In 2007, Israel slammed the blockade gates shut.

The Children of Oslo had grown up seeing images of an entropic world that they had never touched. Some of their peers gave up and fired the rockets, as if their only remaining agency lay in their ability to make someone pay. They were a product of siege logic.

Before I began to meet some of the graduates who persevered against that logic, I brooded over the blank pages of their CVs. They were young parents who had never left the Gaza Strip. They would not have ridden on a train or seen a forest, been immersed in foreignness or driven fast for an hour in a straight line. How did they spend all the hours that I spent in the globalized economy or in nature, or travelling, or reading by unquestioned lamplight? Where did their minds go for privacy? What would they belong to, and believe in?

The Children of Oslo were the pivotal people to work for, I was sure. Demographically, educationally, politically; if they gave up, they would take Gaza with them. Their younger siblings would have less reason to stay in school. But who were they, and what would work behind a blockade?

No answers walked off the page that morning. I wandered early into a management meeting. Finding only a pair of trusted colleagues there, I interrupted their small talk.

'Why was there no Arab Spring in Gaza?'

'Oh, there was, sort of,' the woman said, dismayed by Gaza's poor showing. 'A few people tried. Hamas picked them off. I heard they got arrested, and beaten pretty badly. No one else dared.'

The man shook his head. 'They didn't do the advance work. They thought it would just grow, but they hadn't prepared properly. So then, everyone else saw that it was too dangerous.'

'No,' the woman protested. 'No. You can't blame them. They tried. The problem is that there is no press. You can do all the advance work you want, but no one was watching – that's why it was too dangerous. You know, Marilyn, we have a joke: how do you know a democracy activist in Gaza?'

'I don't know. How?'

'They limp.' My colleague pretended to aim and fire a pistol at her own knee, and looked up grimly. 'You remember, Hamas is not Gaza, and Gaza is not Hamas.'

I paid no attention to the meeting that followed. Instead, I added a piece to my profile. The Children of Oslo grew up knowing that they were unprotected.

Around the December anniversary of Israel's 2008–09 invasion of Gaza, the Israeli Army Chief of Staff bristled that it was time for Gaza to 'feel the pain of Israeli fists'. He declared that the next round of fighting would be initiated by Israel, to be 'swift and painful'. No one around me seemed to register the threat.

Our three-month milestone had passed unnoticed as the team coalesced around their new projects. I thought of them as a John Irving family, walking upright through a tilting world. They fell into subgroups, had rivalries and suspicions, yet they came to work knowing that they cohered. Rasha would look up the new words because she was more conscientious. Ibrahim would blush when singled out.

'I'm pinkening,' he would groan.

A group of us went out for a fish lunch on a bright morning. Randa wore a new shawl around her shoulders, a creamy knit that made her teeth whiter and her eyes dark chocolate.

I admired it as we left the car. 'That looks *so* good on you.'

Randa stopped on the sidewalk, unwound her new shawl and spent some time arranging it around my neck, humming, fluffing my hair and composing me in the sunlight.

I said, 'My dear Randa, you make it feel like the best part of having a new scarf is seeing how it looks on someone else.'

'It is,' she beamed, spinning me around to show the others.

I shook my head at her while I posed. 'If people like you could speak, all this would begin to change. I'm sure of it.'

She stepped back. 'Why? Why are you sure of it?'

'Because no one would tolerate the blockade. You would make everyone believe in better endings.'

We could not know that we had begun our work together at the peak, the last season before the slide.

Chapter 5

Then it was winter. Gazans warned me about their forty days of winter. In its glittering summer, Gaza was a stretch of the parched desert. In winter, Gaza rejoined the coast; to be pummelled by storms and subjected to all the moods of the sea.

The first January storm encased the Gaza Strip for days. Wind skidded off the slate-blue waves, driving a horizontal rain that was rich with stinging sand. Wind and water smacked into my windows. I could hardly sleep, listening for the glass to break and imagining the rivulets that would be dribbling down Beit Lahiyans' hollow-block walls. The temperature plummeted and the cities began to flood. Mornings, Marjie and I splashed to the car.

Then the electricity failed. Gaza's electricity demand already exceeded its supply by one-third. In February 2012, Egypt cut back its supply of fuels through the Gaza tunnels. The remaining power supply equated to less than 40 per cent of demand. Essential users like hospitals received more, and residential homes got less. Gaza's sole power plant dipped its output to one-third of its capacity. Intermittently, the absence of fuel shut the whole plant down. Sewage treatment failed. Without power, the municipal stormwater pumps gave up, and the floodwaters soon seethed with filth.

Transport diminished, and long lines of cars snaked away from every open petrol station. Hamas instructed its civil servants to carry hitch-hikers in their cars. My team took longer and longer to reach the office each morning. Some, like Hani and Randa, shared taxis. Others, like Ibrahim, who lived in southern Khan Younis, arrived later and colder, after waiting in the rain for multiple rides. The office put fewer cars on the road, and closed earlier so that everyone could find ways back to their unlit houses before dark. Someone photoshopped a donkey to make it a bright yellow, painted 'taxi' on its hide, and circulated the winter's iconic image.

The wind whipped up a sandy berm along the beach. It rose and trickled inland, making Beach Road into a course of sodden sand traps. Few drivers braved it on the black-dark nights. The channels of floodwater converged at the lowest point in the road, which was the T-junction at the base of my building. Murky water swirled and climbed up the corner signpost. Our office car had to wait further up the block each week, and we waded uphill to meet it.

Winter flu circled and circled and drained Rasha's pharmacy drawer. Parents' faces sagged. To their children, a clap of thunder in the dark sounded like a returning warplane. Electricity was most common between 1.00 and 4.00 in the mornings. Parents got up to flush the toilets and do the laundry, and then they got talked into staying up to watch TV with their children. Rasha, already with dull grey smudges on her cheeks, fainted quietly away after too many nights with her girls. Someone found a car with petrol to take her home. She wobbled away with escorts at both elbows, clutching a fistful of forgotten Mars bars.

Arriving home in the afternoons, I exchanged my wet office clothes for sweatpants and warmed myself by squeegeeing the floors beneath my fifteen metres of leaking window frames. Gazans burned once-used oil for heat, but Beirut Tower's electrical heat was useless. I read through the evenings by rechargeable lantern, and then by headlamp. I left all of my electronic devices plugged in, hoping for power to charge them during the night. Then I pulled on my winter coat, wound a spare sheet around my head like a turban to blot out the juddering of my windows, and burrowed beneath both of my blankets to sleep.

One night, I left the light switches on. Electricity woke me up. I scrunched my eyes shut against it, because the most corrosive shortage in Gaza was sleep. The missiles, the storms, menopause; everything conspired to disrupt my sleep. Morose, awake, I towed my blanket to the dining table that I used as a desk, and turned on the computer.

Half the team's names popped up on Skype, as if it were 2.00 in the afternoon instead of 2.00 in the morning. Curious,

I opened Skype. There they were, entertaining too-wide-awake children, catching up on the work they could not complete during our abbreviated workdays, and propping each other's spirits up through the storm. As crisis-level blackouts became standard and were overtaken by more interesting crises, I joined the team's companionable second shift on Skype whenever I felt like I was the only person awake in the world.

The moment each lashing storm slid away from the shore and the windows dried brown with crusty sand, beachgoers hastened back to stroll in the pause. I opened my windows regardless of the cold, to breathe with them and marvel at them.

Gaza could have been anything behind that wall. It could so easily have been predatory, a jungle of all against all. Instead, the beachgoers cheered each night's power cut. When the lights went out, everyone steeled everyone: *we will not be seen to despair*. They cheered louder than I cursed the inconvenience, so that the first sound to reach me in the darkness was their heartening reminder of company nearby.

I mentioned the beach cheerleaders over a morning coffee. Hani flung his head back and his arms out wide, teaspoon in one hand and a mug in the other. For a moment, he looked like Gene Kelly, singing in the rain. 'Existence is resistance! My grandmother, hmm? Old-fashioned – wise. She says that having a chronic problem, a problem forever with no solution, is just like having no problem at all.'

We called that the secret knowledge of Gaza.

***

Randa, Rasha and Laila leaned irreducibly on each other. They had a fourth, Laila's sister, who strolled past my building of a weekend morning, with her little boy and Randa's two. The women seemed as mismatched as the legs of a Hundertwasser chair. Meticulous and incurably obedient, Rasha was the married mother of two girls. Randa was divorced. Laila, seeker of ideas, pursued her career while a man pursued her. Randa and Laila wore their hair loose, taught me to swear in Arabic, smoked surreptitiously on the roof, and tossed off conventions like chocolate wrappers – in a community whose core civic virtue was its crushing unity. I never knew whether to build them a statue, or mount a rescue.

Near the end of January, Randa came to my doorway. Her hair was glossy black and her lipstick fuchsia, but her pallor turned the colours into hard surfaces. She wrung her hands, and I saw that she had been biting her nails again.

'Come, come,' I waved her in and got up to close the door behind her. '*Yalla*, what's wrong?'

'People are talking about me,' she said in a small voice.

'Randa? Dear? People would talk about you anywhere. You're noteworthy. I mean, we're all alive but you're a little more so.'

She smiled but it didn't last. 'I think they're not saying good things.'

'Ah. Let me check around.'

She was right. The office had become fixated on Randa's friendship with Hani. Before I could think of a response, Adham knocked on my door. I waved him in. He huffed into a seat, balancing his lapels. Mohammad, the logistics manager, looked dour behind him. I took a deep breath. They were both procedural and cautious, which was to say, they were not natural fans of our team, or of Randa in particular.

Adham demanded that I change the desks, send one of them on holiday, suspend them if necessary, to prise them apart. 'They are alone too often. In the same office. With the door closed. Together.'

I looked pointedly at my own office door, which Adham had just closed. He followed my eyes, pursed his lips and turned back. 'Hani is married. Randa is divorced.'

'So am I. I'm not suspending anyone for that.'

'The door is closed.'

'Adham, every door in the building is closed, to keep the heat in. I'll bet your door is closed right now, and a man and a woman share your office, too.'

Adham drew himself up in his chair, and looked down his aquiline nose to say with the severity of height, 'They should not be there.'

'Okay, I understand. I do, I understand,' I repeated, deliberately slowing Adham's staccato and my own temper. 'I understand what you're saying.'

Mohammad pressed this opening. 'My drivers refuse to carry them.'

'They do?'

'They arrive in the same car.'

'Oh, come on! Everyone is sharing cars. There's no petrol.'

'Not everyone is sitting together in the back seat,' he said smugly. 'Hani should sit in the front like a normal man. They come in early so they think no one can see them, but everyone knows. Everyone is talking.' He sat back, then leaned forward again to tap one long, large-knuckled finger on my desk. 'Everyone—'

I nodded sadly at the taint on our morning coffees.

'—and someone will tell Hamas,' he finished, and folded his hands.

I fiddled with the things on my desk, in order to look away from him. I liked his arid humour. His family's Beit Hanoun orchard had recently been struck by a missile. I would have preferred to confront someone with whom I could be uncomplicatedly angry. I reasoned with myself a moment, and acquiesced. 'Let me talk to them.'

Adham waved this away. 'No! No. You have to be seen to act. You have to take this very seriously.'

'Seen? I said I would—'

'No-no-no. You can't brush this off. You have to take a strong action. Do you understand? Strong. People are *talking*.'

'Well, then,' I said tartly, 'Let's suspend the people who are doing all this troublesome talking.'

They didn't bother to reply.

I had marvelled at Gaza's tolerance. However, in their faces I saw its limit. They were reasonable men, and they perceived a weighty and threatening matter. When I spoke next, I tried to sound conciliatory. I didn't feel conciliatory, and I could hear my throat constricting with held anger. 'Let me explain how I see this, okay? They are colleagues and friends, but because they are who they are, people are eager to gossip. The gossip escalates a harmless situation to a harmful one. I agree that it has escalated, and we must de-escalate it. I agree with you. But you are also asking me to punish them for the crime of being talked about, and I can't do that.'

'Someone will tell Hamas.'

Mohammad had spoken but I replied to Adham.

'Well, Adham, I think you should talk someone out of doing that. You know as well as I do that nothing is going on, and I see as well as you do, that they should be more aware of appearances—' I paused one heartbeat, to test the truth of that. 'So, let's talk everyone down. I'll be changing the offices around once our recruitment is done. Everyone will see a change soon enough.'

With diminished heat, Adham reminded me that a previous international had departed from Gaza overnight, at Hamas's suggestion, over a similar matter. 'They're putting *you* in danger, too.'

I lifted my chin and bluffed. 'I can't think of a better principle over which to be thrown out of Gaza.'

They shrugged, and left. I nodded into the hallway after them. Hani would be angry, but Gaza's consensus would welcome him back.

Randa lingered in the hallway, watching Adham and Mohammad depart. When she turned around, her contrition could not quite overcome her flagrant fuchsia lipstick. I exhaled and nearly laughed.

She had once sat opposite me at a staff dinner, on the plaza of a local hotel. After her workday, she had picked her two boys up from the babysitter, drilled them on their homework and done a family French lesson. Then she got everyone dressed and hustled them back out the door. She arrived late, sweaty and flustered.

From across the hotel terrace, all the children began to call for her, gesturing insistently. Randa's boys rocked from foot to foot, just as she did. Heaving the universal sigh of the single mother, Randa had pushed herself up from her chair to go and entertain everyone's children. She wore a white blouse and, as she rose, I saw beige foundation smeared on her collar.

I had fought an urge to throw my sweater over her shoulders to conceal it. I wanted to hide the proof that – in conservative Gaza – Randa had no husband to tell her to change her blouse.

Randa dissolved in a flood of tears behind my office door. She crumpled and groaned and her voice grew plaintive. 'I'm not doing anything – why does this happen – I'm just living my life—'

'I know, we know. And it's no one's business.'

'They always *do* this. He'll tell Hamas, and then what?'

'And then – what?' I asked. 'What would Hamas do about a bit of gossip?'

'My boys. My custody of the boys.'

'Oh.' I clamped one hand over my mouth and slumped onto my elbows behind it.

Randa wiped one hand beneath her eyes, assessed the mascara on her fingertips and cried harder. 'A woman can't live – they won't let me live.' Her tears slowly subsided to shudders. She took tissue after tissue from the box at the corner of my desk, and considered her options. 'Should I, do you think I should . . .'

I bit my own tongue. 'I think . . . if you want to choose your battles more carefully and not get hurt, that's okay. If you never want to change a thing, that's okay, too. You're allowed to protect yourself, or to just be yourself. You choose. You'll make a good choice, and we will love you for it.'

Subdued, she left with Laila to be consoled.

I made it home with my teeth clenched, and I began to gouge at the floor tiles with my squeegee.

'This is what we *do*!' I grunted. 'Human beings throw off sparks. That's how we know we are alive – *leave her alone*!'

Finally, I sank into an armchair and stared out at the gunmetal sea, shivering and hating Afghanistan. I thought of the lively women I'd seen snuffed out, and I tried to brace myself for the loss of one more. Randa was wired for only one course of action, and it couldn't end well. Randa in Gaza – it could not possibly end well. I sobbed and I shook and I squeegeed some more.

Randa had to lead a community forum on recycling the following morning in Tal El Hawa, a middle-class neighbourhood of brutalist concrete apartment buildings. She came into the office hallway at mid-morning, with stilted steps. I knew them all by their tread (except for soundless Rasha), and Randa normally sashayed. I jumped up and hurried around my desk to intercept her and ask what was wrong with her step. We nearly collided in my doorway, Randa teetering on perilous heels.

She looked smart and feminine and distinctly sexy in a soft

black suit, lacy-collared blouse with the shape of a camisole beneath, and black patent-leather stilettos. She tossed her hair into a cascade, and gave me a sly, fuchsia smile. My mouth fell open and we stood that way, enjoying the sight of each other.

I pointed to her shoes. 'Yesterday?'

She grinned, and bobbed her eyebrows.

'And how was your forum?'

'It was gr-r-reat,' she said savagely.

'I bet. Half of Tal El Hawa will still be frozen to their chairs, asking each other what just happened. You look . . . recovered.'

By way of explanation, Randa held out both hands and mimed snipping a length of videotape. Then she pressed the fingers of one hand into the palm of the other, to splice the cut ends together. Randa always swore that she had taught herself to expunge embittering events from her memory. I once asked if she could really make herself forget. She replied that she survived in Gaza only because she cut the tape, and refused to watch the news.

Having cut the tape of the previous day's strife, Randa's face wore only the morning's triumph. She turned to mince back to her office.

'You are a natural wonder,' I called to her back. '*Allah yatik el afiah.*'

Randa saluted at the side of her head.

Adham and I soon reconciled. Returning from an aborted meeting in Jerusalem one morning, I walked the 900 metres into Gaza. As I neared the middle of the pedestrian tunnel, the IDF fired the first of five shells over the border walls. There was no shelter. I sprinted forward, telling myself that they wouldn't bomb their own tunnel. Adham stood at the end of the tunnel, having come to the border crossing to drop off some paperwork. He flinched into his collar with each explosion, but he waited for me.

We dashed to the car, laughing with adrenaline and shaking our fists back at the concrete walls. An emergency shawarma smoothed things over between us.

***

We hired the first new recruits, and shuffled the offices. The four senior project managers squeezed into one office. They found smaller desks, so that Ibrahim could join them. Hani dominated his desk like a parent visiting grade school. A season of Randa's work could be undone by one stray breeze across her mousenest. They worked together without ill will, and if you hadn't known that they once leaned naturally toward each other, you would not have noticed that they now listed away. Next to Randa, Rasha's desk was sometimes piled so high with her work and others' that it yielded no flat workspace. When that happened, Rasha folded herself and her laptop into the kneehole beneath the desk, and insisted that it was adequate. Wasim worked against the short wall, perpendicular to Rasha. He was the calm in the team's perpetual brainstorm. Angular and easy-going, he synthesized the discussions of his more voluble workmates. When they ran out of words, Wasim often tossed in the idea that moved things forward. Just as deliberately, he would romance and marry one of the women upstairs, and spirit them both out of Gaza. Ibrahim shared the fourth wall with the files. On the far side of his desk, an empty wading pool served as a sort of Speakers' Corner for anyone who had an idea or a problem to discuss. Two stuffed cows lived on the bookshelves above the pool. They bore a malicious resemblance to real people within the building. I moved into the office next door with a demented little stuffed rabbit known as Procurement Bunny. We did much of our work standing in doorways.

Hani and I continued to discuss relief food, both as a humanitarian stop-gap and as a commodities market for local businesses. After one of our conversations, I printed a sign and slapped it on my office wall: GAZA > RELIEF. It became the team's irate motto.

The first time Hani saw it, he jutted his chin toward it and smiled like the Cheshire cat, 'Do you still think that "strategy" is too strong to describe it, hmm?'

'Huh? No – wait, let's go next door.'

We went to the managers' office, where Laila was visiting. I sat in the wading pool, pulling bespectacled Moo Cow absently into my lap. I paused long enough to take in the flowers that someone had freshly drawn on the whiteboard. 'So, the question is, why should you care if donor states relate to Gaza primarily by sending relief food? What does that mean for *you*?'

Laila's lips thinned and her eyebrows lowered. 'It means they think we're all helpless.'

'They *want* us to be helpless,' Hani corrected.

Rasha said, 'It means that people spend too much time worrying. It makes everyone insecure. Will it be enough? Will it be less than last year? They only hope for things not to get worse.'

They waited for Randa, who looked sheepish. 'It means that I can't get a babysitter.'

'Right,' I agreed. 'All of that. Relief helps today, but it's not designed to fix anything, and Gaza needs change. And that sign on my wall means more, too. Let me ask the question a different way: for what kind of community is relief sufficient? If relief is enough, if Gaza needs only those blockade walls around it and some food, then maybe someone thinks there are only two kinds of Gazans, fighters and the very poor people who truly need food. That's Gaza's image in the world. That's what people know about Gaza, violence and poverty. For sure, those are real, but what has caused them? The cause is missing from Gaza's image. And you – and people like you – you are missing from that image. You don't fight, and you're not poor. And where are the university graduates – why doesn't Gaza stand for 96 per cent literacy?'

They added the entrepreneurs, the professionals, the start-up culture, and the creative artists. The people we worked with were integral to Gaza, and they had all vanished.

'Yes, and what does all this disappearance mean? The missing people are the ones who make Gaza a whole community, a capable community that could govern and work, and manage scarce resources, and resolve problems and co-exist in some kind of justice. You—' I pointed, emphatic, specific, '—when *you* disappear, you take the solutions with you. Gaza's character, its self is gone. The sign on my office wall doesn't mean that Gaza needs more than relief – although it does. It means that Gaza is more than relief suggests it is. Gaza is more than a humanitarian problem.'

Hani squared his shoulders and looked grim, but most of the eyebrows were more furrowed, including mine.

Laila lowered her voice almost to a whisper. More than my own team, Laila queried politics and power. 'But, how could anyone not see us? What do they think we are?'

'I don't know. I didn't see you.' I looked up quickly, but no one had heard my apologetic inflection. I cleared my throat. 'I don't know how it happened. But why? Ask yourself who benefits. That's always a good starting point in political economy.'

Laila had studied computer science in the US, and she continued to study social enterprise and management accounting. She recalled American hospitality warmly, although she had grown tired of repeating that Gaza was not in Israel; that it was unhappily stitched to Israel's side. She had taken to saying that Gaza was Not Quite Israel.

NQI became our byword for absurdity.

In January 2012, the US Congress announced that they would continue to fund the uniformed security forces in the West Bank, and cease funding Palestinian *Sesame Street*. In the interests of security, every inquisitive three-year-old in Palestine would be left to watch violent Islamic Jihad cartoons on TV. Laila and I met in the hallway to shake our heads: NQI.

When Newt Gingrich, a candidate for the American presidency, denigrated Palestinians as 'an invented people', Laila flounced into my doorway, planted her hands on her hips, and snorted, 'Isn't everyone invented?'

'Yes, of course they are. NQI! Look at the number of inventions since World War II. I do not understand why, this time, America should respond by withholding aid and shit-canning Kermit the Frog.'

'Ooh,' Laila giggled into her hand, and rapped, 'Obama's gonna shit-can Kermit the Frog.'

We discussed the lived reality around us, while I hedged on my analysis. We talked about statelessness, but never the fact that statelessness had also been the problem statement of Zionism. Zionism responded to the vulnerability of Jews who had been denied the rights and protections of their states. In a world organized by states in the interests of state power, anything could be done to such dehumanized and unprotected people. Jews knew that statelessness was a precursor, yet, watching Palestinians endure the same vulnerability, Jews turned amnesiac.

We drove to Jerusalem together once, when Laila got a permit to leave Gaza. We stepped out of the car on the Mount of Olives, overlooking the Old City and its sparkling gold Dome of the Rock. Promissory images of the dome hung on countless Gazan walls. Laila faced the real dome for a time, one steadying hand on the car as if the drive had been much longer than a few hours. She turned to me with tears in her eyes.

Politics prevented me from agreeing, *me, too*. Jerusalem was inscribed on both of us.

For months, I had read book after book about Palestinian history and identity. Gaza led me ineluctably to re-examine my own.

Chapter 6

Halifax, Canada

My mother's sister, Pearl Hirsch, had a stroke in the early 1980s. I felt it as a breach of contract. Aunt Pearl flouted medical prognoses, and I assumed that she always would. Scarlet fever had weakened her heart during her childhood, in the 1920s. Doctors gave her six months to live, and although she lived to the age of sixty-two, her life was circumscribed. She could not drive, bear children, or climb the stairs to the modest apartment at the edge of the Dalhousie University campus, where she outlived her parsimonious doctors.

Throughout my childhood, Aunt Pearl lived as an adjunct member of our family, an observer rather than an authority. She lowered herself into easy chairs, knitted and watched us grow up. Mother waved us off to school each morning with the phone in hand to call her sister. A few times each week, Daddy brought Aunt Pearl home for dinner. He carried her up the back steps which were fewer, but trickier, than the round stone stairs up to our front door. My father was stout, but he waltzed Aunt Pearl gracefully around the screen door and stood her upright among the snow boots. We set an extra glass of water by her plate for her medications, and she picked up her glass with arms that were forever band-aided and bruised by her blood tests.

Aunt Pearl survived open-heart surgery and wrung a few more years from each medical advance, until spidery lines ran between the greying hair at her temples, and her girlish figure relaxed. Devoid of bitterness, she acknowledged every kindness shown to her, audited university courses without the pressure of exams, and basked in a solicitous circle of friends.

I loved her thoughtlessly, as a piece of family furniture. Although it prevented any real kinship between us, I considered it a bit of cosmic good governance that my aunt had been born with her retiring nature, and I with mine.

I had left home for university by the time of Aunt Pearl's stroke, but I went to her hospital when I next visited Halifax. It was a raw November night, wind slapping at skeletal trees. I edged into the wrong hospital room, and reached behind me for the door handle to edge back out. In this room was a hag – someone else's hag – with wild hair and a crepe paper neck. She fixed her eyes on me.

'Stairs!' she spat, and my hand hung suspended behind me. 'They bought a house with *stairs*, so I could never walk through their door without their help.'

Physically intact but unlatched by her stroke; I had come to visit a blank, blameless abstract of my aunt. Not this. I backpedalled until I hit the wall. Goosebumps erupted like quills along my arms.

'Abe Garson always resented me – did you know that? Resented the time he spent driving me, resented me anywhere near his family – and she never stood up for me! She *never* stands up to him, never. Your mother,' my mother's sister rasped, 'is weak.'

She said bitter, heartfelt things. She dredged up all the grudges that I would have held in her place, and she swore that she could have lived more fully. They held her back. They – we – preserved her from life.

Guilty, repulsed, I inched closer. Had this always lurked beneath my aunt's gracious surface? Was she finally free to speak her mind, or had it fled? I picked up her paper cup of water, and offered her the elbowed straw. Up close, I could see her familiar needle bruises. The corners of her eyes were pink and raw, as if she cried often. Of the person she might have been, I could see only that my Aunt Pearl had an animating rage.

Drawn by her parched voice or the hour, a nurse arrived. She marvelled at my aunt's unsuspected strength while she fed something into her intravenous line. Gradually, Aunt Pearl's voice flattened, until she sounded more perplexed than angry.

No one, she said, had seen through her gratitude. All those years.

I wasn't sure whether she intended to measure her performance, or our gullibility. Did she want to be seen through? By then, she was blurring into sleep.

I went outside to smoke in the lee of the hospital. I watched the tree branches snap like flies' legs around the parking lot lights until the smoke settled my stomach. Thoughts, illusions – didn't matter. Families were the surface of a lake, reflecting light to hide their depth.

I had stolen my aunt's secrets when she had no power to stop blurting them out. I was sorry only to have learned so late that we were kin, after all. We were both hiding from the polite agreements that governed our lives around my father's dinner table.

***

We were Abie's babies: Joan, Debbie, Carol and I.

Abram William Garson was born in 1918, the third child and eldest boy of nine children. His mother, Mary Garson, held their sprawling household together with love and authoritarian steel. She housed assorted relatives through the Depression, and during World War II, she welcomed the Jewish servicemen who had been turned away from some of Halifax's other lodgings.

The Angus L. MacDonald inter-city bridge ramps were later laid through the site of the Garson home, in the undesirable North End of Halifax. As a child in the back seat of my father's car, I tried to summon Mary's ghost each time we drove through her house. Of all my grandparents, I most wanted to know Mary. My father adored her, and I thought she might have secrets for me, given that I bore her name and her features.

Twenty years later, I looked so much like my grandmother that men around my father's age stopped me in the streets of Antwerp and Singapore. They studied my face, arms out as if to clap me on my shoulders or lift off my backpack.

'Mary Garson,' they each said, one in confusion and the other quite certain. They were veterans. Mary had taken each of them in off the street and, my father being out late, she had given each of them his bed for a night. She had made such an impression that, half a century later and continents apart, they recalled her in a passing stranger's face.

By all accounts including his own, my youthful father often came home late, on his way to a life in music or in trouble. Those choices vanished when his own father disregarded medical advice and died young, in 1942.

Overnight, my father inherited financial responsibility for the household. From that moment, Daddy's repertoire of growing-up stories narrowed to the ceaseless pursuit of money. He worked any reasonably legal job, sold blood and boxed rounds for cash. Mary caught him expanding the family's scrap metal business into underwater demolitions. While helping to raise and support his siblings, my father grew particularly close to Mary and to his youngest brother, Saul, for whom he was a surrogate father. My father's reserve amplified those intimacies, for although he made avuncular conversation, Abe Garson had few confidantes.

By the time his responsibilities eased, most of his Jewish age group, and all eight of his siblings, had paired off and married. My father was considered old to be a bachelor. I have never heard a more romantic founding myth for his marriage to my mother.

Before each of his children was born, my father loudly pronounced that he was due for a basketball-loving son, with a boxer's timing and perfect harmonic pitch. He publicly arranged for the ceremony that would accompany the birth of each son. Instead, four baby girls tethered him forever to duty. From *Monday Night Football* to the *NBA Game Of The Week*, my father hollered alone into a household of women, 'Look at him go, *lookatimgo*!' Between touchdowns, home runs, layups, slap shots, and knock outs; he let loose only at the piano. There, for a few hours, anyone could see that Abe Garson was born a blues musician. Each time he rose from the piano bench with one final riff, he willed himself to be a wholly dedicated, honourable father of girls.

Mary Garson neared her death as my sister Carol neared her birth in 1958. My parents asked the rabbi to postpone naming the baby, as Jews are not named after living people. The rabbi refused to taint the celebration of Carol's birth with the anticipation of Mary's death. Far from invoking grief, Carol's Hebrew name – Shira, or song – epitomized our family's joy.

Then Mary's death devastated my father and his marriage. I was born into Mary's name three years later. My parents were both in their forties, and I had no inkling that anything had been lost between them. On the contrary, through the eyes of a small child, Abe Garson was just about perfect.

Daddy carried us everywhere, seated on his shoulder or the ample shelf of his belly. He played with us for hours on the floor of our Beech Street house. Weekday mornings, he shouted up the stairs, 'Joan-debbie-car-mar *break*fast! I fried the guinea pigs!' Washing the dinner dishes, his baritone underscored our harmonies. He loaded us into the car at weekends and took us to any place that might ignite a child's imagination: concerts, construction sites, skating rinks, the illuminated fountains of the Halifax Commons, apple orchards, container piers. Then we trooped into the library for armloads of books, and on to the Public Gardens, to feed the ducks and wash our hands in the fountain because Joan was allergic to the ducks' peanuts.

He took me once to Africville, a neglected Black settlement built on land that had become strategic to the city's expansion. It would soon be demolished, its residents relocated from their homes into public housing projects. I remember him impressing mildly, firmly upon me, 'This is part of your city, too.'

Mother was often tired, so Daddy became the tireless weekend custodian of our curiosity. In return, we understood that he required us to excel. He willed it, and my father's will exerted the kind of transubstantiating pressure that squeezed the life out of plankton and – not content with manufacturing rock – crushed the rock into oil.

I made it my childhood mission statement: Daddy only loves you when you come in first. Being the youngest, I had arrived late to the contest. My sisters had head starts of three, five and eight years. Everything worth doing had already been done. I drove myself with an excoriating voice that still lurks within me, and a fear of falling behind, slipping from view, and vanishing altogether.

As the sole arbiter of our march to law school, Daddy's approval was our currency. I craved it as much as my sisters, but I could not seem to fix my eyes on his path. My eyes travelled.

I parked myself at the television as a small child, absorbing the Vietnam War, Cambodia and Watergate with the cartoons. Nixon resigned when I was thirteen. By then, I recognized the shapes of power and exclusion.

Thickset American soldiers dwarfed the Asian defenders. The villagers, who were never dressed for war, lost everything. I felt no immunity from the waste of war; from the villagers' sudden, irredeemable losses. Or, rather, I saw that the villagers might have believed they were safe, too, until they weren't. It happened all at once, leaving them freshly bewildered in each image. I could see them thinking that it wasn't supposed to be like this. I felt no safer than they had probably felt last week.

Adults assured me that it couldn't happen here, and it would never happen to us. They were demonstrably wrong. Canada instituted the War Measures Act and suspended *habeas corpus* in 1970, in response to domestic political violence. For months, I dreamed that the army took my sister Joan away in an Irving furnace oil truck, to investigate her role in student politics.

When adults mouthed their rote reassurances, I imagined other mothers telling their children the same thing, at breakfast, on their last day of having a hut in a village. At noon the war washed into their dirt yard. Then they joined the columns of empty-handed villagers, walking away as night fell. The children walked barefoot, and I worried that they would cut their feet.

Adults confused distance with immunity. They noticed endangered people only long enough to catalogue all the insulating ways in which they differed from us. I wanted to bring the endangered people closer because, to me, we looked alike. Only our clothes distinguished us. How could anyone mistake it? We smiled, our mouths puckered into a little 'o' of realization, and widened when we wailed. Barefoot, the soles of anyone's feet would soon be bloody. Vulnerability was our human condition.

I grew up fearing our ability and our willingness to harm each other. At home, Daddy's absolute power of closure kept us safe.

He told us when someone was in trouble, and he told us when it was over. Outside our home, fights in the yard of Sir Charles Tupper School upset me. I wanted a referee on site, in case one boy wanted to stop and the other did not. Ice hockey, with its consensual rules and padding, worried me not at all. I reserved my fear for people who did not choose their violence, as Vietnam must have been full of children who were terrified and wanted it to stop.

I was a porous, insomniac child. I knew a faraway world, a magical realism more compelling than the competition at hand. But then I wanted to be as robust as my family. They shared some structural understanding that eluded me, as if they had all been listening when the instructions were read out. I tried to join them, pushed away their confinement, lay in bed for hours dreaming of escape, then recited from *The Golden Book Of Poetry* to replant myself among them.

In the sixth grade, I ran with the cool kids. Membership was affirming and it kept me busy. Other people made the plans, and I happily went along, just as I naturally dated the only Jewish boy in the group. A number of us followed a girl home from school one afternoon. I took part because my friends did. Our group was never violent, but we outnumbered and intimidated this girl. As we walked toward her home at the edge of the baseball field, I felt a creeping dread of the threat we posed. I couldn't look at the sports field. Its rules disgraced me. So did the two pink spots that bloomed on the girl's cheeks as she let herself into her house.

I made an excuse, left my group on the sidewalk, went home and closed myself into my bedroom. I had made those incriminating spots on her cheeks. In a group, for the comfort of belonging to the group, I had the same capacity for harm as the people around me. If love happened in the heart, then I decided that ethics must reside in the pit of the stomach, where the actions of a group proved to be indigestible alone.

Even I could see that the story was more compelling from the solitary girl's perspective. Had she also felt like throwing up? I lacked the courage to apologize to her, so I never got to ask how she had acquired the poise to walk so steadily home, and walk back into school the following morning. My shame cured me forever of the cowardice and approval of groups. Instead, I began to notice how often the figures of courage walked alone.

My mother would have understood that day as a character study, if I had considered telling her.

My mother, Lily Michele Hirsch, grew up in a gentle home, as studious as the Garsons were rambunctious. She would launch her middle-aged comedy career by writing about her family's uneasy fit into the Coke Ovens, an immigrant slum near the coal mines of Cape Breton. Her father, Joseph, was a rabbi and Talmudic scholar. He had studied for years across Europe before booking his passage to New York, and disembarking by mistake in Sydney, Nova Scotia. Perhaps English-speaking communities were all the same to him. Fluent in half a dozen scriptural languages, he would never bother to learn English. Unlike Ancient Aramaic, my grandfather demurred, English had yet to produce much scholarship worth reading.

Bella, later his wife, made the most promising start of all my grandparents in the New World. She worked as a Communist labour organizer in the garment factories of New York. She softened as she aged, and because she lived well into her nineties, Bella was the only grandparent I ever met. She was a silvery wisp by then, from her gleaming hair to her long-handled cloisonné brushes.

Bella and Joseph raised four modern children who spoke Yiddish at home, and English while they served at the counter of the family's corner grocery store. Although Joseph was disinclined to collect overdue accounts from his impoverished neighbours, the Hirsch family saved enough to send three children away to university. The fourth child, my Aunt Pearl, cultivated her rich interior life at home. It did not occur to anyone that physical frailty diminished the value of her mind, or that education might be less essential to three girls than to a boy.

My mother moved to Halifax to attend university in 1936, at the age of sixteen. She asked her father what she should study. He advised her to choose a subject that would still interest her in old age, or in solitude. Disregarding his advice, my mother studied nursing in order to help support her parents financially.

People have told me stories about the vivacious young Lily

Hirsch, before she stopped working to marry my father. The Lily Garson of my own memory dressed in beige and accepted a recessive role in our household. Our stronger temperaments overshadowed hers, and our debates drowned out her humane observations. From a young age, I knew how to work around her, or run over her. I associated her defeatism with the two shelves of pill bottles, behind the sliding doors of her wardrobe. Pill bottles were the stock in trade of stifled housewives in the 1960s and 1970s. I didn't know what they were for, but they hinted that life with us was not turning out as Mother had envisioned.

She asserted herself only as a strict grammarian. 'Like' was no surrogate for 'as' in her home. Swearing was lazy and imprecise, lacking explanatory value. Daddy handled the rest.

***

My sisters and I went to Hebrew School two weekday afternoons and Sunday mornings, to Jewish youth groups on Sunday afternoons, and Jewish summer camp for six weeks of the summer. Saturday mornings, we went to the synagogue.

Especially during his tenure as president of the synagogue board, Daddy introduced Jewish rituals into our home. If they meant little to us in the abstract, we looked for meaning in their enactment. We tried out the Jewish dietary laws, but banning bacon just made it taste like breaking rules. I still gorge on it at hotel breakfast buffets, although I cannot bring myself to prepare it in my own kitchen. More successfully, we made Sabbath dinner our essential family ritual.

When I was four years old, we moved into a house on Bloomingdale Terrace and inherited the previous owners' bold décor. They left us a glass slab dining table, so fixed and monumental that I believed the house had been assembled around it. Flecks had been chipped from one mitred, lengthwise edge. A truck, perhaps, or a missile; nothing less. Eight people could sit comfortably around the table, and it required as many, in two rows like casket bearers, to shuffle it sideways for buffets. An ornate chandelier speckled the glass.

We were a family of six, but in my childhood, we rarely ate alone. Sometimes a second table jutted into the checkerboard hallway. Relatives joined us, and visitors to the Jewish community. Musician-cousins and law students came for dinner and lived in the attic through graduation. My father's paternal risk radar was no match for the prospect of a Jewish pseudo-son willing to watch sports with him.

When Mother covered her hair with lace to light the candles on Friday evenings, when Daddy blessed the braided *challah* bread, the house grew still around us. Brothers-in-law blended into us then. We sang the blessings in unison, making them last, standing behind our chairs with wine glasses extended. In that suspended moment, I belonged most organically to our inner circle. The moment passed in a clink of wineglasses, and a chorus of 'Shabbat Shalom'. Then we slid the headcoverings back into the telephone table drawer. One or two sisters joined Mother in the kitchen to serve, and we dispensed with the decorum.

Vehement debate was the music of our dinner table. Daddy presided. Equally, he deferred to American presidents and disdained Canada's Prime Minister, Pierre Trudeau. (In case anyone doubted the Prime Minister's status in my father's affections, a gold-framed copy of Trudeau's hallmark Charter of Rights and Freedoms hung upside down in the bathroom.) Defending even Nixon, Daddy often argued alone. He thrived on it, clutching the sides of his head and rocking like a Hasid – 'oi-oi-oi' – in mock horror at the liberalism of young people.

Our debates could turn into trials by ordeal, as Daddy eviscerated anyone who could not substantiate an argument. However, if you disagreed, studied up and held your ground, dinners could also end in mutual victory.

My father's Judaism walked. Almost daily, he took the shortcut past the sports fields, to help make up the Orthodox prayer quorum of ten men at the Beth Israel Synagogue. Winter storms and others' vacation schedules might require him to go twice a day. In those seasons when the sun set at dinner time, the phone might summon him from his plate. No matter. Daddy would open the telephone table drawer, pull out the blue velvet bag containing his *talis* prayer shawl, and walk out the back door with his car keys. He took his turn on the synagogue boards and committees, and sat up countless nights with the bodies of deceased Jews awaiting burial.

Decade after decade he prayed, although my father did not believe in God. He found all the heaven he needed in the spirituals of Mahalia Jackson. On this earth, he knew that Jews had a responsibility to maintain the rituals for those who did believe, and for those in mourning. The principle was neither abstract nor convenient: responsibility walked.

As a child at his table, I could not have explained where Judaism ended and Garsonism began. I knew that our acts of prayer were Jewish. My father and God had somehow co-authored the rest.

Consistent with the public face of Canadian Judaism in the 1960s and 1970s, our home was unreservedly Zionist. Israel was a present guest at our Sabbath table. Tangible Israel had replaced a tarnished post-Holocaust God as the repository of our Jewishness. To be a Jew was to have Israel, and to be a good Jew was to build upon it. We underwrote each family occasion with a donation certificate, 'A tree has been planted in your name in the State of Israel'. I beheld this State of Israel with awe, as both a religious state of being and as a country established by avowedly secular Zionists.

Gentile children sometimes asked, 'If Israel went to war with Canada, who would you fight for?' I gave them withering looks. They didn't get it. Canada didn't go to war with Christianity, so why would it fight with Judaism?

Palestinians were unknown to me. It's not that I exempted their dispossession from my political scrutiny. I was not aware of any dispossession, only of the threat posed by Israel's Arab neighbours.

In our book-lined den, four Naugahyde recliners surrounded an accordion-sized shortwave radio. We sometimes tried to name all of the staticky languages that inhabited its axes. For a week in June 1967, men from the synagogue bustled in and out of the den. While they clutched the arms of the recliners, six invading Arab armies collapsed. Wasp-waisted Israel tripled its size. In one epochal week just twenty years after the Holocaust, the Israel Defense Forces arose as the fierce New Jews.

Zionist Judaism was a generational progression around our dinner table. My grandparents had left Eastern Europe because they saw that Jews had no future there. I did not view them as victims. Rather, they were adventurous agents, makers of their better lives. The cataclysms of the Depression and the Holocaust shaped their children's – my parents' – timid sense of Jews' place in the world. My parents were the kind of unwavering, committed members on whom every small Jewish community relies, yet they did not feel secure enough to socialize readily with non-Jews.

The Six Day War was my generation's inflection point. I was six years old, and I did not fear being Jewish. I feared the human capacity for violence; but Judaism meant blessing the wine, standing one's ground on matters of principle, planting endless trees and enacting responsibility even when it snowed. Except in summer, Jewishness was my asset.

In summer, it became the bane of my life. An hour and a half from Halifax, Camp Kadimah espoused the Zionism which cast Jews as history's eternal victims. Banners from the team competitions juxtaposed the barbed wire of the concentration camp with Israel's Star of David, and a dove or a fist – or both, keeping our options open. Camp sometimes primed the kind of ganged-up behaviour that I most feared – not because it was Zionist but because we were aggrieved teenagers. I still remember the summer when we simulated life in a Nazi ghetto. Victims and guards inhabited their roles so fully that someone had to call it off.

Camp had no referee, and I pleaded not to be sent. In 1974, I staged a bloodless coup, hoping to get kicked out with my co-conspirator. We failed. The camp director may have worried that sending me home would cost him his room in our attic, before he could graduate from law school.

Public Judaism consisted of incendiary elements – victimhood, menace, defence, grief, outrage – so different from the acts I saw at home. I struggled to reconcile the incongruent faces of Judaism. Slowly I came to see them as responses to different world views. Fortunately, someone had told me in childhood that a Jewish God accepts the terms of each dialogue with Him. They may have been trying to explain free will, but I took it as permission to place Judaism's complexity on hold. I grew up belonging firmly to a fuzzy category called Jew, and it could wait.

***

When I became an adolescent, my father had four teenaged daughters.

His right eyebrow was the leading edge of his temper. It alone hopped within a still-placid expression, offering an errant daughter one chance to behave or recant. As children, we generally did. We knew how fast his boxer's anger could heat a room.

As teenagers, we exercised his eyebrow more often. Its deterrent power might have held out long enough to get us all into university, if not for the death of his beloved youngest brother in 1974. Uncle Saul was eighteen years younger than my father, still square where my father had gone roly poly. Uncle Saul was athletic and upbeat while my father was balding into middle age, yet it was my uncle's heart that failed. Everyone agreed that his fitness would pull him through, and then my parents were coming home from the hospital, cheated of him.

We sisters arranged ourselves around the dining room table, seeking contact with something heavy and familiar while we listened for the car. We had no experience of grief, but Daddy comforted bereaved families all the time. He would know what to do and say. I heard them close the back door and trudge through the kitchen. The chandelier cast criss-crossing shadows across Daddy's puffy, unshaven face. Mother gripped a chair back, looking lost, looking away. They were severed from each other, brought up short in a way that made me wonder what they'd said in the car.

My father said, 'I've lost everything. My baby brother. My best friend. My business partner – and my only son. No one will ever mean that much to me again.'

First as eulogy, then as warning. He surveyed his four daughters and repeated, 'No one.'

Mother reached for his arm. She may have needed to steady herself, facing a reprise of the death of Mary Garson. Perhaps she reached out to console him. Or to make him stop. Either way, he evaded her. He angled away and went to the garage to grieve without us.

Daddy-after came downstairs for breakfast the following day. I searched his face for a signal so intimate that only a daughter would recognize it, but there was nothing to find. He had moved on from us. We sat still and obsolete, outliving his resources for us.

Joan lived in Toronto by then. Debbie and Carol were older teens, both with more thoughtful and accommodating dispositions than mine. I was a wilful thirteen-year-old with years of demands still to make on him, and no strong connection with my mother. I was Abie's baby.

One evening not long after, I refused to do the dishes and wandered away from the dinner table. I cannot remember why, as the consequences long ago eclipsed the cause.

I retreated to Mother's acid-yellow recliner in the den. Someone tried to turn him aside in the hall, and I heard him brush them off. Daddy burst in with a dishtowel draped over one shoulder. I had never seen him so red-faced, breathing raggedly. I could feel his urge to hit me and I would have bolted but he loomed over the low recliner, jabbing one finger at me and blocking my escape.

Anger choked his voice. 'You – you are more trouble than you're worth. Until you smarten up, I'm finished with you.'

He wheeled and walked out, leaving me stranded at the terminus of childhood. Relieved at first by his exit, I fingered the cool Naugahyde as I began to tremble. What did he mean – was this still my home? Was I really that bad? Yes (that was easy, but the others were older), probably. And how, in practical steps, did one go about smartening up?

There followed a pitched, unspoken war. My father's nebulous word was his bond, and he did not sustain unnecessary conversation with me until after I left his house, more than five years later.

One sullen dinnertime, the salt shaker sat in front of me. One sister after another folded her arms and refused to pass it to my father. Thwarted, he rose and walked around the table to get it himself. Everyone stared at me, with pity and a hint of weariness as if I should give in and move on. Give in how – smarten up how? My father's blueprint lacked a placating reverse gear and, in his home, closure had always been his sole prerogative.

For a while, guests still brought debate to the table. He spoke in front of them, maintaining the carapace of my family's standing in the community. I sometimes sat on the stairs where I could listen while they sang. If I tried to join them without guests present, I thought he might lift his fingers from the piano keys.

I strained to hear an intelligible message in his silence. Finding none, lacking the subtlety to probe for weakness or the sense to run away from home, I fortified myself and fought with the weapons I had. I took a firestarter's glee in trying to make him talk. I withheld every school report for the balance of my education, silently daring him to ask me for the grades that had mattered so much, but he never did. Nothing worked. If he missed me in the aching way that I missed him, he concealed it flawlessly. He never explained what he wanted, and I concluded that he wanted someone else.

They healed over me. My sisters moved out, and the dinner table crowds tapered off. The air of the house grew stale and doughy with loneliness. I traded up through the larger bedrooms as they emptied, until only my parents and I remained in a house far too large for us. They slept on the second floor, and I in the furthest bedroom on the third.

I left home as soon as I finished my high school exams. Mother came up to the attic while I packed for the flight to Toronto. She offered to come to the airport. Her averted eyes told me that he had refused to drive me.

I threw things at the suitcase. She sat at the foot of my bed, stoic and uninvited. She had once sat through David Bowie's *Ziggy Stardust And The Spiders From Mars* with the same posture. When the album was over, she said that she liked the orchestration, although the desperate people made her sad.

Mother unrolled a stocking and poked her finger through a hole in its toe. She cocked her finger and told it that she was thinking of leaving my father, once I left the house.

I stood still, examining the back of her head for clues. Should I stay or go? Ignominiously unable to smarten up, had I brought the roof down on us all? At the nape of her neck where the comb would not reach, her curls were furrowed from the rollers. I never understood why she put rollers in hair that curled naturally.

What do you want from me? I thought at her neck. *What do you want me to say now?*

We had never been the other's first choice. I learned from him, and so I showed her all of his indifference. 'Do what you want, but don't blame it on me.'

Her head jerked as Mother recoiled. Whatever she had expected, it was not that.

I returned to my suitcase, wanting only to get out of the path of falling brick.

My mother did not leave. My leaving obviated hers and for four decades, she enjoyed a very different Act Two. She wore bright colours and wrote comedy. I scarcely knew her. They never came to New Zealand but when I visited Halifax, she repeated that my upbringing was her greatest regret.

When he was ready, my father found his voice. He never explained, and no one required him to. I found myself reading both volumes of Richard Nixon's autobiography on a beach in Mexico, laying the groundwork for a dinner table debate, and I realized that we had recovered.

I applied for law school although I had never wanted to be a lawyer. A few weeks before the 1986 law school semester, I went to Europe. From there, I thought I would talk myself through the law school doors.

Instead, I absconded. From the moment I saw that the world around me – the gritty, tactile, motley, political, unmediated, glut of worlds around me – required nothing more than a one-way ticket; I was on my way to Cambodia.

Chapter 7

New Zealand and Cambodia

Vietnam invaded its neighbour, Cambodia, in 1979. They rescued Cambodians from four years of isolation and butchery at the hands of the Khmer Rouge. Ghoulish testimonies poured forth. Some called the killings auto-genocide, because the definition of genocide assumed there would always be an ethnic or national line to distinguish the genocidaires from the people they killed. People didn't slaughter their own. The Khmer Rouge invented an ideological Other. Then they killed and starved and worked to death one-fifth of their own nation in four years. Maybe a quarter; no one knows. The Western press painted the Khmer Rouge as an inexplicable evil, alien and therefore safely beyond our comprehension.

Finding it most important to punish the Vietnamese, Western states embargoed aid to the grief-stricken Cambodian survivors, even as famine stalked them. Denied our help and far from our headlines, Cambodians continued to suffer and starve, while Western diplomats shook hands with the Khmer Rouge at the United Nations.

The whole of my childhood was outraged by the decontextualized portrait of the Khmer Rouge years. They were not aliens. Both the killers and the killed were the villagers of my childhood. Something had happened, and it was continuing to transpire, because such epic crimes were living structures until people acted to resolve them. We – I – had to understand it, and the survivors would need help.

Cambodia would be my gateway drug.

For some time, I inched around the world like a serendipitous snail. Periodically I surfaced in the long-distance call booth of one Central Post Office or another. When I hung up, I skipped off the map again. Before there were cellphones, AIDS, email or George W. Bush; travel was a permissive, portable privacy. In foreignness, I found the unblighted learning that others found in childhood.

I hitch-hiked around the circumference of New Zealand in 1987, saving the less-travelled, subtropical north for last. On my final morning in the country, the car wound through the coastal villages of Opononi and Omapere, and climbed Pakia Hill. We idled at the summit, poised between its three distinct outlooks. State Highway 8 veered inland through the windscreen, swaying through farming valleys and on to the primordial kauri forest. Through the rear window, the Hokianga Harbour spread itself below us, opening onto the Tasman Sea. Sandhills rose and glittered three hundred feet above the harbour's north shore. Through my passenger window, one unpaved lane hugged the heights of the hills, and vanished around their first fold.

I read the street sign. Newton Road – no exit.

I knew it utterly. I felt the summons of the next bend in that lane, and I heard it in the taffeta waves: *I could live here*. Onward flights abandoned, I shouldered my pack, walked back down the hill to the village, and met my husband.

I immigrated to the Hokianga, but I was drawn irresistibly back to the unsettling questions of Cambodia. New Zealand is the only place where I have wanted to live; Cambodia was the first place where I encountered and learned from my whole-body questions. Back and forth I went, from my new home to my old search. Each time Asia's moist, reagent sun opened all the pores of my skin, I knew I was close.

For a decade after the Khmer Rouge fell, occupied Cambodia remained the world's poorest country, with an annual GDP of $40 US per person. The Western embargo held it down. I came and went through the silent shed of Pochentong Airport. A few antiquated cars lurched around potholes on the unpaved road into the capital city of Phnom Penh. Frangipani bushes lined the road like sweet white ghosts.

Late one afternoon in 1989, I stopped to change money at the illicit street rate of 17 riels to the dollar. The shopkeeper tried to interest me in three triangular sections of *La vache qui rit* cheese in his plexiglass-and-duct-tape display case. In a corner, a wary toddler and his grandmother sat on their heels and stared at something I could not see.

I stepped into the dusk of Achar Mean Boulevard (since renamed Monivong). Its buildings were largely uninhabitable beyond their first floors, and many were still in the act of falling down. Lacking electricity or nutrients to stay awake much beyond dark, people were already settling in for the night. Shadowy figures strung hammocks and spread sleeping mats between eruptions of the concrete sidewalk. Men shifted in their cyclos to sleep at the curb. Although there was no confident supply of food for them yet, a crop of babies and toddlers was sprouting. They were wide-eyed but hushed. Without machinery to hum, all of Phnom Penh was hushed because there was no point in complaining.

I heard rustling nearby, and a man materialized. It was too dark to see his features well. His silhouette used a walking stick, and his gait was older than his story.

'Excuse me,' he said softly in French, 'if you would?'

Sibilance, whispered translations in their cooing language.

'I was studying engineering when Pol Pot drove us out of the city. I worked like a slave.' He paused, freshly bemused by this. 'Twenty hours a day. We dug canals that always fell in. Pol Pot killed my father. Then my mother starved. I have a brother – I had a brother, but I don't know where he is. It's finished for me now. If there would be a university again, I could not afford to study. I repair bicycles by the side of the road.'

I nodded. A few men had squatted at the side of Pochentong Road with bicycle pumps, a roll of tape, or an upturned military helmet for a bucket.

'I don't understand politics. Would you explain, please, why has the world forgotten us? What have we done?'

As they gathered to bathe at the river or to listen to the news on a radio, Phnom Penhois always asked for an explanation they believed I could bring. Sadly, they were wrong. As often as we had the same conversation, I never found a dignified reply.

The French philosopher, Emmanuel Levinas, wrote about 'the epiphany of the face'. How do you take on the endless obligations of one face? How do you look into a face with all the features of your own face, and tell one human being that his children's hunger is rational to others, and newsworthy to no one? The man's question dishonoured me, for I could neither explain nor help. I was driven to be there, yet I was of no more use to him than the indifferent world.

I visited Cambodia for the last time in 1991. I resolved not to return unless I had something of practical value to bring. Without that, I could no longer be a voyeur at human suffering.

***

After my marriage ended, I built my house on that Hokianga hillside, near the end of that unpaved road. There were so many things I had never done! I had never distinguished the birdsongs that made up the sunrise chorus, started a fire, grown my own salad, planted a tree or shot the possum that chewed on it, drawn squares on graph paper to build a house, or caught rainwater from a roof. I named my property Surreal Estate, astonished that anything so beautiful could be my home. I stocked it with a dog, cats, cows for steak and a goat for a lawn mower. I planted trees and trees and trees and trees, and gradually I learned to select and plant species of trees that would flourish on my exposed hillside. I saw how other people formed their standards and resolved their arguments, and the apprehensions of my childhood dissipated.

The South Hokianga was in its heyday, scantily populated by people whose lives were more spacious than structured. The national phone grid had not yet found us. Police travelled our unpaved roads reluctantly. Neighbours relied on neighbours, and the parties went on for days. I felt finally at home.

Mother phoned on a chilly winter morning in June 1993. As I reached for the phone, I saw the low bank of sunrise fog gliding down the harbour. Something cold wrapped itself around my spine. No one called that early with good news.

My father, who still worked and walked to the synagogue at seventy-four, had had a minor heart attack. Mother hastened to assure me that he would be fine. She had driven him to the hospital –

I interrupted. 'You drove him? *You* drove *him* – he let you drive him?'

'Yes, I—'

I didn't hear the rest. It had to be life-threatening. I told mother I was on my way, and I called his hospital. A nurse named Kathy said that the cardiac intensive care unit had no patient phones. She offered to bring him a cellphone, once they had raised his blood pressure to a stable rate. She assured me that he would be fine.

'Kathy,' I implored, shivering so violently that my voice shook, 'please. Believe me. All my life, every time he has been in a room with me, my father's blood pressure has spiked. If you want to raise it now, please bring him this phone. I swear to you, my father will want this phone.'

She did. Sounding tired, he assured me that he was not in pain. Then he cleared his throat. 'So, you and I, we're okay, aren't we?'

'Yes. We are. We're fine, you and I. I'm coming, I'm on my way to the airport. I'll be there in twenty-four hours.'

He died while my plane flew over the Pacific. Gravity sputtered, as if the planets might break free and collide. It had never occurred to me that forces like my father's will could end.

I became a weaver in New Zealand's thriving artisan industry. Kissinger Cat and The Buddha Cat dozed on either side of the loom's treadles, blanketed before lunchtime by glowing threads. Weaving was Zen, and business was fun. Hilltop Handweaver sold across New Zealand, and exported to Australia and Japan. I had no lofty artistic pretensions, but I did have an original eye for colour, and I had a million boisterous greens outside my studio window. Soon I noticed that artisans with finer talent felt less confident about paying their mortgages. In fact, talent weakly predicted business success. Curious, I studied other operations and decided that the real variable was pricing. Either a thousand bits of information had been distilled into a strategy, or they lay scrambled all over the kitchen table. When that happened, breakeven and profitability were anyone's guess.

Neoliberalism gripped New Zealand through the 1990s,

gutting the services available to remote communities like the Hokianga and blaming those worst affected. There being no ready-made jobs, I tried teaching compact, intensive courses for unemployed people to employ themselves. We imagined small businesses backward from straining household budgets, and we calculated the hours and sales and pricing that equated to school uniforms, or a registered car that could be driven on a Thursday when the police came through.

Income gave people choices, autonomy. The vision and design of small businesses (each with its bespoke pricing strategy) became my creative protest.

In 1997, a large marine farm was proposed for our harbour. For much of the year, I neglected my own business to do research for the community's opposition. The applicants withdrew their proposal after a rowdy, acrimonious fight. My partner of four years walked out, accusing me accurately of being unwilling to commit to a second marriage. I lost the dog to a fast-moving brain tumour.

My idyll had been unsettled and my house felt too still, even before I read the advertisement in *The New Zealand Herald*. Rehab Craft, a production NGO, employed eighty people with disabilities. They sought someone with experience in weaving, manufacture and export, business and professional development. In Cambodia. Leaning on my elbows on the kitchen butcher's block, I raised my eyes from the newspaper to tell the omnipresent sandhills, 'There is no need to shout. I'm right here.'

Then I phoned a friend and told her I was going back to Cambodia. Seven years after I had left it, I had something useful to bring. Starting with a VSA stint, I resumed my old enquiry: what happened to the villagers?

***

Rehab Craft's staff had been children under the Khmer Rouge. The men had been child soldiers in various armies. Each of them survived alone and viscerally distrustful, inured to violence but not to humour. Over three years, we made a broke income-generation NGO into a business that would now be called a social enterprise. None of us had done anything like that before.

One afternoon, about a year into our work together, I stood baffled by a whiteboard:

Profit = (income – costs)

It should have been the well-trodden preface to the day's actual topic. Inexplicably, we had run aground. Khmer-language spellings took up so much space with their strings of silent letters that I had drawn the equation. The management team was squirming at images of a vegetable seller with dollars in his pockets and a pyramid of red-circle tomatoes.

I waited. Through my office window, I watched two rats frolic on the sacks of rice in our lunchroom. Last time I'd gotten impatient about sharing our food with rats, someone had brought in a three-metre boa constrictor to consume the rats. Instead, it ate up all the little white bunnies that we were breeding for sale. Then it settled down beneath my desk to digest them and wait for me. I found it there, loudly. It took two men to coax it out and bear it away. Since then, I had learned to wait more philosophically for unforced solutions.

At length, one man spoke up and asked to be drawn with the tomatoes.

'Excuse me?'

He explained as patiently as when he edited my Khmer spellings. 'I sold vegetables in the market. You put my inventory way over there. That's not the way – I would never leave my inventory. I slept beside my inventory.'

I inspected the tomatoes, until I heard it.

Duggaduggadugga: algebra! There was more than one way to write a business equation.

I juggled the elements of the equation to place him with his inventory. And then I erased the whole board, muttering in Khmer, and began to draw again.

'My mistake. You're right! I drew – that was a Western kind of business. We would call it capitalist—' I composed in Khmer for a moment and then flapped my arms, '—never mind. Now let me draw a Cambodian business. That's what you were trying to tell me. Here – see?' I surrounded the business owner with faces instead of static dollars. 'Family business doesn't put profit in its pocket, does it? That's not what it's for. Cambodian business succeeds by employing more relatives. That's its purpose, it profits by supporting more family. That's what you were trying to tell me, right? Income minus expenses equals employment.'

We visually transplanted the sample business to Cambodia. Then we drew our own business, which also existed to maximize employment. By configuring the business around its aims, we drew our first social enterprise, long before any of us had heard the term. We learned to weigh management decisions in units of employment.

One man was an especially astute reader of our volatile building. After three years of work and trust, he walked into my office on a steamy afternoon. He smoothed his pants and, *a propos* of nothing in particular, told me a story that could only have been told by a Khmer Rouge soldier. A civilian would not have had that experience, in those years.

We sat in thick silence. Outside, the songbirds napped.

I strained for some other explanation. For twenty years, I had been insisting that the Khmer Rouge were not aliens. They had to come from somewhere – but they didn't have to be him! I negotiated – they could be a *little* alien. I studied his face for any tic that would distinguish the Khmer Rouge killer from the man I knew. I would have given anything to find some other face responsible for murder.

He smiled and waited for me to catch up. When I did, when I let my head droop and looked back up at him with Daddy-after resignation, he resumed.

He said he had volunteered, left his family at the age of fourteen and walked into the jungle to join the Khmer Rouge. He went in search of something to admire, and he found a discipline to which he could belong. He escaped the humiliating, disproportionate power that was killing Cambodia's villagers unreachably from the skies. He fought until the country was theirs.

'And then?' I swallowed hard. All those skulls. He was going to make me say it. 'Did you . . . did you do the things that I associate with the Khmer Rouge?'

'I did what everyone did, until I became an amputee. Then I couldn't do soldiers' things anymore.'

Survivors spoke with undiminished remorse about their inability to protect the people they loved. Yet my friend was at ease. We talked for a long time.

I asked, 'Would you do it again – or, what if your son wanted to fix politics with violence?'

He frowned and thought out loud. 'If my son wanted to go into the jungle because he felt humiliated by being weak . . . being called beggars because we are poor . . . being treated like children because we are disabled . . . if he went because of the corruption . . . I could not stop him. I could tell him that it doesn't work, but that would not stop him.'

He was the root I had refused to unearth. His killing was as human as the dying – and that, I believe, is why he told me.

Chapter 8

Gaza Strip, 2012

When I first arrived in Israel, I had waited in Jerusalem for the permits to enter Gaza. A Jerusalem newspaper editor passed me on the terrace of the Ambassador Hotel. He called an acquaintance to ask what Joan Garson was doing in East – Palestinian – Jerusalem.

Although she wasn't in Israel just then, my sister travelled to Israel several times each year for meetings. I left Gaza to visit with her in February 2012. She was a semi-stranger with a crisply labelled Judaism. I was unable to define my own Judaism at all. It was just there.

'Are you a Zionist?' she asked me.

I swirled the wine around my glass as if splashes could be read. 'Last time I heard that word, it was a secular way to be a Jew. Now it's this combustible settler-messianic thing, some kind of zero-sum battle for square inches. I'm not that, if that's what it means, but Israel has always been a part of me.'

It satisfied neither of us. Zionism was, she explained presciently, one of those things that you had to declare.

I brooded into the hotel mirror, later that night. I had not lived within reach of a synagogue since I left Canada, and I had spent more time in the company of Muslims than Jews. What did that make me? I could not even be a lapsed Jew, because I had no practice from which to lapse.

In Gaza, I began to hunt for Judaism by night. Lacking any theological starting point, I searched the keywords of my anchoring principles. I winced each time I downloaded, fearing other eyes on my email. No keystroke in Gaza went unrecorded. I read by my windows, and then by rechargeable lantern. Some read beneath my blankets, trying to ignore the wind.

A footnote led me to Maimonides' taxonomy of charity. In twelfth century, Maimonides had assigned the greatest value actions which gave others the means to support themselves. I had never thought of my work as Jewish work. Then I found Avraham Joshua Heschel, the rabbi who could be seen marching with the Reverend Martin Luther King Jr in Selma, Alabama. Someone had castigated him for leaving his synagogue to join the protest for others' civil rights. Heschel had replied, 'When I marched in Selma, I was praying with my feet.'

I found ethical principles that I regarded as scaffolding. They told me what Jews should do, but what was the structure within that scaffolding – what really made one a Jew?

On a calm night between storms, I began to read about Prophetic Judaism. The prophets placed an unfinished social and political project above ritual. They told people to do more than just pray. Justice, they said, was divine and God's covenant was its performance bond. Their Judaism was the portable practice of a dispersed minority. They critiqued power and exhorted the community to protect vulnerable people.

I had been searching for something proscriptive rather than aspirational, something that would make me balk even as it made me a better person. Instead, I heard the unmistakeable sound of our back screen door swinging shut behind my father. I heard my mother's humane interjections into our shouted debates.

I felt the tingle of stepping into a cool, flowing brook. Its current had been flowing right past me. I had turned away from the questions raised by the Intifada. I could not reconcile my understanding of Jewishness with the inequities of occupation and my bedrock belief in the indivisible value of life. The Prophets spoke from that bedrock: Judaism was my source. When I understood that, I saw that I could rejoin its current. My current.

'Who knew?' I admitted to the fishermen's lights through my window. 'All this time. I came to Gaza as a Jew, after all.'

I doodled marginalia in my journal by lamplight, and clicked my pen nervously. What happened when a dispersed people recovered their specific place, and when a minority enjoyed majoritarian power? If we were instructed to love the stranger and care especially for the powerless, then what was a Jewish occupation?

There, I deliberately closed my notebook for the night, turned off the lamp and went to bed. I had uncovered an object of beauty. I did not want to lose it again.

My study widened the contradictions around me. I found a social ethic that I had to hide. Even as my team accepted what they knew of me, I withheld identifying information from them. I lied to them by omission. I had to decline many of their weekend invitations because they lacked the facts to consent to the risk of me. If I spent time in their homes, with their children, they would be less able to disavow me later. So I mumbled excuses, and they always looked down and said politely that they understood. Seeing them downcast and hurt, I promised myself that I would tell them on my final day.

They searched for information that I wanted them to find. Rasha slipped into my office on a warm spring day, smiling victoriously. She held out a printed copy of a Khmer-language booklet that I had written in the 1990s.

I ran my finger along the lines and read, '*P'kot p'kong kluon aing* – it means to support yourself. What a relic! This was the handbook for a workshop about micro-business. Where did you dig this up?'

'I found it on the internet. We're interested in anything about you.'

If Rasha could not connect me to my sister online, then I told myself wryly that I was safe.

One Gazan did know. We were sipping tea late one afternoon in my flat, feeling small before a sea of milky foam on steely ultramarine. My subterfuge sat between us until I blurted out the truth.

My visitor was incensed, glancing at the front door as if the battering ram had already struck once. 'Are you crazy? There are people here . . . there are crazy people here. Do you have any idea what they would do to you?'

I blanched.

Months later, the same person asked casually if I had a religion.

They paused, remembered and lowered their voice. 'Oh yeah. I guess I forgot. Huh,' they wondered at it.

I felt an urge to giggle. 'You forgot?'

'Yeah. I guess it didn't matter.'

***

In August 2012, the shadow of Afghanistan withdrew. Outside my windows, the pixelated sea sprang into a sharpened sunlight. I craved colour. I longed to walk. I spent a weekend in Paris, drinking in the life and the motion of the abstracts in the Pompidou. I stood a long time in front of a Jasper Johns painting of the number 5, agreeing with a stranger that it was the most replete, self-satisfied 5 we'd ever seen. I sent emails to friends from a bench in the gallery, telling them I was finished with war. I had already extended my Mercy Corps contract for the second and final time. Beyond that, I saw no way to launch an enterprise in Gaza's blockaded logistics.

A fellow social entrepreneur invited me to apply for his job in Cambodia, and I did.

Hurry, I wished at them. I didn't want to see what was coming.

A year earlier, the IDF and Gaza's militant factions had exchanged fire three or four times each day. By October 2012, the daily average had risen to eleven. After each spate, the militaries allowed Egypt to intercede and usher them back. Thus far, they were playing chicken.

In Gaza, it was a core competency of occupation to subdue that knowledge, normalize that deterioration, and keep moving. We awoke to explosions and cancelled our plans more often. Week by week, some people grew more solicitous, while others tried more imperiously to control any aspect of their lives. As a group, my team tried to savour normalcy. We sucked slowly on melting chocolates, and inhaled Hani's fragrant coffee. We remembered to say 'goodbye, dears!' at the end of each day.

'Daddy, what is that lady doing?' a child's voice cut like a piccolo through the gloom of our vegetable shop.

Marjie, my Mercy Corps colleague, frowned at the two bananas in her palm, and seemed to doubt herself.

The girl's father smiled an apology over her head. He took her hand, knelt down and replied in the English of a teachable moment, 'She is buying two bananas. That is her culture. We are Palestinian, and our culture is hospitality. We feel polite when our table is covered with food, even more food than we need. This lady's culture tells her never to waste food. She is politely buying only what she needs. She is leaving the rest of the bananas for us! We should thank the lady.'

We left them exploring cultural tolerance in full sentences. I thought of them often as we dawdled to war.

The firing spiked again on November 9. I downloaded *Natural Born Killers* to camouflage the noise. Then I left my phone (and therefore my security texts) mute, burrowed into bed and slept soundly through 49 rockets, 11 air strikes and 9 tank shells.

In the morning, Randa and I slipped out to visit the housewares factory that bought recycled plastic from the women of Beit Lahiya. An Islamic Jihad rocket had fallen short overnight, and descended through the factory's roof. It left a hole in the roof, but it held no explosives and no one had been hurt.

Working horse-carts outnumbered cars along the roads. Gazans were staying near their families. If people had to leave home, they hastened through the streets with pursed lips.

Egypt stitched one more ceasefire together.

Families flocked to the beach on Wednesday, November 14 to enjoy a sunny midweek holiday. I threw my windows open to the warmth and the sound of the road. The owners of the Shalehat hall had just painted diagonal parking lines along the length of their curb. Ever polite, Gazans left the white-striped field pristine. They parallel-parked beyond the ends of the painted lines, cramping Beach Road traffic into an even narrower lane. I enjoyed the traffic jam for a few minutes, did the housework and drafted some documents for Wasim to find when he returned from his wedding leave.

I stepped onto the treadmill at mid-afternoon, turned up the volume of my iPod, and ran with my eyes fixed on the frilly, azure sea. I stepped down an hour later, perplexed to find the beach and the road deserted. I swung my head along the length of my windows: no one. Beach Road had never been empty in daylight before. The skin prickled on the back of my neck as I reached for the BBC.

Israel had assassinated the head of Hamas's military. Hamas had sworn that the killing would open the gates of hell.

Israel had not mobilized its reserves and the afternoon had gone silent. I thought in terms of retaliation, not war. Hostages – Hamas's perpetual threat and Israel's phobia – were a likely retaliation. The sweat chilled against my back, as I wondered if I would be one of them. I squinted through the peephole in my door, and I wondered if they would knock. I didn't dare endanger a Gazan by calling them. Instead, I busied myself doing useful things. I showered, packed a bag. Positive that any Gazan mother's son would allow a fifty-year-old woman to bring her purse into captivity. I put a comb into my purse, and I pulled out my Kindle.

It stopped me. I scrolled through the archive which revealed and incriminated me, and I glanced at my doorway again. I could delete the Jewish books and be left with an enquiring, non-denominational library. My hand hovered, but I couldn't do it. Deleting books was repugnant, and somehow more frightening than the prospect of accounting for them. At least I could account in my own voice. Without my books, I would become a stranger.

Better, as Joseph Conrad wrote, to be faithful to the nightmare of one's choosing. I had chosen this. If they came for a Jew, they would find one. I slotted the Kindle back into my purse, and turned up the news on the hour.

The IDF had struck around thirty initial targets. Israel called it the opening salvo of a wider assault, and began to call up their reserves. Then I understood that a war had begun, and my thoughts turned outward.

Palestinians would be out visiting for the holiday. Wasim had been married only two weeks. Ibrahim's wife was seven months pregnant. I hardly knew our six new team members.

Not now, I thought. *Not today*!

The planes closed in with the night. Each time one engine disengaged from the chorus overhead, I held my breath and tracked it across the ceiling.

My windows had blast film, but Afghanistan had left me with a persistent fear of flying glass. I opened the windows a little, to make it less likely that glass would blow inward. Still, I wanted something solid between myself and my windows. I made a little burrow within my heavy, chest-height kitchen bar. I plugged in all of my electronic devices, to charge them while the electricity lasted. I set each device to a news feed. Cursing the Hamas facility next door, I jammed the car keys into my pocket. I popped popcorn – Garson comfort food – for dinner, and wondered where to go if they attacked the Hamas compound. By the bottom of the bowl, I had not thought of a single refuge in the Gaza Strip that would not be adjacent to some kind of target.

A bomb detonated just up the road. My building shuddered. Fourteen floors up, it lurched and corrected more than I would have guessed. My stomach followed it like a pendulum. Then my chest constricted, because Randa lived a few blocks inland. I went to the windows and leaned out, feeling as quaint as a housewife checking her birdfeeder, but I stared into solid blackness.

In Gaza, the bombs had names on them. Berating myself for not thinking of it sooner, I opened a list of my team's addresses, and I plotted our new colleagues' homes in my mind.

Light blinked in, then *crrr-ump* with a syncopated echo. Through my sea-side windows, the Israeli navy began to shell Beach Camp; a thickly ingrown, urban refugee camp north of my building. Beach Camp had no weapons to return the fire.

Crrr-ump-rrrump. Crrr-ump-rrrump.

I looked at my phone because it was instinctive to call for help, but who would make this stop? The sky was filled with busy, dispassionate lights and the roofs of Beach Camp erupted in bursts of firelight.

The bombing of Beach Camp worked like aversion therapy. Every last bit of my sneaking, subcutaneous pride of ownership drained away, because it took no courage to fire explosives into a refugee camp at night. Abruptly, I left the window and slapped the car keys back onto the bar. 'Target' meant nothing in Gaza. There was nowhere to drive.

I opened Skype and found my team, Skyping through the first night of a war. Social media was their assembly point. People joined the conversation when the violence lulled in their neighbourhood. They announced their survival, read their colleagues' updates, and cheered each other unselfconsciously. It fortifies me to care for you, they seemed to say.

Hani was distracting his children by teaching them to dance to the distinctive backbeat of the naval bombardment. Randa and her two boys were safe with an uncle, although their apartment up the road no longer had windows. Ibrahim was shepherding his family from room to room, keeping as many walls as possible between his pregnant wife and small son, and the bombs that were falling on Khan Younis.

Not seeing my name, they had assumed that the internationals had been evacuated. When I signed in, they asked about the mood in Jerusalem. I wrote that I didn't know, because I was at home in Beirut Tower.

Instantly, the two nearest men offered to leave their families and come for me. They could be downstairs in three and ten minutes respectively, to bring me to their homes for the duration of the war. One of the men had enduring professional differences with me, yet he urged me to join his family. No one, he wrote, should be alone in a war. I thanked him many times, then and later.

I left Skype open after that.

I sat and waited for the planes to fire. Mine was the view of the fish in the barrel, waiting to be shot by incomprehensible weapons, with nothing to do but flap its stupid fins and look up. My light fixtures trembled each time the planes flew low. Dots of chandelier light jiggled on my ceiling in a way that recalled my family's dinner table.

When they explained their wars, Israeli civilians spoke of listening anxiously for the sound of the warning siren. It gave them only seconds to dash to the nearest shelter before a rocket fell. They said they had to be perpetually aware of the steps to their nearest shelter.

In Gaza, there were no sirens and there were no shelters. There were no seconds; there were everlasting hours. I sat and watched my light fixtures, I listened to the jet engines, and I waited. I had always read about asymmetry as a relative measure of strength. Sitting and waiting for the planes to drop their bombs at will, I learned that asymmetry was absolute. It meant being defenceless every damned time.

The Israeli planes circled and circled. They took their time because they had the luxury of time, and because they knew that protracted anticipation compounded the punishment. Why else did the IDF bomb at night, when they were perfectly safe in daylight? Darkness exacerbated children's fears. It impeded the rescue of survivors, and deprived everyone of sleep.

When they bombed near enough for me to guess the neighbourhood that had been struck, I consulted my address list. Then I sat glued to Skype, until that person checked in, alive. For all the other bombs, I had only to close my eyes. Seeing Gaza's conurbation behind my eyelids, I knew that each bomb was inscribed with someone's name.

***

Another rocket launched from our right. Parked at the edge of a neighbourhood known as Rocket City, Marjie and I nodded sagely at each other. In theory, the NGO security office was evacuating the foreign staff of agencies which had no emergency response role. In fact, the morning had not gone well.

Around thirty of us had mustered in the UNRWA parking lot in the centre of Gaza City. Our instructions were simple: drive fast and don't stop. Unfortunately, our convoy included one fellow who had snubbed all contact with international organizations on principle, until he needed rescuing that morning.

'What if someone shoots out a tire?' he asked the convoy's UNDSS security lead, Vlad.

'Drive on three.'

'What if the person sitting next to me gets shot?'

'Drive faster! I'll be there with first aid at Erez. Do you understand – I mean, generally, right? If someone is shooting at you? You want to keep moving, don't you?' Vlad glanced around for validation, his ruddy complexion turning a deeper red. If this stranger lacked the sense to drive away from a person who was shooting at him, what else might he not know?

Marjie prodded me with her elbow. 'In this man's dream, who, exactly, is doing the shooting?'

Undeterred, the man asked, 'What if the driver's dead?'

Vlad crossed his arms and spoke with menacing, idiot slowness. 'Roll him out of the way – out of the *way*, not out of the *car*, get it? – and drive the car yourself. Right? Would you like me to show you how to drive?'

We sped to Erez, and no one fired as much as a dirty look toward us. Then we parked our column of soft-skin vehicles in a wide open area, midway between two belligerent armies, because no one could contact a Hamas official senior enough to consent to our departure. Everyone that senior was safely underground with his phone turned off, to avoid Israeli hacking and detection.

Voices rose into a shouting match outside the cars, while from the cellphone in Marjie's lap, a senior colleague's voice squawked advice from Jerusalem, 'Run! They won't really shoot – run!'

Marjie muted the sound and massaged her temples.

A half hour passed before the convoy retrenched to its curb at the edge of Beit Hanoun. The rockets launched with gusto around us until we sped back to the UNRWA compound in Gaza City.

There, Robert Turner, UNRWA's Gaza Director, strode past on long legs. He took the exterior stairs to the security office several at a time. Two Close Protection officers loped behind. He froze on the landing, startled to see us snacking in his canteen garden, hours after we had been dispatched. Bob Turner took it well. He counted – forty or so, by then – scratched his head but appeared to conclude that his questions did not matter, and extended his hands like a slow-motion stop sign.

'Wait here,' he said, unnecessarily, and dashed away.

My niece texted from Israel that our convoy was poised on the cusp between urban legend and breaking news.

I could see the sidebar behind my closed eye. In The Middle Of More Important Things, Hamas Holds World Zionist Org Sis. I gave my niece a single family talking point: not-leaving did not equate to being detained by Hamas. I was not being detained. I was eating pretzels.

We set off for the border again around 3.00 in the afternoon. Gazans rested on their stoops in the lowering sun. Their faces showed resentment, amusement, weariness, boyish bravado and mild disgust at our third, ignominious, high-speed passage of the day. This time, we trotted shamefacedly though the tunnel and reached Israel at dark. Photographers waited for us in the Erez terminal. I spun on my heels, raised a hand to my hairline and skirted around them.

Oxfam's minibus would not be sufficient for the column of people straggling toward it. Three of us apologetically commandeered the back seat of the only taxi in the parking lot. We gave the taxi's original passenger the whole front seat, and we paid his fare. I knew him slightly, a middle-aged Gazan businessman.

'They won't let me back in,' he said dejectedly, kneading his hands. 'Too late in the day. I've got to get back to my family.'

The first rows of tanks silenced us. Dozens of tank hulls lined the verges of the highway to Jerusalem, all pointing at Gaza.

Chapter 9

Israel bombed and fought a second, message war. The IDF dropped 200,000 leaflets over Gaza, warning people to stay away from all places of militant operations – a physical nonsense in walled, interspersed Gaza. Tens of thousands of phone calls followed, and text messages that drove people this way and that ahead of assaults that might or might not materialize.[18] The messages stoked fear and confusion. Once they had issued warnings, the IDF treated neighbourhoods as if they were empty of civilians. They regarded all remaining Palestinians as combatants. After each war, human rights reporting would protest the illegality of their tactics.

Hamas fired rockets and ordered Gazans not to answer the IDF's calls.

For seven leaden days, I lived through my phone, fed it spare batteries, stared at it, slept by it and woke to consult it. We scooped our new hires into the team by phone. Wasim phoned around each morning, and Randa called to buoy everyone's spirits before the nightly bombings. Those daily proofs of life became my fetish. I waited on tenterhooks to hear that all seventeen were well, and I chased anyone who had not been found. Once everyone had been accounted for, I sat at my desk and waited to be texted by anyone who felt like talking. Then I called them back, and I rambled with the phone through the olive grove outside Mercy Corps' office, until they had talked enough.

18 For more detail, see the *Report of the United Nations High Commissioner for Human Rights*, A/HRC/22/35/Add.1, https://www.ohchr.org/Documents/HRBodies/HRCouncil/RegularSession/Session22/A.HRC.22.35.Add.1_AV.pdf (accessed April 2, 2019).

The newlyweds were blasting music videos on the stereo they had been given as a wedding gift. It played loud enough to rival the noise of the bombs.

A man who lived near the prison watched the prisoners file out to care for their families. 'They'll be back,' he assured me. 'They have no way out of Gaza either.'

Randa was unhoused a second time. She reasoned that she would be safest with a relative who lived near a hospital. No one would bomb near a hospital.

A colleague went to buy milk for his children. He returned to claw through the rubble of his neighbours' home, hunting for the remains of eleven members of the Aldalou family.

A few people missed their morning calls while they were escorting relatives across the Strip, positioning them so that the family unit might survive the destruction of any one home.

At the ends of the days, I ran mechanically on the hotel treadmill. I counted off the fuggy swamp-time of long-haul airplanes, and tried to imagine distributing my sisters' children among the targets, and living with the consequences.

Everyone knew that the bombing would end when Obama and other leaders required it to end. They were slow. Hiding behind language, states egged on an attack against Hamas as if that were something other than bombing Gaza's neighbourhoods.

Day by day, my team's voices grew wearier. Doubt slipped in with fatigue. Our calls shortened as their electricity dwindled. I got sick of repeating platitudes. Inadequate truths. I wanted to throw the phone away but I could not let it go.

Randa phoned, agitated, while I was walking down the steep, gravelly cut beneath the Middle East Quartet's compound.

'I can't do it!' she panted. 'I'm too tired. Only I have two hands!'

I skidded on the scree and pitched forward without letting go of the phone. Lying on the ground, I listened with the phone clamped to my ear. The planes were striking near the hospital, making her third shelter unsafe. Randa had two small boys and four bags, all needing to be carried. She blurted until she had caught her breath enough to keep moving. Then she ran.

I rolled onto my back, too drained to sit up. I traced the tattered edges of clouds with the corner of my phone, wishing for a word more futile, more thuggish and intimate than 'war'. War was the purposeful campaign of armies. This was just violence, battery with a foregone conclusion.

The following day, the IDF prepared to invade Gaza by road. I read their declarations at my desk, breathing through the nausea that rose with the memory of the ominous rows of tanks. I could hear the crunch of the tank treads, and it sounded like the grinding of bones.

Randa called again. She had slept a little during the morning, and spent hours answering her boys' questions about the war. Yet she cut me off curtly. 'Don't worry about me – but you must call to Hani. He won't ask you this. He thinks it's decided. You have to call to him, right now.'

I got up from my desk and went outside while she explained that Hani's home sat along one of the IDF invasion corridors. The streets around him were filling with people, abandoning everything they owned and hurrying toward the centre of the city. UNRWA was opening emergency shelters to receive those who had nowhere else to go. A ground assault was imminent, and Hani stood squarely in its path. He had refused to leave. If they invaded, Hani would be one of those people the IDF treated as a combatant. Hani and his children.

'He refuses to move,' Randa repeated, spacing her words. I pictured her, leaning intently forward. 'Do you understand? He has to move. His children are there.'

'I'll call him.'

'If the Israelis get in, Hani's house will be a hill.'

'I'll move him,' I said more decisively. 'You look after your boys. I'll move Hani.'

Our morning host was a proud man being told to surrender, and a father being bullied in front of his children. Hani would be digging in his heels. I texted him, and I called after he replied that he did want to speak. Exhausted beyond sentences, he vowed to defend his home.

'I will fight—'

I said, 'I know that you would. I know. But your children are there with you.'

'Let them see—'

'No-no, please, don't think that way. Please move, Hani. Move for your children. It has nothing to do with being afraid, it's for your children and for us. We care about you, and we think you're in danger.'

'I'm not afraid.'

'I know, but we are.' I swallowed a lump. 'I am. I am very much afraid for you. You must get your children out of the house, in case . . .' Drifting between the olive trees, I braced one elbow against my hip bone, and rested my forehead on my fingertips. 'You can always go back, if you decide that you must. But please, please bring your children out in case they invade. Okay? Bring your children to a safe – er, a safer place.'

Hani let out a troubled breath, while I held mine. What did I know? What was I making him do?

I shook my head and pressed for the one action that had to be right, 'Bring your children out of the path of the army.'

'Okay – but I will – wait—' I heard snatches of Arabic, too muffled and rapid for me to understand beyond the word for 'house'. Hani spoke in a rush. 'My neighbour – they called – his house—'

'Oh Hani, go. You have to go now!' We had all heard reports that the IDF warning times were very brief. Both of our voices rose.

'No! It's too late. F16s – not my children, not in the street!'

'But they can see you in the street – they will not see you in the house! Go – go where they can see you!'

His voice jerked as he ran. 'Ten minutes – less – I will call – wait for me—'

I balanced in mid-stride, as if any movement might change his mind. I held my phone directly before my eyes for news of Hani's safe arrival.

It happened so suddenly, and then it was quiet enough to hear the breeze swishing through the long-haired olive trees. Trees? I blinked at the trees and back at the phone. What did I know, to be issuing orders from Jerusalem? I wasn't there. Where was he?

Had I pushed him into the path of the airplanes?

It was his home. Who was I to tell him not to fight for it?

Ten minutes passed.

Would the walls of his house have protected him?

Twelve minutes.

I scrolled through headlines and texts that threatened invasion. I found nothing from Hani's neighbourhood. My hands began to tremble. It was taking too long.

Why did the whole Middle East lack my Western, literal sense of time? Everything here was ten minutes.

Why were West Bankers so eager to fight to the last Gazan?

Why did the world egg this on?

Had I been wrong?

Why wasn't I there?

Where was he?

Twenty minutes.

I walked myself deliberately out of the grove and back to the row of parked office cars. From there, I could see the Old City with everyone's sacred places. I begged for anyone's god to save him.

He called after twenty-three minutes. I laid the phone on the boot of a car, put it on speaker, and crumpled forward over it. I spoke between heaving breaths as if I, too, had been running for my life.

Hani had arrived at his sister's door, only to find her holding another leaflet in her hand. She, too, had been ordered to abandon her family's home. Now a larger and slower group of three generations, they would have to move yet again. The streets were clotted and chaotic, the afternoon nearly over.

Hani was whispering. 'Not one more step – not until I sleep—'

We agreed to talk in the morning.

I lingered on the office hillside, weak-kneed and weepy with subsiding adrenaline. At the base of this very hill, the stony Old City had withstood total wars. Siege had deprived people of water and food and light. They were shunted with their children through the streets ahead of invasion.

No, I shook my head; this was not medieval. In Gaza, I moved among individuals, but from my Jerusalem elevation, I could see that the Gaza blockade belonged to the new wars rather than the old. Israeli strategy lumped all of Gaza into a single enemy object. Hamas blurred into Gaza, and two million human beings became one biopolitic. The Gaza blockade mobilized the land, air, sea;

the built environment and limited natural resources; the humans and their economy, information, and communications; the robots and the data; all of it to dominate a battle space.

Indeed, this was not purposeful war. This was total, endless, futuristic conflict management.

US Secretary of State Hillary Clinton arrived in the region, and a ceasefire was announced for 9.00 pm on November 21. In my hotel room, I watched the news channels pan around Gaza's quiet skyline. I wondered how long to withhold my belief.

At 9.14, Ibrahim Skyped, 'Congratulations!'

I let my breath out. 'Happy ceasefire!'

All the names began to pop up.

Two Israeli soldiers and four civilians were dead. The bombing had killed 174 Palestinians, 55 of them civilians.[19] Nothing else changed, because change had never been at stake.

Not long after, the team's bachelor wrote to declare that he would seek an engagement as his way of affirming life after the war.

19 https://en.wikipedia.org/wiki/Operation_Pillar_of_Defense (accessed April 1, 2019). The number of Palestinian combatant casualties is always disputed. Wikipedia's chart of casualties illustrates this well. I have used Palestinian figures.

Chapter 10

I drove back to Gaza with the head of the office, and kilos of brightly wrapped chocolate wafers. Our narrow hallway pressed everyone together. People embraced and smiled tearfully into their friends' faces, and then trailed after each other from room to room, to hug once more.

Every strong-fingered woman took a turn easing Randa's bruised shoulders, although Randa could not sit still for long. She bounced up from her chair to locate Laila every few minutes. The radio news had used the name of Laila's apartment building as a proxy for her neighbourhood. Each time they reported that the neighbourhood had been bombed, Randa heard the name of Laila's building. She heard the words that would have announced her friend's death, and she felt the possibility of that loss every time.

Hani scuffed through the litter of chocolate wrappers at mid-morning, bearing a stack of pizza boxes for breakfast. We ate our way through the whole day.

The very next morning, I leaned out of my apartment window, aghast. Three units of Hamas had fanned out across the beach like invading lobsters, doing push-ups with their feet in the tide. Up and down Beach Road, the runners' full-throated chant sounded gloating. Hamas was basking in the approval that any community shows its defenders.

I was fuming at all the armies. I did not equate their roles, or their options, or the extent of the actual violence they inflicted. Still I seethed at the unreachable pilots and the leaders of Hamas who hid underground; at Israel for choosing to wage war in the cities among civilians, and at the world leaders who winked and turned away. None of them had protected my colleagues, and neither had I. And already on that beach, before anyone could catch their breath, they were training for more.

***

Randa and I drove to Beit Lahiya. We found the elderly Ghabins in front of their tiny cottage. They matched, both stout and dressed in starched white shirts, both seated on white plastic chairs at the edge of their lane. They did not budge when our car passed within inches of their knees. They did not stand up or greet us as we walked around the car. Even when we stood with them, Mrs. Ghabin could not unclench her fingers from the arms of her chair. She was shocked beyond hospitality, staring out of a waxy face. Her husband tipped his head diagonally, issuing us into their house.

Inside, the walls were engraved with deep fissures. The roof sat overhead, despite having parted company with the walls. The window and door frames were parallelograms, but no longer rectangles. I backed out on my tiptoes, before a breath of wind could knock the thing down.

Mr. Ghabin followed us with his eyes. Those plastic chairs might have been the most solid things the Ghabins had left.

I pointed across my body and then at him. 'You were . . .?'

He nodded fractionally although I don't believe he spoke English and I could not recall a word of Arabic.

Beyond the Ghabins, not ten metres from the wall of their home, two craters had churned the dirt and tossed their scrubby fruit trees aside. Squinting into the craters, I tried to imagine the ear-splitting noise, the stagger of a house coming unglued. Like a sea of small tragedies, the fields and side yards of Beit Lahiya were riddled with such craters.

A few kilometres away, the Rajebs stared into a crater the size of a pond. Tatters of plastic fluttered up. Of their greenhouse, only a twisted rebar sculpture remained, knotted around twenty thousand citrus trees. Fifteen families had shared the nursery business, and their trees were ten weeks short of maturity.

Hugging himself in a thick sweater, the elder Mr. Rajeb confided to Randa, 'It would have been better if they bombed the house. That way, at least, we would have some income to recover. Now . . .'

Still they filled our hands with clementines. Leaning against the car before we left, Mr. Rajeb rubbed his whiskers and absently ushered his sons forward with more. They heaped clementines in our laps, while Randa listed the factories which would buy and recycle what was left of the plastic greenhouse covers.

Winter storms would catch the Rajebs and the Ghabins and their neighbours standing in lines for the materials to replace their windows, greenhouse covers, cooking oil and rice, and the thousands of home-industry chickens and rabbits that had died of fright from the noise of the bombs.

A few days later, I listened from the wading pool, hiding my worry behind Moo Cow. Sunny Wasim had joked about killing an irritating colleague. Ibrahim repeated words three times with his new stutter.

Randa talked about leaving Gaza, and then dismissed her own words with a crooked grin, 'But I won't do it. A few days – I say this every time.'

She exhaled slowly, parcelled out spaces precisely with her hands and gazed into each space while she spoke. 'I spent . . . every minute . . . knowing exactly where they were. They were not allowed to go away from me. Not ever, not where I could not reach them with my hand. You know how hard that is for little boys? I was very hard with them. In the last hour? Before the ceasefire? I would not let them go separately to the bathroom. The last hour is always bad and I could not stand to lose them right at the end. Every minute, I knew it was this far . . . or this far . . . but . . .' She cautioned us with one finger. '. . . but, I kept asking myself, if the bomb comes now, do I grab this one or that one? Which one do I save?'

She waited for an answer, because the question had never been rhetorical. 'They're too big now, I can't carry them both. Tell me which one to save.'

I swallowed hard and thought how different the boys' hair was, one with unruly curls and one straight. 'But you did. You got them both through the war. You protected them both, and they will know that's why you were strict. And what did you tell them? How did you explain?'

Rasha had been sitting dreamily, with her chin on her folded arms. She sat up to answer, with a nod to the others. 'We discussed it together. This is not easy to explain. Just we want our children to know that they have a right to live in their homeland, but we don't want them to grow up feeling anger and hatred. I said to my girls that Gaza is full of good people. But we have an angry government. On the other side of the wall, Israel is like that, too. There are good people there – and they asked me questions about Israel. "Do they have this and do they have that? Is it as good as ours?" But, I told them, in Israel there is also a very angry government. When the angry governments fight, everyone is afraid. But the angry governments will fall. We must not hate, or we might forget how to live together. We are refugees from our home, but all humans deserve to live in peace and with dignity, regardless of their religion. What do you think, is that a good explanation?'

'I think you're wise, and very generous,' I said.

'Thank you. It was easier when they were smaller. It's getting more difficult to answer their questions.'

Ibrahim asked me what I thought of my twenty-four hours of Gazan war, by comparison with others.

I frowned, and I folded my arms over Moo Cow. 'I've heard loud noises before. But I have never thought of war this way. Two armies stand still and throw two completely different scales of explosives at each other's people. The weapons on that side are big, and the civilians on this side are locked in. It's madness. There is no purpose, and there is no change. Still those walls. I want—' Rasha was pointing at my stomach. When I glanced down, I saw that I was pulling Moo Cow's ears. I let them go, and straightened his spectacles, '—I want a different word for it. When people hear the word "war", they won't think of this.'

They looked affirmed.

'It's egregious,' I concluded, using our insiders' code for bureaucracy.

Next to the remaining chocolate wafers on my desk, I kept a box of tissues. Nearly a week after the ceasefire, one mother stole in and closed the door. Her eyes were still on high alert, too round, and her hijab was carelessly pinned.

Her house had been destroyed in the previous invasion, and she said that she had faced this war nearly inconsolable with the prospect of her next loss. Each time she saw pictures of dead and dying children on the news, she began to see her own children. She saw them in detail; dead, reduced to found pieces, or horribly wounded and screaming in pain.

Kneading her tissues, she let tears roll down her face. Then she excoriated herself in a low, growling voice for being so selfish. She tore the tissue and I reached for her free hand.

'Oh no-no! I don't think you're selfish, not at all. It sounds like you were actually feeling each family's pain.'

'But I made it about me,' she whispered, shuddering and gripping my hand. 'Something is wrong with me. I should have been grieving with all my heart for the other parents, only for them. Honestly, I was crying for me. I'm so ashamed.'

'It sounds . . .' I was ignorant. I drew a breath deep into my lungs and composed reluctantly. 'Listen, I think you were showing that you have a great, big capacity for empathy. Don't you think? A huge, big heart that was actually feeling each parent's loss, over and over, and I think, maybe you are still feeling it. Have you slept yet?'

She shook her head, desolate and undeserving of rest.

'Well, you cannot punish yourself for the size of your heart. That can't be the right answer. Maybe you need to let yourself sleep. How might you do that?'

Most of all, they were tortured by their inability to keep their children safe.

After a week or so, their bodies decided that the danger had passed. One after another, my team members crashed. Some arrived late, after sleeping twelve or fourteen hours. Everyone's English degenerated, and all their tempers frayed at once. Thirteen additional workspaces had been squeezed into our suite, most of them no more than desks in the hall. All day long, we called to each other over their heads. The noise level strained tolerance and concentration. I went home each day and ran without pleasure.

The sea stared stonily up, more grey than green.

On the afternoon of Hamas's formal victory celebration, Marjie and I shopped early for our vegetables. Workers were unstacking the last of thousands of white plastic chairs on the Katiba field opposite our produce shop. A crew was lashing an enormous, phallic mock-up of an M75 rocket onstage. At least, I hoped it was a mock-up.

Leaning against the car, Marjie shifted her grocery bag and fingered her iPhone. 'I s'pose it wouldn't be too smart to take a picture. "And this is me and my little green apple, standing in front of the M75."'

I shook my head, 'And in the next frame, all that's left is the little green apple. Y'know, all those plastic chairs are making my fingers itch. I want to recycle them. Do you think anyone'd notice?'

Our driver slid his sun glasses over his eyes, Hollywood-cool, and said, 'I heard Bob Marley is playing.'

Because I was still enraged on their behalf, I waited for anger to follow the team's crash. Instead, it was as if someone declared the post mortem closed. Four weeks after the war, they told each other that it hadn't been so bad. Wars lasted only a few days, every few years. They pointed out that the ceasefire agreement had extended the fishing zone, as if that had been the aim of the whole exercise. Randa edited the tape of her memory, and stopped talking about getting her boys out.

Bewildered, I found moments to close my office door and ask them individually, 'Aren't you angry about the danger you've lived with?'

'This is our fate, as Gazans,' said one.

I asked another, 'What about the Hamas leaders who hid underground while you were in danger? Aren't you angry at them?'

She wrinkled her nose. 'That's Hamas. "We fight for you; you die for us." But at least they fight. No one else cares what happens here.'

'They fight, but what do they gain?'

'Nothing. But when they don't fight, the world forgets that we are here.'

'That's true,' I conceded.

I asked Hani, who since the war had sat ramrod-straight with both fists clenched. He declared, 'Who cannot live this way, I think he must leave Gaza.'

He added that he could no longer digest eggs. 'First the Israelis bomb the chickens, or they die from fear. Then they sell us Israeli eggs, and then they tell the press about their nice, humanitarian act to let in their Israeli eggs through the blockade. Their eggs are making me sick.'

The blockade felt most successful when they internalized the low value it assigned to their lives. I tried to explain that to a soft-spoken engineer across the hall. 'I think . . . I think I am just more indignant than you can afford to be.'

He asked me, 'How many times have you voted? Once in my life, I had a vote. I had two choices. I could vote for or against corruption. That was my issue. It has to come first, do you agree? Nothing else will work until . . .'

He stopped himself, catching the passion in his voice and tamping it down. 'Anyway . . . I voted against corruption. I did, I voted for Hamas. Hmph,' he grunted, still a little amused by it. 'What did it get us? Two wars and a siege. What a mess. Now everyone says they need to call another election. But here's the thing: if we had another election today, I would have exactly the same two choices. I could vote for or against corruption. So, what should I do – please, tell me – what do they expect me to do?' He pressed his thumb and forefinger together and punctuated his conclusion with them. 'We. Are. Not. Moving.'

Mauled and weary, Gaza restarted. The beachgoers returned to the Mediterranean shore between winter storms, and resumed cheering the blackouts. Months later, parents were still counting the number of their children who only felt safe enough to sleep beneath their beds, and the number who refused to sleep much at all.

***

I took my final break in Phnom Penh, to attend my last interview for the Cambodian job in person and meet up with old friends around the city.

Months earlier, I'd had a glancing ankle injury on my treadmill.

I had run a thousand kilometres since then. Disembarking in Cambodia, the pain made me stagger. I hobbled into an emergency clinic, wondering how I could have broken a bone in flight. The ultrasound showed that my right Achilles tendon had swelled around the tear. It was now 3.5 times the diameter of my left.

'A thousand kilometres – didn't it hurt?' the doctor asked, incredulous, as he cut lengths of tape and hung them from one edge of his desk. 'I mean, literally, how did you get that far? Pain is supposed to stop you.'

'I work in Gaza,' I explained absently, disoriented by the orderly, sterile, bright, quiet, consulting room. When the doctor didn't reply, I turned to fully face him. 'Maybe I didn't notice it because my ankle hurts less than watching Gaza.'

The doctor shook his head. 'Don't walk,' he said flatly, cupping one hand over the hen's egg that protruded from my ankle. 'Not until every bit of this swelling has gone down. Don't think in months. Think in seasons.'

'Right,' I replied, thinking instead of the Erez pedestrian tunnel and the two flights of stairs up to an office suite that was stitched with acutely angled desks, and the third flight up to the operations departments. And the fourteen flights up to my apartment, when the elevator was grumpy. After those, I could minimize my walking – except for the coffee, every hour or two.

Chapter 11

When I returned to Gaza, the sea had hardened to pewter for the winter and the city was flooding again. One morning, the car's temperature gauge read six degrees. I warmed myself steadily with coffee. In the office next door, the managers were cramming for their project management qualifications exam. Unable to balance crutches and coffees, I hobbled past their doorway with each hot cup. At mid-morning, I heard them dispatch Randa to reason with me.

She planted her hands on her hips in my doorway, and asked sternly, 'What did the doctor say?'

'I'm hardly moving.'

While Randa threw a glance down the kitchen hallway and then back at my crutches.

'What did he tell you?'

'He said "don't walk", but he didn't mean it. "Don't walk" is not a serious statement.'

'Really? And is it getting better?'

I made a face at her. 'Don't, don't give me that look, because only Rasha is allowed to look that innocent. You and I, that look doesn't work for us.'

Randa grew mischievous. 'You don't know, do you?'

'Know what?'

'Oh, let's just say that everyone has very, very good study materials for their exams.'

'What kind of materials? You read a stack of PDFs and you take a sample test online, right?'

'Yes, a sample test online. *So* good to work with IT people,' Randa teased with the upcast innocence that she and I were supposed to forego. She imitated me. 'Don't you think?'

I thought this through. 'You're telling me that Rasha hacked the testing site? Our Rasha – Rasha The Good?'

Randa's mouth curled into the smirk of an angelic child's sibling.

We held eye contact long enough to confirm. Then I threw back my head and sang, 'Ra-sha! Oh Raaa-shaaa!'

Rasha slipped in front of Randa. Randa burst into gleeful song in the hallway, and Rasha's smile drooped.

'Rasha? Dear. Have a seat.'

Within her parka and a scarlet hijab, Rasha's eyes flattened. 'How are you, are you better?'

'I'm very well, thank you for asking,' I said. I tried to look severe, but I was far more intrigued by Rasha the rule-breaker than I was by the rule. 'Rasha, is it possible that you hacked your employer's testing website?'

'Hack,' she hiccupped. Her eyes found the corners of my office and she nodded.

'Rasha, you did something against the rules – you!'

'But not very wrong,' she said in a tiny voice, and chewed on her lip.

'Not very? You hacked your employer.'

She nodded.

'And you downloaded all the tests?'

There was stagecraft involved in being caught. One assumed a pose of bravado or conviction or denial. Rasha merely nodded and stared, stricken. I felt a twinge of doubt.

'Did you download the answers?'

'Oh no,' she breathed.

'Did, Rasha, did you download the actual tests, or just some study sample tests?'

'The samples, only the samples! All the samples. The test – that would be cheating and you know I could never do that.'

'So, you— I don't get it.'

Rasha blushed. 'I didn't— Just it was— Just we were all going to register for one test each and then share all of our tests but you know how busy we are. So, I studied the whole material. I answered all the questions by myself, and I cross-checked all the answers. I downloaded every question during the test running times, to create a complete questions reference matrix with every possible answer to every question on every version of the exam. Then I shared it with everyone to be sure the others could prepare fully without doing my whole process. Just I made this tiny shortcut. Why should we have only one sample test to prepare?'

'Why? I'm not joking now, I don't understand what you're telling me. Why do you all need to do, what, six times the recommended preparation?'

'You know the answer. It's because we are from Gaza.'

I cocked my head. 'Do you think that you learn more slowly than anyone else?'

'No! Of course not. But to come from Gaza, it means that we must do more than anyone else. We need to get the very highest scores. There are no jobs here and no one else wants to hire us because it's too complicated to get us out. So at least we must show them the very, very best marks on our qualifications, and at least we must do every possible preparation to feel confident.'

I shook my head at the sign on my wall, Gaza > Relief, and composed a companion: Gaza Tries 6 x Harder. I saw no wrongdoing, but Rasha's nemesis was also taking the test, so I asked her pointedly, 'Did you share this matrix with the whole team?'

'Yes, of course. Even . . . you know, everyone. And Laila, of course. Am I in a lot of trouble?'

'Nearly, but your team spirit saved you.'

After she left, I had a silly urge to call her back and listen to more of her breathless syntax. We had so little time left.

We went for a team lunch at Mazaj. I sometimes ordered their lunch salads for delivery, always with the dressing on the side. When I ordered the same thing in the restaurant, '*sauce lahal*', our waiter let his notebook fall to his side.

'Marilyn! Is it you? "*Sauce lahal*" – we all try to guess what you look like!' He turned and announced to the room, flourishing his notebook at me, '*Sauce lahal* – Marilyn is here!'

The lunch rush ground to a halt as all the waiters crowded around to say hello.

How could I leave?

I Skyped with the members of my prospective Cambodian employer's board, and counted the days until the birth of Ibrahim's second child. The baby's February due date came and went.

One year earlier, Ibrahim, Wasim and his future wife had applied for exit permits to attend a Start-Up Weekend in the West Bank. They lived and breathed start-ups. On the day before the event, Israel's permit liaison office decided that Ibrahim could not leave Gaza. The others could.

Ibrahim congratulated them, listened to their plans, and returned dully to his desk to absorb his refusal without undermining their celebration. He held up his hands to ward off any consolation, and instead chided himself, 'I should never get excited. I should never believe it.'

An hour later, the liaison office reversed itself. Ibrahim could go and one of the others could not. When they changed their minds a third time, all the air went out of Ibrahim.

For eleven months, Ibrahim had been attending security interviews. Finally, shortly after his second child's due date, he received a permit for several days of work outside Gaza. The whole team surrounded his desk, cheering and pinkening him. Then they compared this season's permits with other seasons. They told each other that the restrictions might really be easing.

I took a step back. *Passports,* I thought, *not permits.*

Hani had also stood back, with his lips pursed in one straight line. I caught his eye, and went back to my office.

Ibrahim found me punishing my keyboard.

'Do you think I should go?' he asked.

Distracted by the task of relaxing my face, I could only ask, 'Why wouldn't you go?'

'Rula,' he reminded me. 'My wife is past due.'

'Oh, of course! Of course – but I can't answer that. Rula's vote is the only vote that matters.'

Ibrahim nodded.

'Were you at Suleiman's birth?'

'Yes, I was.' He brightened. Ibrahim's toddler, Suleiman, was a tolerant, wise-faced boy. I looked for him aloft at social gatherings, being flown hand to hand. 'But that hospital is closed now. I think they will not let me be in the delivery room this time.'

Ibrahim went to call Rula, and returned uneasily. 'She says I must go. But my baby – what do you think?'

'I think Rula is very supportive and I know you are, too. Come on, then, *yalla,* do what you're told. We'll ask Islamic Jihad to be quiet while you're out.'

Since the war, Israel had begun to close the Erez crossing in retaliation for rockets, as if the rocketeers were the ones left stranded.

Ibrahim wrote his project management test (which they all passed), and left Gaza the following day. He blogged every step of his trip and returned, still the father of one. Eleven hours after he returned, at 3.13 am, Ibrahim emailed as the father of two boys.

I found his desk empty when I went to congratulate him in the morning. Wasim murmured without raising his eyes from his monitor, 'He's in jail.'

I squinted at Wasim. 'You're joking. You're not joking?'

Wasim chose from his options. 'Not.'

Late the following day, a haggard Ibrahim arrived to explain.

'I knew they would not let me see my baby's birth. My mother came to take my place. But the delivery room wasn't clean. They did not clean the room from the last birth. You would protest, wouldn't you? I know how important it is. My mother argued with the doctor, and you know that I don't like to argue, but I agreed with her, because this is the room where my baby will be born. The doctor said it was late, and she was tired. A nurse could deliver the baby, in a room with blood on the floor. For me, this is not just a question of being professional. This is a human thing. A doctor has an obligation to help *every* baby. I would say the same thing about an Israeli baby, because they are humans. I needed that doctor to help my baby to begin its life.

'When my baby was born, they wrapped him in a towel with another baby's blood on it. Ohhh,' he hung his head, anguished that he had already failed his baby. 'That towel was the first thing my baby felt. And before I could see him, they told me to wait in the parking lot. Two hours, they said, before they would let me see my baby, and I was not allowed to come back into the building.'

I had never heard Ibrahim say so many words. He rested his

arms over the paunch where his son would now perch, and kept shaking his head with moist eyes.

'But they lied to me. I saw the police coming. They arrested me because they said that my mother had been disrespectful to the doctor. They brought me to jail. And Marilyn, it was terrible. I didn't know how bad they were. It was filthy. I saw faeces on the floor. And it was full of fear. We are educated people, how did we let the hospital and the jail get so bad?

'The first police weren't bad to me. They knew my father's name, and I think they knew that I didn't do anything wrong. Later, the second shift of police treated me more like a criminal. But my baby – I was in a nightmare. I just kept saying to them, please let me see my baby, my baby needs to know his father from the first minute, you have to let me go and be with my baby.'

He began to rock in his chair. 'Do you know, it's not just a feeling. It hurted, like something physical. It hurted me so much. They kept me away from seeing my baby for twelve hours, and I talked to them the whole time. Please please please.'

I took a tissue and handed one to him.

'Please please,' he remembered.

Emissaries from Khan Younis brokered his release and vindication, late in his son's first day.

After a few days, Ibrahim joked weakly that he had learned his assertiveness by trying to make himself heard between Rasha and Randa. Then firstborn Suleiman concluded that his baby brother was not living up to his advance billing. Ibrahim sought the advice of parents with larger families, and took on the patient, hourly task of reconciling a toddler to an infant.

***

The winter storms ran their course, and by spring, the team had recovered its momentum. Each project manager was trying to focus the next phase of work. Few projects could be scaled up effectively in Gaza's tiny, closed space. They had to keep evolving, and that posed creative challenges. Where was the pulse point of each undertaking, what was its underlying value? I swivelled my chair from one query to the next.

Ibrahim was preparing to supervise the next income-outcome

courses, from helpdesk to the sale of digital images. On a February afternoon, he asked, 'How do I make the next courses better? How can I work better with the trainers?'

'Aaaaahhh,' I stalled, because the course contents were well beyond my technical range. 'I don't know . . . what are they really . . . I mean – what do I mean? Ibrahim, is programming an art or a science?'

Ibrahim's hand went straight to his beard, a gesture that reminded me of letting the sliver be drawn out across my palm, to spin into wool. The hardest part of learning to spin had been the need to master every motion at once. Until all of the actions were integrated, there was no result.

I said to Ibrahim, 'Wait, let me ask that another way. What are you really training? You, when you're programming, before there is a product, how do you know that you're doing it well?'

'Yes, yes,' Ibrahim nodded vigorously, needing nothing further. He walked away without another word. I had no idea what he thought I'd been suggesting.

Each of his supervisory relationships promptly degenerated. I fielded complaints from trainers whose preparations Ibrahim rejected. Then one trainer got it. He deconstructed his own learning, and recreated it within his course. His students expected to receive a list of instructions. Instead, he challenged them to work at a deeper level, to examine how they learned. The trainer told me that it confused everyone at first. Then he said he would never train in the old way again.

Ibrahim set out to train more trainers.

Randa danced in after Ibrahim. An international evaluator had commended the recycling project. Once they saw their wives' stable incomes, husbands took part. The families had negotiated new, more finely differentiated prices for the plastic they sold, effectively dismissing us as intermediaries.

On our final visit, the woman with the chicken coop held up the eggplant that she had been preparing. 'My children eat vegetables. They don't have to look for edible weeds by the side of the road, so they can come home from school and do their homework. This is good. Now, please, do something for the young men. We have to keep them away from the fighting.'

Randa had thrown herself into the home-based manufacture of fuels from recycled ingredients. In my office that afternoon, she ran her finger down columns of piston costs and capacities. She showed me laboratory comparisons of the units of heat generated by the most recent fuel samples.

'Why are the results so different?' I said cautiously, pointing to the images of patty- and ring-shaped fuel samples. 'Same ingredients?'

'Doughnuts always make more heat than patties because they have more services – surfaces – to burn.'

'Ah. Remember to add some coffee grounds, so that the fuel smells like Gaza when it burns.' I slid the papers back to her side of the desk, and said, 'Tell me something. You said that you always talk about leaving Gaza after the bombing, and you said that you never would. Why not?'

She took a while to remember something. Randa had been a child of nine in Kuwait when Saddam Hussein invaded. She and her brother had foraged for food in the streets. A part of the adult Randa still seemed to tend that child, who was afraid of spiders and inhabited emotions so fully in the present tense. Something flitted across her face – the prospect of escape or of the unknown – and left a pensive smile. 'Where would I go? Gaza is where I belong. I walk down the street and everyone knows me. Where else can I give my boys that feeling? I don't want them to grow up with strangers.'

'And the danger to them?'

Randa shrugged, drawing her eyebrows up and the corners of her mouth down. 'It's only a few days.'

'I don't get it. After what you went through? Why don't you want a bomb shelter, as much as I want a bomb shelter for you?'

'Because the Israelis would just drop bigger bombs.'

Chapter 12

My final task was to write our study of Gaza's information technology companies and computer science graduates.

Gaza pinned its hopes on the prospect of high-value IT exports through the blockade. Families steered their promising children toward the industry. Women flocked to its merit-driven prospects. The West Bank IT industry, with its links to Jordan, grew steadily. Microsoft and other technology companies had offices in Ramallah. However, Gaza's IT industry was static. Aside from the branch offices of Ramallah-based telecoms companies, IT was not adding new jobs or new value to Gaza's economy. One thousand Gazans were graduating each year with computer-related degrees. They had studied three, four or five years; and most had studied partly in English. Only a quarter of them were finding paid work in their field.

Gaza's few economic donors studied the technology companies' lack of growth, and they funded the things that worked for firms elsewhere. We believed that they were all looking the wrong way.

Notwithstanding Gaza's chronically high unemployment, both IT employers and graduates complained about failed recruitments. We called this red flag the Gaza Paradox. Companies would not grow in size or sophistication, if they could not recruit. Graduates' skills would not mature without the experience of work. For some reason, the graduates and the companies had each other at an impasse.

We placed the graduates – not the companies – at the heart of the Gaza Paradox. Why should such an eager workforce be unemployed? Our project team and a local research firm spent the winter of 2013 researching the first granular labour market analysis for Gaza's digital economy.[20] The study found significant gaps between graduates' skills and the international industry's entry-level requirements across a range of competencies: technical knowledge, language, soft skills, project management, and others.

When we saw it from the graduates' perspective, the reason became clear. Gazan graduates studied and took every available training course, but they hadn't had the part-time job experience or the applied-science focus that gave graduates elsewhere exposure to their industry. Without real work, Gazan graduates lacked any practical way to apply the theory they studied. Without practice, theory did not become a skill. Without progressive professional learning and responsibility, skills did not ripen into judgement. Graduates were stuck on the far side of their skills gap. They were educated, but they had no chance to make themselves employable.

We were convinced that the industry's impasse would be broken when graduates had a way to catch up with the experiences of their overseas peers. They needed an intensive practice-learning step between university and private sector employment. A social enterprise winked at us. We toyed with names for the concept – a learning workplace, a practice platform – but we had no buyer, no client, to try working that way. Who would take the risk of contracting real commercial work to Gazan nearly-employable graduates, when the world was full of more accessible, ready-made competitors? I had no answer for that. If that client ever materialized, we hoped that our study would save them many months of figuring things out.

In the course of our research, an Egyptian court ordered the destruction of the Rafah smuggling tunnels, to prevent militants from entering Egypt underground. Gaza's graduating class of 2013 began to worry about their exams, while their parents began to worry about the rising prices of cement and industrial materials.

***

20 Much of the study investigated and expanded upon the insights of the project team leader, Taysir Shaqalaih. https://www.wamda.com/2013/04/overview-of-gaza-s-ict-labor-market-report

My phone rang as I was driving home. I didn't recognize the number.

A foreign woman's voice said, 'Hello, I'm looking for the economic director of Mercy Corps. I hear that you're the go-to people for questions about IT in Gaza. If you have an hour, I have a question.'

'Of course, I have an hour,' I replied. 'Why don't you come to Beirut Tower?'

I hopped to the door when I heard them knock, and my face fell.

A blonde woman passed one hand over her make-up, and held out a pinch of her silky blouse. 'This – sorry! It's my last night in Gaza. I'm on my way to a thing. I'm Leslie – this is Philip – and I do *not* always dress like this.'

Philip frowned down at his suit jacket and tie. 'Actually, I do.'

I introduced myself and offered them the couch. I tugged my feet beneath me in the easy chair, surreptitiously poking the frayed cuffs of my sweatpants out of sight. Leslie noticed, and we both laughed at the tyranny of first impressions.

Leslie explained that they both worked for UNRWA, the largest actor in Gaza's economy. Although UNRWA procured locally whenever it could, its local IT procurement lagged noticeably behind other industries. With a $40 million software conversion project underway, UNRWA's Gaza director had much more work to offer.

She hesitated. 'Listen, there's no way to say this very delicately. The director needs to know, if we offer more contracts, will the companies' performance improve? It's not really good enough now.'

Duggaduggadugga.

'Hmm.' I scrunched my forehead said a silent ode to the gods of serendipity, while I tried not to look gleeful about UNRWA's misfortune. 'Hmm. It might improve, but I don't see why it should. We – the go-to team? We think there's a structural problem. We call it the Gaza Paradox.'

I described the recruitment impasse. 'Did you know that Gazan universities have dozens of theoretical computer programs, but not one that teaches IT as a practical, applied science? No one studies the application of IT to medicine, or marketing, or design. Graduates can't practice and specialize on the job, because there are no jobs. Donors fund three-month internships and employers recycle their funded interns, so the workforce is perpetually inexperienced. Graduates don't advance, so their skills don't improve, so their employers don't have improving work to sell you. With the best of intentions, donors are reproducing the problem they're trying to solve.'

Leslie and Philip exchanged a glance that might have been doubt or confirmation.

'If we're right about all this, then a few scattered UNRWA contracts won't change it. To change it, someone's going to have to break the whole cycle. Someone's going to have to contract real projects to a training workplace that gives graduates a really intensive work-study-experience time. Then they will be able to do more-skilled work, and then their employers will show you better results. But what kind of buyer is going to speculate on a blockaded, war-prone community that they can't even visit?'

I leaned forward. 'Get it? If you bundle some of your contracts together, then UNRWA has workflow.' I crooned, 'Work*flooow*. A pipeline of sustained, paid work to prove the value of working differently. You're the missing link, you can break the cycle. You're the buyer!'

I settled my chin contentedly onto one fist. 'Do you know what a social enterprise is? It's a business, established for a social purpose. Imagine some kind of training business . . .'

'I'll be the devil's advocate, if that's okay,' said Philip. He ran his hands over the stubble on his jaw. 'Wouldn't this enterprise just compete with the existing companies, and maybe put them out of business?'

'I agree, that's the risk. It has to be a bridge that leads into the companies.' I thought for a bit, and conjured with one hand. 'Somehow.'

We talked long enough to make them late for Leslie's farewell.

I sketched the concept for the managers on the following morning. We played with it some more, before we tossed it wistfully into the gulf of UNRWA.

Randa asked, 'If it happened, if UNRWA gave its contracts to this . . . thing, would you stay and do it?'

'With UNRWA? I can't imagine it. I mean, UNRWA – business?' I juggled them in my two hands, testing their weights. The mismatch sunk one hand. 'Can't imagine it.'

Philip called a few days later. 'Would you come in and continue this with our director? He's interested, but he's not convinced.'

I made an appointment and told the managers. No one knew what to say. As if someone had put a stronger bulb in the overhead light, we looked fusty and settled to each other.

***

On the day of the UNRWA meeting, I drove into Gaza City from the north. Passing the empty edges of the Strip, I tried to picture wave after wave of dislocated Palestinian refugees, straggling across those very fields with the possessions they could carry.

Israel established itself in the war of 1948, at the expense of catastrophic Palestinian displacement. Eighty thousand Gazans took in at least 160,000 refugees. No one could have intimated that 1.8 million Palestinians would one day cling to civility and dignity in the same space. Towns expand as they become cities; Gaza had not.

We drove into the conurbation. UNRWA's whitewashed, blue-trimmed buildings were often the only painted buildings on the streets. UNRWA's logo was ubiquitous because UNRWA built and operated its own health clinics, schools and food distribution centres. That made UNRWA's size deceptive among the UN agencies that merely contracted for service delivery. Teachers, not bureaucrats, made up the largest group of UNRWA staff.

In 1949, the United Nations created a temporary, single-issue agency called the United Nations Relief and Works Agency for Palestine Refugees in the Near East. No UN member-state opposed UNRWA's creation. It took state-like responsibility for the Palestine refugees who had been displaced to Syria, Jordan, Lebanon, the West Bank and Gaza Strip. Critically, UNRWA's unified mandate recognized them as one nation, waiting in several places to return home.

As its single issue languished, the unpronounceable UNRWA

became the bureaucratic evidence of Israel's ongoing occupation of Palestinian land. States began to react to the occupation, in part, through UNRWA. Primarily, they did so by renewing UNRWA's mandate every three years in the UN General Assembly. Each renewal reflected the world's collective refusal to normalize the occupation, or to let Palestinians' needs be subsumed into hundreds or thousands of NGO programmes. UNRWA held their needs together. A much smaller number of states treated UNRWA with hostility, again because UNRWA rendered the occupation visible.

UNRWA was a puzzle to me. Occupied, blockaded, governed by an unrecognized authority; the people behind Gaza's walls needed some kind of dedicated service mechanism. Someone had to help, but why UNRWA? Having imposed for-profit neoliberalism upon Afghanistan, why did the same donor states overwhelmingly vote to maintain and fund the UN's most superannuated agency as their channel to assist educated, skilled, entrepreneurial Gaza? The rest of the world got disaster capitalism and Chinese neo-mercantile infrastructure. Gaza got Ban-Ki Moon's viceroy.

I passed through the turnstiles of UNRWA's Gaza Field Office and asked where to find the Gaza Director of Operations, the senior staff position in Gaza. The compound felt like a small college campus, its footpaths lined with date palms and bright flower beds. Its distinct clusters of low-rise buildings told of donor cycles of headline and forgetting. Paint had flaked since the last influx of funds, and junk furniture was finding its way back into corners.

The Front Office building was an unadorned concrete square of three storeys, less inviting than the offices that opened onto greenery or breezeways. Thick security doors divided the floors. The tiny second-floor vestibule was shared by a stationery cabinet and a burly, shaven-headed Close Protection officer of similar proportions.

He nodded me through the glass door of the director's L-shaped suite. Three square workstations dominated the suite. Each square looked larger than the offices along the opposite wall. Three young Gazan women presided. Deftly they juggled screens, papers, phones and voices in two languages, while passers-by addressed them in acronyms. Visitors' chairs were propped between the side office doorways, making visitors into spectators at the assistants' work.

The director's office was unusually long. He waved his phone, and returned it to his ear to finish a call. I cocked my head at a wooden conference table, so absurdly long and narrow that speakers would have to lean in and swivel to make eye contact. The whole suite's proportions and abrupt angles stiffened the flow of people and conversation, although the offices' inhabitants no longer noticed. I wondered in which era this design had made sense.

To my relief, we met around a well-worn rattan coffee table and chairs.

Scott Anderson, UNRWA's American deputy director, jumped up to shake my hand. His square shoulders and haircut marked him as ex-military. Scott had springs. Motion was his milieu and he toyed with his necktie as soon as he sat down. I guessed that he was in his mid-forties. Kirstin, seated next to him, was around ten years younger. She was drawn in straight, trustworthy lines: long hair, nose and wide smile. She introduced herself with broad Australian vowels. They were both easy to meet, both people who knew that others wanted to be included. They asked a string of open, inviting questions about our labour market research.

Robert Turner finished his call and walked around his desk to join us. He slouched in his seat, propped his feet on the base of the rattan coffee table to make a desk of his knees, and although he remained the tallest person in the circle, he had closed the gap. He had researched social enterprise business models and wanted to discuss financial viability rather than gestures of goodwill.

My surprise must have showed.

'I'm not a career UN person,' he explained factually, his eyes smiling rather than his mouth, 'Also private sector, NGOs, consulting.'

I liked him. Smart and spare, he leaned on his ideas. He wrote a couple of lines in a palm-sized notebook, shook blond hair out of his eyes, and said that he would give it some thought.

We met regularly through the winter and spring of 2013. Kirstin returned to her own desk when Bob's permanent Special Assistant arrived. Uta was German, white-blonde and coltish. She made effervescent conversation while steering purposefully. That, and her towering heels, made her an ideal foil for Bob.

Around the coffee table, we set out the first vision of the

social enterprise that would become the Gaza Gateway, and then the GGateway. The Gateway social enterprise would take on commercial contracts for IT projects. It would hire teams of recent graduates to carry out the work, and it would run intensive on-the-job training for its teams while they worked. Graduates would learn in the Gateway's sheltered, business-like workplace for a limited time, becoming more qualified to succeed in Gaza's private sector. At the end of their Gateway stint, graduates and employers would have more to offer each other.

It fell to Rasha, Laila and Ibrahim to ground the airier aspects of our design in technical reality.

UNRWA would be the Gateway's first buyer. No one else in Gaza had a pipeline of work sufficient to anchor and prove the concept. UNRWA would contract labour-intensive, entry-level IT projects to the Gateway social enterprise, starting with blocks of work from its own software conversion. The Gateway would use UNRWA's pilot projects to figure itself out and establish a track record of project delivery. Then it would market more widely.

All we needed was an organization willing to house the Gateway's pilot phase. Complex, time-consuming obstacles prevented the Gateway from immediately opening its doors as an independent social enterprise. A new Gazan business law was then in the works. We knew that it would not contemplate an operation like the Gateway. The registration of a social enterprise would require extensive legal work. The Gateway also needed logistics to cope behind the blockade, a legal capacity to employ and contract, bank connections to receive payments, and start-up funds – not to mention a generator and a source of fuel for it, and permits to import the computers. We sought an existing entity to handle all that, while the Gateway concentrated on proving that Gazan graduates could make themselves employable, fast.

Would the UN's largest and most elderly agency be able to act like the kind of initial buyer the Gateway needed? United Nations procurement regulations weren't known for their agility. I made up my mind on a spring afternoon, when Bob set aside a bothersome regulation with an infinitesimal shrug. The regulation meant nothing to me, but I knew a skunkworks shrug when I saw it.

Scott recognized it, too. 'We'll apologize later,' he said amicably to the bottom of his tie.

Clearly, such apologies had been made before, and letters of policy variation had been signed. After the meeting, I chuckled as I picked my way down the stairs on my crutches (down was so much more precarious than up). If you needed your bureaucratic insecurities stroked, Bob Turner was not your man.

My job offer arrived from Cambodia. I emailed Bob and offered to stay in Gaza instead. Bob replied within moments, 'please stay'. He wrote me a three-month consultancy to set the enterprise in motion.

I declined the Cambodian job, and finished writing the study for Mercy Corps. Leaving my crutches to be donated to a medical NGO, the driver brought me to Erez with my hands free at last. I held my unencumbered arms out to the sunshine before I picked up my bag, leaned on my phantom crutches for balance, and toppled straight over the suitcase. A friend in her twenties and a nun in her eighties manhandled me and my gear through the pedestrian tunnel for the last time. I had traded in my NGO car keys. When I returned from a holiday, I would be driven down the diplomatic lane in the white armoured vehicles of the United Nations.

Chapter 13

A wave of sound woke me and jolted me upright. The sound, the room, everything was strange. I was . . . I was in a temporary apartment on the first floor of Beirut Tower, and still the roaring did not subside. I reached for my phone – of course! I kicked the sheet away – of course! It was June 22, 2013 and Mohammed Assaf, the wedding singer from Khan Younis, must have won the *Arab Idol* singing competition.

Gaza was cheering! Exultant, delirious – and dancing! I found my journal and began to cheer with them, and to bop and scribble on my terrace, a few feet above the boiling T-junction:

> . . . daredevil joy broke out on Beach Road. Every young man in Gaza was there, racing and dancing in every direction at once – hanging out [of] car windows, and who knew there were so many sunroofs to jump through, and standing in the boot, or just clinging to the back windscreens and being hurled off at the speed bumps. Or, can it be, standing on the car window ledge, braced by nothing but their knees! . . . Tonight, all of Gaza is a boy racer while Hamas is tucked up sourly in their beds. Cars going in all three directions through the T-junction, some spinning in circles, all of it going way too fast with crowds streaming, running, weaving through. Flags flapping, horns, drumming, chanting, reckless, chaos – if you hadn't grown up on these roads with no stop signs, you wouldn't dream of it at these speeds, racing each other, navigating like bats with Gazan radar to make them swerve at the last moment . . . We won – Gaza won something beautiful – it could not be this sweet anywhere else because the odds could never have been this steep . . . Gaza is celebrating *music*! 'This is Gaza, we dance here!'

Later the same morning, a meticulous Gazan notable bounded down the stairs to his office waiting room on the ground floor. Pyjamas would not have startled me more than the flapping tails of his napped-in shirt. He had not shaved, and he used both sets of thumbs and forefingers to peel the puffy lids back from his eyes.

'Gaza won – we won something.' He let his Adam's apple bounce, revering it. Then he let his eyes snap back into slits, took a prosaic breath and led me up the stairs. 'And you could hear the politics in the street, couldn't you? Oh-h-h yes. Gaza said to Hamas, "We love to dance, and you can't really stop us." They stayed home! For one night, Hamas stayed home. Very sensible.'

Reliving it, inhaling it, he began to chortle on the landing. He yanked his tie further askew and slapped one thigh. 'I'll tell you how we won. Can I? I've thought about this. You see, I think that all those Arabs – hehehe – who've never done a *thing* for Palestine before? I think that every one of my Arab *brothers* sent five well-earned votes for that fine young man's talent. What a voice! He deserved to win. *Yalla* – ha! And then, and then? Then I think they squeezed off five more votes to *SOOTHE THEIR GUILT* – and – *hahahahaha*!' he doubled over with glee, and pumped his elbows like bellows to take in the air he needed to holler, '—strengthen the *BONDS OF SOLIDARITY with their Palestinian brothers*!'

***

For two years, I had known Gaza as an intimate, young, hopeful, ambitious place. On my United Nations induction rounds in the summer of 2013, I encountered UNRWA's Gaza. My first stop was a concrete block room in Jabalia. It had, just then and perhaps often, no electricity.

'Eighty tons of rubbish,' I repeated. I verified the translation in Arabic – not eighteen? I measured rubbish in donkey carts, or by counting broken plastic chairs for recycling. 'Weekly?'

Salah replied, 'Every day.'[21]

Salah had been removing rubbish from the Jabalia refugee camp for twenty-six years, battling mosquitoes and rats for

21 The Palestine Central Bureau of Statistics calculated that Gaza produced a total of 716 tons of rubbish daily in 2015. http://www.pcbs.gov.ps/site/512/default.aspx?tabID=512&lang=en&ItemID=1454&mid=3171&wversion=Staging

possession of each alley. Towering and cadaverous, he tipped his chair back and reached through the doorway to pluck one white jasmine from his wall outside. He smelled it and smiled, displaying his equanimity. Then he handed me the flower and went to boil water for more tea.

'And through the wars,' he said again from the kitchen doorway. 'That's important. We must work through the wars, or there would be disease.'

My driver followed a swelling sound to an UNRWA school nearby. The schools were staging Summer Fun Days (a budgetary comedown from the Summer Games of better funded years). With the exception of the kite-painters in the art room, everyone was screaming. Across the Gaza Strip, 150,000 schoolchildren were shrieking from trampolines, inflatable slides, volleyball courts and *debka* dancing yards; determined to deafen their 4000 hardy activity supervisors. The supervisors popped aspirins and got paid. That made them lucky among the 180,000 Gazans on an UNRWA waiting list for temporary work.

Jobs were more scarce than ever. In July 2013, Egypt's General Abdel Fatah el-Sisi accelerated the destruction of the Rafah tunnels. He closed the Rafah border exit, rendering all of Gaza entirely dependent on Israel's fickle permission to leave the Strip. Unable to leave Gaza, university students were prevented from completing their international degree programs. Builders felt it next. With the exception of UNRWA's supplies for its own activities, all of Gaza's steel, cement, and 94 per cent of its construction gravel had come through the tunnels. The construction industry ceased, wiping out 20,000 jobs and silencing the gritty background hum of machinery.

Gaza's economy – already one of the world's most volatile – began to fishtail from such rapid, grievous losses. Overnight, Gaza lost 65 per cent of its non-UNRWA supplies of flour, 98 per cent of its sugar and 52 per cent of its rice.[22] The disruption of food supplies revived Gazans' arterial fears of scarcity.

We drove to the Jabalia relief food distribution centre, where

22 For statistics on the tunnel closure, see https://www.al-monitor.com/pulse/originals/2013/07/hamas-financial-crisis-gaza-egypt-morsi.html (accessed April 1, 2019).

temporary workers were unloading pallets of food and filling family-sized sacks. Across the Gaza Strip, the family representatives of 800,000 refugees were collecting their seasonal portions of rice, flour, sugar, cooking oil and tinned meat in similar concrete yards. The men hoisted their sacks with resignation, but the women were edgy, fidgeting, hands restless. The women had to cook. They had to make it stretch. Some families had lost a $10 cash grant from their seasonal bundle of relief supplies – exactly the kind of discretionary grant that would have insulated women's household budgets.

A ruddy, pot-bellied man soothed one woman's agitation near the wickets where coupons were being checked. All in black despite the heat, the woman flapped her coupons in his face, insisting that something was wrong, or that there should have been more, or maybe the numbers on the coupons were accurate but she could see already that these meagre quantities would not suffice. The man was listening and absent, removing his hat to swipe at his bald spot, one ear for the woman and one eye for the currents of people and flour sacks moving around him. He doled out his attention with an easy authority. He had probably been presiding over this concrete yard for as long as Salah had been fending off rats. The yard showed him nothing that day which he had not seen before.

As I got into the car to leave, a passing hand flicked a tightly folded scrap of lined paper through the open car door. The driver inched toward the gate while I unfolded the note. I read the phone number and sounded out the name in Arabic. There was no other message. I looked back, but the arm had been swallowed into the motion behind us.

The driver nodded at me in the rear-view mirror, and held out his own hand.

'Mr. Robert Turner.' He pantomimed writing on his own palm. 'Is trouble, is problem, Mr. Robert Turner to help.'

'Oh.' I hesitated to let go of the paper, having taken on this hand's situation.

The driver smiled and named the Front Office's PAs. 'You give. They help,' he promised.

'Okay,' I said, and wadded the note back into my palm. It rested in my hand like one little counterweight to the confounding scale of UNRWA's Gaza. I handed the note to a PA when we got back to the office, and she assured me that someone would call the family.

I leaned out of my apartment window at the end of that afternoon, flapping my notebook in lieu of a breeze for my neck and chest. A muggy, fretful stillness blanketed the city. The sun was liquid punishment on the horizon. Beyond it, Syria was sliding into calamity. Opposite my window, a billboard promoted Hamas's summer camp with images of boys doing military-style exercises in black track suits and balaclavas. A tubercular yellow taxi parked beneath the billboard, and eight people of three generations unfolded themselves from within it. The parents and the taxi driver unloaded beach and baby supplies from the boot. Two small children got impatient and rambled into the gathering crowd, knowing that any adult would show them the way back, if their own parents got lost.

Only a few nights remained before Ramadan. Its fast days would be exceptionally hot and lengthy in mid-summer. Hamas's teachers, bureaucrats, police and fighters were wondering how to cope with the extra expenses of the holiday, having received only a fraction of their salaries.

In August, Egypt bulldozed the border fuel pumps to cut the supply of smuggled fuel to Gaza. Side streets became derelict as cars were abandoned and reclaimed by sand. Ambulances parked when their tanks ran dry, and hundreds of water wells were decommissioned. Food prices spiked and cigarette prices tripled as the cheap Egyptian stocks ran out.

The destruction of the tunnels threatened Gaza's power structures no less than its economy. As Hamas lost its tunnel taxes, it had to balance the demands of welfare, administration and resistance – and a payroll of 42,000 – with 40 per cent less revenue. Hamas found itself boxed into the role of preserving Israel's quiet because it could not afford trouble, even as Gazans bore the escalating hardship of that quiet. When it appeared quiescent toward Israel, Hamas became vulnerable to challenge from Gaza's more radical militants. They had nothing staked on the status quo. They accused Hamas of collaborating with the occupation, and they agitated for a more violent resistance. Hamas clamped down in response. Hamas police began to spar with Islamic Jihad gunmen. Nocturnal checkpoints appeared throughout the Strip. Rockets flew overhead more often at breakfast, test-firing into the sea.

They could clamp down, but Hamas couldn't make payroll. From August onward, even the most non-ideological Gazans waited with sweaty palms to hear the fraction of salaries that Hamas would manage to pay its fighters and police each month. When would the armed forces begin to extort their salaries, and from whom? I listened intently to the Hamas joggers beneath my window, in case the discipline of their salaried chant should devolve into a seedier, self-interested sound.

UNRWA was part of the deterioration. Gaza was slipping down the donors' to-do list, outpaced by crises in the Ukraine, Libya, Syria and the growing number of people crossing the Mediterranean Sea in small boats. UNRWA's expenditures constituted 16 per cent of Gaza's GDP, and UNRWA's payroll, purchasing and liquidity were essential to the economy. Therefore, its budget shortfalls reverberated systemically.

I was beginning to understand UNRWA's invidious political position. Two things happened when UNRWA met its humanitarian obligations. Some anti-occupation activists – Gazans among them – accused the agency of implementing Israel's blockade. UNRWA, they said, relieved Israel of the cost and responsibility that an occupying power should bear. No less vigorously, Israel's defenders blamed UNRWA for relieving Hamas of the cost and responsibility that Gaza's government should bear, whether it enjoyed diplomatic recognition or not.

The Western states wanted the Arab states to fund more of UNRWA's budget, as a gesture of regional solidarity. The Arab states required the West to fund UNRWA, as the cost of indulging Israel's occupation.

UNRWA was a 360-degree target of opportunity, and the Gaza Field Office was its largest mass at which to fire.

Because it provided services in Gaza's eight teeming urban refugee camps, UNRWA also confronted the meaning and the inadequacy of intergenerational refugee camps. A camp was, by definition, supposed to be temporary, but four generations of Palestinian refugees had lived in that suspension. Their camps were physical proof of the world's as-yet-unmet obligations. If UNRWA normalized or improved the camps in any way that made them seem more permanent, it might suggest that the refugee issue had been shelved and justice had been given up. The camps' built environment was sub-standard, crumbling and difficult to service – but the camp residents were deeply conservative about change. Their caution extended, explicitly, to the visibility of UNRWA's logo.

My induction rounds had helped to explain why donors didn't contract Gazan services, as donors did elsewhere. Why wasn't food being distributed by a for-profit company, and why weren't a hundred different NGOs operating schools and clinics? The donors preserved UNRWA, partly because UNRWA's continuity proved that they had not forgotten about Palestinian refugees, and the occupation of Palestinian land. If UNRWA's logo were to disappear from Gaza's refugee camps, it would be taken as a sign that the donor states were neglecting their obligations.

The great preponderance of UN member states mandated the single agency of UNRWA – not a hundred NGOs or contracting companies – to assist the single community of Palestine refugees. However, they did not fully fund refugees' rights and burgeoning needs, nor act effectively to end the occupation of land. In lieu of a political solution, UNRWA's job was to graft a little global welfare onto the blockade's deprivation.

Every other Sunday, after the local statutory workday had ended, UNRWA's 35 international staff (among 12,500 Gazans) met in a utilitarian room. We dragged tables into a ring beneath promotional posters. Meetings opened with Bob's updates on the agency's fundraising and budget shortfalls, and the cancellation of unfunded activities: the $10 cash grant, packages of school supplies for children of the poorest families. Week by week, the ring of faces fell and retrenched.

One August staff meeting opened with the press release for the rigorous, biennial study of Gaza's food security. The report found that, even after they received their relief food, 57 per cent of Gazan households remained food-insecure. Very poor households were spending up to half of their income to buy the additional food that they needed to survive. It was hard to imagine how they were getting by. The meeting room hushed as we reminded ourselves that the study covered the years 2011–2012. It reflected Gaza's food insecurity before the tunnels closed, before the demise of the construction industry (whose skilled workers had become the new poor), and before food prices began to spike.[23]

I placed the press release on the table before me, and tried to catch Kirstin's eye. The part in her hair wagged slowly as she read. Around the ring of tables, I took in the hair, glasses, water bottles, sandals beneath the tables, the Close Protection row of shaven skulls. UNRWA's international team had never looked more pedestrian to me. I glanced over my shoulder, hoping to find someone more visibly outstanding there. My eyes found only the wall at our backs.

***

Philip, whose enquiry had brought me to UNRWA, transferred to the Jerusalem office. He offered me his apartment in the Tiaba building, a few blocks up Beach Road and directly opposite Gaza's little seaport. With a few weeks remaining on my consulting contract, I unpacked and enjoyed my new outlook. Fishing boats moored by day in the rectangular lagoon, thick and sociable as old Hong Kong. A breakwater of recycled rubble encircled them. Early in the evening, the fishing boats puttered away, top-heavy with banks of overhead lights to attract the fish. Whole families arrived to stroll along the parapet, above the blackening waves. Laila had said that she walked by the port when she urgently needed to be alone. Alone? The walkers congealed into a single mass. From my window eight storeys above, the women's black hijabs and coats turned the crowd into a clump of metal filings, all drawn irresistibly toward the promontory's fresher air. Hunger drew them all back a few hours later for dinner. I tried to imagine vertical Gaza as they saw it, in the moment when they turned from the flat otherworld of the sea.

23 https://unispal.un.org/UNISPAL.NSF/0/B08CF027A9C9A2AF85257BDE004975EE For more current information, search the Palestine Food Security Cluster or SEFSEC surveys.

UNRWA forbade its internationals to walk or drive those precious few hundred metres. Because it was denied, the breakwater took on a quality of longing. I called it Ultima Thule, the limit of the known world.

It didn't take long to unpack and inch the dining table up to the window, where I would use it as a desk. The Tiaba building was not yet two years old, but Gaza's unforgiving seafront climate already scarred it. Watermarks flowered on my living room wall, and a crop of livid aquamarine nodules sprouted wherever the salty, chemical water met the pipes. My boxy rooms lacked the charm of my old apartment, but Kirstin lived overhead in 902. I heard her step out of her shoes when she came home from the office. She would hear Uta, Bob's Special Assistant, who lived in 1002. They introduced me to Swedish Jenny, who lived in 602.

The column of Tiaba 2s enabled my passive-aggressive accommodation of the international culture of UNRWA. I was dismayed to find a few garden variety bigots among its international staff. I was not willing to confront them, when a single internet search might have undone me or my team. I resented their comfort and my cowardice equally. Yet I was drawn to UNRWA's mission, and to the Gateway. The real risk to Gaza lay in the world's disengagement. I wanted to prove that Gaza > Relief.

But how? The Gateway's launch timeline was sliding languorously to the right. After nearly three months, we had found no organization willing to house the pilot phase of work. Donors had given us a slew of reasons why they had no funds available for social enterprise in Gaza. Anywhere else it might have appealed, but Gaza was a humanitarian problem, wasn't it?

Deep in the miasma of last resort, we had that day agreed to conduct our whole proof of concept under UNRWA's own roof. The Gaza Gateway social enterprise would be a special project of the UNRWA Gaza Field Office. We were already straining UNRWA's procurement policy. Now, our hourly operations would depend entirely upon policy exceptions.

From the outset, we had sworn not to do this. Within UNRWA, it would be difficult to emulate a private sector workplace. It would be harder to convince prospective clients that we carried out our pilot projects at arm's length from our buyer. Everyone in Gaza knew the terms and conditions of UNRWA employment. We would need HR to create new terms that were comparable to the private sector – and disillusioning to every incoming member of every project team. IT staff would notice that UNRWA had sprouted a second technology unit. And so on.

Bob had sighed, 'People do not understand. The absence of choice is not a choice.'

Front Office, back pocket, I warned myself grimly as I left his office. Despite UNRWA's proliferating demands, the Gaza Gateway social enterprise had unabashedly jumped the queue. We would never be popular.

***

I arranged the last of the wires beneath my dining-desk in time for the power to fail at 10.00 pm. Electricity rarely lasted beyond that any more. A cheer rose from the port to welcome me to my new neighbourhood. I brushed my teeth in the beam of a torch, and sat down to compose. I felt obliged to disclose my sister's Zionist offices before I extended my consulting contract. Whether or not they posed a security risk, her titles certainly risked embarrassing my employers.

We met around the rattan table, in the lull before a visiting delegation went to Bob's place for dinner. Scott took his seat last, having briefed and seen the visitors off to their cars. He would have made them feel welcome, and in the moment when he reached for his necktie, I admitted to myself how much I wanted to do this job.

I hummed and hawed long enough to build more suspense than I intended. Scott's hand froze on his necktie, and Uta clapped one hand over her mouth. Her eyes were huge.

'You know that I'm a Jew. I'm, ah, I'm also one of four sisters, and one of my sisters is, well, she chairs the largest bloc in the World Zionist Organization. And she's a committee member of the Jewish Agency – ethnic land use, immigration. And, oh, there're a few more, but those would be the headlines.' I closed one eye and took stock with the other, and then I remembered, 'We look alike.'

Scott barked, 'Haw!' and fell silent with his mouth open.

Uta said into her hand, 'Well . . . at least . . . she hasn't killed anyone.'

'Not that I know of.' I paused, and apologized silently to my sister. 'I'm quite sure.'

Everyone turned to Bob. His height ebbed away as he subsided behind his knees. He checked his forehead for fever with the front and the back of his hand, before he said weakly, 'If it comes out, we can always say that you were just a consultant.'

I slunk away, feeling my employment sinking into quicksand. I emailed Uta that Bob's response had been hard to read. I offered to skip the delegation's dinner if he felt awkward. Uta guessed that Bob had probably been making a joke, although it might not hurt to check.

Late in the afternoon, I plodded up to the tenth floor of Tiaba, and knocked on Bob's apartment door, braced for *ex post facto* dismissal through the peephole.

Bob pulled the door open and said pre-emptively into the hallway, 'Joke – it was a joke. Not one of my best.'

He stepped aside to wave me in.

I sighed. 'Thank you, I am glad that's done. Do you have siblings?'

'A brother.'

'Does he ever complicate your life like this?' I exuded empathy, hoping for a confession to bind us.

Bob swung his head in slow arcs to frown over one shoulder and then the other. 'Nothing like this.'

Scott assigned me an office that opened onto a strip of garden, overlooking the parking lot and the main compound gates. He sounded me out in a pleasant voice from the doorway. 'I'm a deputy, and you're an adult, and this enterprise is Bob's big thing. You work it out with him, and you report to me to get things done. Just think how badly that could go.'

I nodded. 'It's got that triangular informality, huh?'

'It does, it so does. So, let's be up front here. I didn't really ask to be your manager, and I mean this in a good way but you don't seem like a person who wants much managing.'

'True. We sound complementary when you put it that way, don't you think?'

'Mm hmm,' he sighed, dubious, and scratched his chin as he turned away.

My office was one box in a contiguous single-storey row; quiet, as the adjacent offices were rarely used. I left my door and window open onto the garden because flowers were more refreshing than any air conditioning.

A technician set up my computer. He left as UNRWA's security deployed for a demonstration. Protestors had recently climbed the walls and run straight at Front Office. I leaned against my door-frame to observe, expecting a heavy hand and prepared to dislike it. Instead, middle-aged, unathletic desk-dwellers sauntered past and waved from the footpath. They took up lounging positions near stairways and shortcuts. They fanned themselves, chatting through the break in their morning's work. Through the heavy bars of the compound's vehicle entrance, a crowd began to clot the street. Pickets bobbed on a few shoulders, and someone blew into a microphone.

I imagined some young hothead scaling the compound wall, rounding a corner, bent on piracy and coming upon . . . his uncle, suppressing a heat-induced yawn by the daisy bed.

There, I smiled to have cracked the code. Right there lay UNRWA's flabby genius, and its value. UNRWA really was the hotheads' uncle, and the screaming children's big sister, and the distressed woman's pot-bellied neighbour. UNRWA reflected Gaza's unwieldy self: 12,500 average folks thrown too close together, repurposed, and brandishing the mandate that time forgot.

Chapter 14

A stranger held the apartment door open for me to join the henna party. I thanked her as I stepped past, and she teased, 'Do you think we look different?'

I turned back. The voice was Rasha's, but hair altered all of her proportions. Whose nose was that?

Swirling, thrown-back heads of hair filled the room, and then turned into women I knew from Mercy Corps. Their vivid, sparkling party dresses were less disorienting than their heads, which were merely brown and black. They took up more space, they performed and demanded to be noticed. Only Randa remained her daylit self. She grabbed my hand and towed me into the overpowering music, breathless dancing and singing and whirling, the heat and the joy of having lived long enough to celebrate Laila's engagement.

At the formal engagement after the henna party, Ahmad and Laila waltzed beneath white fairy lights in a hotel reception room. Ahmad, a dancer who walked with an activist's minor limp, had pursued Laila for years. He looked ready to treasure every non-conforming bone of her.

I nudged Rasha beside me. 'Would you look at his face – he adores her.'

'*Tammam* – perfect,' Rasha sighed.

Randa kept jumping up and chasing after her boys, whose stiff party clothes might not last the night. A woman nearby leaned over to me. Her silver eyeshadow glittered as she closed her eyes to shout into my ear, 'She is checking on Haneen. Laila's sister, do you know her? She's pregnant, but she has a flu or something.'

It wasn't the flu. Haneen, the fourth member of their inseparable circle, had hepatitis. In the hours and days after the engagement dance, Haneen lost her baby, then her liver function. Then she lost consciousness. To reach a specialist, she had to be gotten through the Erez border crossing on a humanitarian emergency permit. Her hepatitis was unnecessarily advanced by the time Haneen made it to a well-supplied, brightly lit Israeli hospital. Just as her friends were assuring each other that it would be all right, Haneen died.

I had known Haneen only on sight, yet I arrived at Laila's shady apartment block feeling scraped raw by her death. It was easy to be galvanized by exhortations and volumes of human rights. The secret knowledge of Gaza – the fullness with which Gaza lived and fought from its corner – could draw the eye away from the blockade that was killing people one at a time. Haneen's death shredded my insulation. No one had to die of hepatitis. The blockade severely limited her treatment within Gaza, and impeded her exit. It worsened her odds. Haneen had also died of delay.

The apartment windows were closed to the heat, yellowing the front room. A dozen women reclined quietly in a circle of chairs and couches. Randa left the kitchen where she had been filling a serving plate with dates, and came to meet me. As she led me to Laila's mother, she said quietly into my ear, 'Laila can't sleep at all. I'm worried about her.'

I held Laila's mother's hand for a moment before I found a seat in the circle. Laila joined us; her eyes pink from crying and her face grey and slack with betrayal. The elders were accompanying each other through the latest visitation of something they had seen before. Laila, in her mid-twenties, had not been braced for this at all.

We met at Mazaj for coffee a week later. Laila tilted, leaning on air. The waiters were more solicitous than usual, knowing the family or recognizing the tilt.

Laila stirred her coffee for an extended time. 'We put off the wedding. Maybe a year.'

'I'm sorry. Ahmad'll wait for you.'

'I have to help get Haneen's son through this. And his homework, I have to be there for him after school. He needs stability, because he can't understand this.' Laila drooped, until she was addressing the table in a whisper. 'I don't understand it. I doubt everything now.' The fingers of one hand patted the table.

'Laila? I'm sorry this is so, so hard, but you ask questions – that's just you.'

'It's not okay. Not here.' Laila swallowed and straightened halfway. Her face always flushed easily, and did so with this admission. 'I had doubts, and I said so on social media. It's not okay, here, to say that you doubt.'

I thought of the nightly, defiant cheer along the beach: enforcement.

'Some people, even some people I knew, they were very angry at what I wrote, and they said so.'

I closed one eye. 'Ouch.'

'I'm deleting my accounts. At least for now.'

'Good. Do that. Just feel what you feel for a while.'

'I don't want to be bitter. The doctors were very good to us, and I know that they did what they could. But my sister should not have died.'

'No, she should not. I'm glad – it feels important that you know the doctors all did their best. I'm just sorry there's not more support for you.'

Laila took a deep breath but could not quite straighten up. 'Exactly. That's why I need to go back to work.'

'Are you ready? It's very fast.'

'Yes. That's where my support is. I can't just think about this or I'll go crazy.' She stretched her lips as if smiling were a necessary physiotherapy. 'I'm coming. UNRWA – *yalla*.'

While Rasha and Laila served out their notice at Mercy Corps, we short-listed applicants for the first enterprise project team. Eighty recent university graduates took technical tests, and I pored over the CVs and test papers on my office stoop. I felt a tickle of warning, because their CVs contained less white space than I typically saw. They were high achievers, some already with titles from Gaza's tech start-ups.

I shook it off and interviewed over two days. I was replicating the English advantage I had disliked at Mercy Corps, but both the industry and the project itself seemed to require it. The pilot project team would use English materials to learn and work within UNRWA's new software systems. In so doing, they would illustrate Gaza's bilingual potential to future clients. Rasha, Laila and I reviewed the results and agreed on the two dozen graduates who would prove the Gateway's concept.

***

Our pilot project began at an inauspicious moment. Flatbed trucks crisscrossed the Strip, ferrying fighters and rocket tubes to the parades that marked the first anniversary of the war. Israeli planes increased perceptibly overhead. Rocket launches, explosions and indeterminate rumblings were interspersed with the chants of demonstrations, as Gazans protested the death throes of their economy. The price of rice had risen by a third, and bread by 11 per cent. The Palestinian Authority in the West Bank (dominated by Hamas's rival Fatah faction) had fuel to sell, but Hamas would not – or by then, could not – pay their taxes. Without fuel, the lights of Gaza were blinking out. The power plant shut down. Electricity dwindled to a few hours, in the middle of a few nights, each week. Hospitals went dark. The sewage treatment plant shut down, leaving sewage to run through the streets. Of the fishery that normally supported 4000 Gazans, one lonely clump of half a dozen fishing boat lights still broke the black night horizon. I felt the mounting, caged pressure as a tightness in my chest. Gaza must erupt, but would it turn on Hamas, Israel or UNRWA?

Laila still looked wan when she and Rasha arrived for their first day as UNRWA consultants. Their arrival coincided with a protest by UNRWA contractors, who were unhappy with the organization's pay and employment terms. Someone had already disclosed Laila's salary, and UNRWA staff were calling her fiancé to complain. Seeing Laila and Rasha in the parking lot, the contractors broke off their chanting to declare in no uncertain terms that the Gateway enterprise was unwelcome, and to accuse the Gateway of diverting funds that UNRWA should have spent on relief food.

By the time they reached my door, Rasha had tugged the sleeves of her jacket over her hands and was slowly disappearing herself. I pulled them in and closed the door to hide their doubt.

'Welcome to UNRWA,' I said. 'Sit, sit. We're not being paid out of the food budget. You know that, right? We're not. I hear it, too. We're a bit of an easy target in a difficult moment, that's all.'

Laila worried, 'You hear it, too? Everyone hates us?'

'I hear from the foreigners who would like to revise some priorities. I guess you'll hear it from Palestinians who've been told that we're in financial competition. It's just a stressful time. I'm sure they'll all love us when they get to know us,' I added drily.

'Yes, of course,' Rasha mumbled automatically.

Scott gave Rasha and Laila an office above the directors' suite. They shared the third, top floor of the Front Office building with the Close Protection team. The CPs, as they were known, had been assigned to UNRWA's Gaza Director following an armed kidnapping attempt, and they stayed because the security concerns never abated. While the CPs waited between Bob's appointments, Rasha and Laila fed them cups of tea, and kept a list of everyone's favourite cookies. By the time I moved into the office next door to them, Rasha and Laila had domesticated the third floor and amassed an encyclopaedic knowledge of their office neighbours' lives.

The Gateway's pilot project team of graduates worked in a large room across the courtyard, near the back gate of the UNRWA compound. They sat in a ring, which devolved into a lived-in shambles. Their originality struck me at once. They saw globalization on the screens of their phones but they could not touch it, so it had not consumed them. They were veterans of an occupation, two uprisings, two wars and a future-eating blockade; yet Gaza contained hardly any formal workplaces. Knowing only Gaza's family-based economy, they extrapolated globalization as one big, informal, tightly bonded neighbourhood. They lacked cynicism, or the sameness of H&M, and they were fairly sure that policy meant less than inclusiveness. Community meant as much as profit.

Although I preferred their vision, we began with a course in more conventional business. Those who passed the course would take on the project itself.

Competition turned them predatory. No one could afford a wrong answer, nor a good answer outdone by a better one, nor a great answer that was attributed to a group. Individuals began to withhold from, or disavow the results of, their breakout groups. They wanted to express individual views that earned individual credit. After every review or quiz, the whole project team huddled to agree on the names of those who were at risk of being winnowed out. Then they clamoured to have all their scores read aloud.

'That might not be a good idea,' I began, sounding more parental than I intended.

'Read the scores,' they chorused from between and behind monitors.

'Let me say that a different way,' I began again. 'You each choose whether or not you want to discuss your results with others. Your results are not public unless you choose—'

'As long as you compare us, they are,' a woman insisted.

'Not really, no. You may choose to share yours, but—'

'We do.'

'—but maybe not everyone feels the same way.'

Laila, leaning against the wall, passed one hand before her mouth to hide a smirk, and tugged at her cardigan to complete the motion. I laughed at myself for having erred so quickly. The graduates read each other like stonewalling twins. Of course they felt the same way, or would vow that they felt the same way. They were Gazan.

'If you don't read them, we will,' the woman informed me.

Laila and I shrugged. They were adults. I picked up the sheet of test scores, and read them aloud. The person with the highest score threw his arms up, and everyone said congratulations. The person with the lowest score looked baleful. Then they gathered to recalibrate their rankings.

The dynamic grew so combative that we gave up and started work with the whole group. We completed the business course and waited eagerly for the real work to begin. A system manual arrived for us to study, and then another. The manuals were abstract but not highly technical, so I could share the unexpected training load.

Chapter 15

The worst storm in a generation struck Gaza in December 2013. Randa and her boys scraped up enough snow to press a sandy, foot-high snowman onto a dinner plate and wrap a keffiyeh around its head. Then torrential rains displaced thousands. Fishing boats sailed inland from the lagoon. They rescued door to door along the inundated streets, while UNRWA dispensed bedding and supplies from its emergency stocks. The international press covered the arrival of a special shipment of Qatari fuel to restart the power plant. They did not pause to ask how a blockaded community was supposed to adapt to climate change, nor did they return to see the power plant close again, two weeks later. The remaining electricity supply met only 20 per cent of demand. Municipalities parked their rubbish trucks and left the collections to donkey carts. Informal rubbish dumps sprouted, and toxic waste again began to burn.

Israel imposed an indefinite closure of the Kerem Shalom goods crossing (the only entry point for goods through the blockade), after an Israeli Bedouin was shot and killed while working on the fence that surrounded Gaza. 'If there is no quiet in Israel, there will be no quiet in Gaza,' the Defence Minister warned.

Four babies and children froze to death in the quiet that followed.

Hamas had gone frankly broke, imperilling Gaza's civil and economic order. Civil servants had not been paid since October. Demanding unity, Hamas made it known that non-conformists forfeited their community's protection, including women who did not cover their heads. As the month progressed, I knew of uncovered women who stopped shopping in the main marketplace, taking the bus or walking on the beach. Others began to cover their heads in the street, unwinding their scarves as they crossed the UNRWA parking lot. Laila already donned a long coat and hijab each time she went to the Islamic University's graduate courses in management accounting. However, her fellow students knew that Laila walked uncovered in the streets, and they felt increasingly free to disparage her.

As she left to do errands one lunchtime, Laila asked in passing whether I needed anything.

'A little peace, a little justice,' I always said.

'Me too,' she always replied.

She returned that day and flopped into her chair. Puckering her lips, she patted her hair as if the attention might console it, and warned, 'The longer this goes on, the more normal it feels to young people. Hamas is all they hear, just that one voice and it starts to sound normal. And it is not.'

The software systems manuals and the stormy darkness leeched morale from the Gateway's workroom. No one had enough electricity to charge their phones and read through a whole PDF manual at night, so we processed a budget revision comprised solely of boxes of paper, and we began to print the manuals. The Gateway's practice platform was bogging down in theory. Worse, from the moment they left each afternoon until the moment they returned taut and humming with stress the following morning, the project team lived with cloying frustration. Nothing worked any longer. Nothing. I had begun to turn on my apartment lights – when there was light – by banging my head against the wall.

One morning, a mother attempted to stretch her blue lips into a smile while she shook the rain from her coat in the workroom doorway. She was a logical woman with degrees in computer science and business, an inclusive and disciplined leader by nature. She cared for us so warmly that we called her Mama. On the day that we had driven to Khan Younis, Mama brought two dozen pastries along, because a half-hour drive was long enough for someone to get hungry.

'I'm sorry I'm late,' she enunciated. *Lay-te.*

'That's okay,' I said from the front of the room, looking for something warm to throw around her.

She dismissed my words and stood on the threshold wearing her malfunctioning smile. 'There was no water, so I couldn't give my daughter her bath. I mean, I knew that. When there was water last time, there was no electricity for me to pump it, so I knew there would be no water. A neighbour said he would bring me some water, and he did. Carried it up all the stairs by hand, because of course there was no power for the elevator. The water was cold, so I had to heat it for her. The neighbours had fuel, so I warmed up the water there and gave my daughter her bath. I got her dressed, I made a cold breakfast for her and my husband. The dishes, I left them – no water. I got her to kindergarten in the clean clothes I ironed when there was power. And there was a sign on the door. My daughter's kindergarten has closed without notice, because they have no fuel.'

'Ooh, that sounds—' I began.

Her voice climbed one notch and her smile widened to compensate. 'No-no, I planned for all that – I'm more organized than that! Everything until the kindergarten, I do that every morning. But today, I took her to her grandmother, except that she couldn't . . . I planned for everything up to that point, but I did not have a back-up babysitter. There I was in the street, calling people to find someone who could keep my daughter for the day. And my daughter, of course, she started to cry and then she started to scream because she knew I was upset, and I can't just leave my screaming child – and *that,* that was just a little more than I'd planned for. That's why I'm late.'

She stalked stiffly across the room without acknowledging our sympathy, jammed a cable into her phone, plugged in her charger and plunked herself into a seat wearing her sodden raincoat and that robotic smile.

She excused herself to the room in general. 'I'll have a Plan B next time.'

Plan B; we said it so often that they wrote it on my birthday cake.

I hung my head to give Mama some time to settle into her seat. Across the floor tiles, I saw one fellow's bare ankles poking out beneath his flood-soaked pants. He had spread the morning's printed pages over his table to photograph them with his phone, because he preferred to read from his small screen for as long as his battery lasted.

Click – frown, *click* – frown. His hands were shivering too violently for the camera to focus.

I wanted to throw warm blankets over them, and then I wanted to scream.

I got home that evening, dropped my gym bag and my bag full of printed systems manuals, and banged my forehead against the light switch. Tiaba's generator was maxed out, and the added demand of my light blew a fuse. I reset the fuse, and tried the heater. It blew all the fuses. I went down to the guardroom, where they reset the master switch. Deciding against the elevator while fuses were making the whole building wink, I walked up the stairs. As I opened my door, I heard Kirstin's door close upstairs. A moment later, my light decayed from the shade of dry sand to the shade of wet.

I had neglected to heat water during breakfast, so there would be only cold water to wash. Shivering already, I wet a facecloth and sponged cursorily at the gym sweat. Then I pulled on a sweatsuit, layered a bathrobe and socks over it, flapped a blanket around me like a cape, and tipped my work bag over the desk.

The manuals exceeded 2000 bone-dry, stilted pages. I suspected that we had taken on the wrong project, but we had no other. I read and wrote summaries while the light deepened to a raw umber. Then I moved to the easy chair in front of the window, where my knees could hold the pages nearer to my half-charged lantern. I slumped and squinted, but as the descriptions of storage architectures became more technical, I understood less. I tried to call Rasha or Laila, but their phones had finished for the night.

My lantern flickered out. The words swam and merged and went dark. Wrapped in my blanket and warm, amniotic self-pity, I stared at the outline of the binder, and then at the low-slung, cheesy orange moon which shed so little light upon it.

I asked the moon, *What good is an IT degree without electricity and running water?*

It smirked at me and I scowled back.

None of them has ever fired a rocket.

I shook my binder at the moon, but the moon was used to me by then.

You can't tell me that the immiseration of Gaza makes anyone safe.

I was stuck. I could not reconcile the world as I understood it, my beautiful abstract religion, and the exercise of Israel's power to squander my project team and torment the people around me.

No label held my pieces of belief together. I had read clear across the Zionist Left. They asked how little Israel had to give up, as if they could find a computational theory of quiet. They did not see, let alone see equally, the people around me. I had read to the edge of the Jewish spectrum as I knew it, and for months, I had been rattling its bars, unable to reach beyond them. So I remained in pieces, daring the moon to justify the superfluity of Gaza's suffering.

***

Early in 2014, UNRWA announced that it anticipated a $65 million budget shortfall for the year. The militant factions united, urging Palestinians to blame UNRWA for their hardship. Within the occupied territories, UNRWA served as the stand-in for its donors' choices, and sometimes for the injustice of occupation itself. For fed up Gazans, UNRWA was the most accessible piece of a deteriorating status quo.

Gaza was laid out in a row of five governorates: North, Gaza, Middle, Khan Younis and Rafah. That winter, graffiti flowered outward from Middle. The motif placed the letters 'UN' within a Star of David or a swastika, or both. Printers cranked out banners, blaming Bob in the most personal terms for failing to raise more money. We passed through a morning gauntlet of blame at the compound gates, as Gazans demanded more from UNRWA.

More? UNRWA may have been as broke as Hamas. We were all tumbling together in a slow, bruising, cartwheeling crash.

The Gaza Gateway's pilot project slid off the rails without real work to do. Software systems manuals piled up like rocket tubes on the Mediterranean seabed. Understandably disgruntled and bored, the project team of graduates responded in their lexicon of power and resistance. They manned the barricades against us.

They learned how to hound Laila out of the room. I would find her at her desk, wrapping her ringing head in a Libyan-style turban. Rasha lasted longer, but she often left the workroom speechless, blinking in the sunlight.

My Tiaba 2 friends commiserated over endless thrown-together dinners.

'Hell,' I bellowed across Uta's dinner table, 'has a room full of under-employed computer programmers, with their faces full of that co-o-osmic disappointment – and one condemned soul who has to stand in front of them!'

I sought exhaustion in the gym. Not fitness; oblivion. A number of us raced 10,000 metres on the rowing machine, straining so hard for so long that rowers sometimes keeled over into a flattened crouch on the cool, dirty floor afterward. I left UNRWA in the evenings, around the time that Ismail Haniyeh, the leader of Hamas's de facto authority, shuffle-jogged along the boulevard with his entourage. He looked as unhappy as everyone else.

Chapter 16

As winter gave way to spring, I whiled away the warmer evenings with Bob, sipping single malt whiskey with our feet on his terrace railing. We were both removed from UNRWA's social mainstream and tolerant of some conversational slack.

The enterprise team called him our marketing manager. Even as he briefed himself hoarse to warn visiting delegations of Gaza's impending disaster, Bob kept touting young Gaza's potential and seeking start-up funds for the Gaza Gateway. He cajoled every visitor, 'Gaza needs half a billion dollars for the status quo, and one million for change.'

Bob brought out pita and hummus for dinner around midnight one evening, set the plate down and reclined into comfortable shadow. I held a corner of pita at eye level and remembered, 'The funny thing is, I always thought I would volunteer one more time. Deliver the rice.'

'Why?' he grunted, bemused, having seen a great deal more of relief food than I had.

'Because there are hungry people.'

We left it quiet for a moment.

'Why volunteer?'

'I guess it's a kind of immunity. I volunteered for two years, and I just worked without pay for another four. The best work happened to have no money to offer. It's sort of liberating to step outside the whole status-obsessed structure and think about different things. And maybe a little fuck-you-ness, too. You should try it.'

'Don't think so. What's wrong with what you do?'

'Oh, nothing. It's just so political now. In the nineties, strangers used to say, "You must be Christian to do this." Now th "You must be the neoliberal batshit Right." Rice is . . . ric blameless.'

A snort came from the darkness.

'*We're* not blameless but the rice is. Rice is the truest thing I know.' I toasted Bob with my glass. 'So, thank you.'

He had appointed me to the poverty survey task force.

In the year 2000, before there was a blockade, one Gazan family out of ten was food-insecure. UNRWA provided relief food assistance to 80,000 Gazan Palestinians. As we spoke on the terrace fourteen years later, 800,000 Gazans needed UNRWA's relief food.

Their need was not caused by a lack of food on supermarket shelves. Proponents of the blockade periodically circulated images of supermarket food, as if supermarket shelves precluded hunger in Gaza or anywhere else. The images were irrelevant. The Gaza Strip did not lack food, it lacked livelihoods. The blockade prevented poor Gazans from earning income to buy the food in the pictures.

UNRWA's donors funded food relief for the two poorest categories of refugees. The poorest received foods roughly equal to 65 per cent of their daily caloric needs. The next-poorest received the equivalent of 40 per cent of their caloric needs. The categories were bounded by income, say, those earning less than $1.60 per day, and those earning between $1.61 and $3.50 per day. Anyone who earned more – even if she had only $3.51 per day – was classified as non-poor. Although $3.51 was far from a sufficient income, and Gaza lacked livelihoods or social welfare supports to make up the difference, non-poor households were not entitled to food assistance.

That kind of food relief was not designed to fix poverty. A sack of flour helped a family to cope this month, but it contained nothing that might improve the family's future prospects. On the contrary, UNRWA's financial ill health reminded everyone that funding was not keeping pace with need. Next month might be worse.

UNRWA's relief food – and therefore its system of assessing poverty and assigning food entitlements – was gravely important to poor households. However, the system was obsolete, and the community had dwindling faith in its equity. Gaza's circumstances could change overnight. UNRWA urgently owed the community an assessment system that could respond swiftly and transparently to such volatility. Bob had resolved to create that system.

The Gaza Gateway automated a complex survey in partnership with a New Zealand company, while UNRWA's own IT department wove the results into its in-house systems. I had been appointed to the poverty survey task force, which would devise UNRWA's new relief policy and operations. For sixteen months, the task force ripped apart every cobbled-together process. We nit-picked through the fiendish variations of household composition. Could a child be poor, if her non-poor father provided inconsistently for multiple wives – and if so, how would each of the resulting households be composed and classified? We argued most passionately over privacy and protection. If a parent lied to ensure that her borderline household would be classified as poor and entitled to relief, what policy response would be fair to her children and the children next door?

We could debate the content of fairness and write an algorithm. But would there be enough money to buy the food?

Gaza heard about the new poverty survey while its unpaid fighters were flirting with war. Already jittery and angry, some people feared that any new poverty assessment system would be used to save money by eliminating people from the relief rolls. They mistrusted change even more reflexively than they mistrusted the current system. 'Change' had meant 'worse' for such a long time. The daily demonstrations grew noisier and more acrimonious.

In a conference room, a genial European chided Bob for his alarmist briefing. After all, this visitor reasoned, their delegation had driven all the way from the Erez Border Crossing without seeing marauding gangs of naked or neglected children. Twenty minutes they had driven, without seeing blood puddles. Gaza looked so civilized.

Bob swallowed hard. His jaw twitched. He filled his lungs with air and said levelly, 'We are alarmist, because we are alarmed.'

'Can I pour you a whiskey or ten?' Bob texted that evening.

On his terrace, we ranted at the donor world's preference for emergency response over prevention.

'Jesus, Bob. Why did you want this job? The more you try, the more someone hates you for it.'

Feet on his railing, Bob blew a ring of cigar smoke from within the palisade of his knees and observed clinically, 'I must be doing a really good job.'

***

I joined my sister for a weekend in Israel. I slept a night on her couch, and we drove to Tel Aviv the following morning.

There were two roads from Jerusalem to Tel Aviv. Route 443 ran alongside the reviled wall which separated Israel from the West Bank, and swallowed up many acres of Palestinian land in the process. Fencelines, watchtowers and checkpoints intruded upon Route 443. Joan took the forested Route 1, driving between some of the 240 million trees of our childhood planting certificates.

I traced the outline of a tree on the window of my sister's rented car. In shadeless Gaza, I craved trees. Not 'trees', but the serrations of one supple, breathing leaf. One, multiplied by the million settled greens of Canadian leaves, and the boisterous young greens outside my window in New Zealand; and that primordial green to which all other greens aspired – the emerald of a Cambodian rice paddy in January. Instead of trees, Gazans had gates – and they were not wrong to accuse the poverty survey of apportioning scarcity behind those gates.

'Mar, you look uninspired.'

I sat up straighter. 'I'm . . . disturbed. This poverty survey is very unsettling.' I described UNRWA's humanitarian task. 'We have to make wise use of insufficient resources. We have to—' I snuck a sidelong glance at my sister, '—apportion the scarcity in some way that is fair, in a context that is not. I mean, dig it: income of $3.50 per day qualifies your family – your children – to receive 40 per cent of their calories through relief food, while income of $3.51 per day makes you wealthy enough to find your own sack of flour and your own bottle of cooking oil . . .'

Joan lifted one hand from the steering wheel. She pressed her fingers over her lips to prevent something from being said.

'Well? There have to be cut-off points, and if it's not $3.51 then it's $3.74, right? Someone has to be the gatekeeper.'

A pained grunt issued through Joan's fingers.

'I know,' I said. 'But UNRWA gets only so much money for food—'

She spoke through her fingers. 'But, Mar, you make it sound—'

'I know,' I repeated with some vehemence.

We eyed each other. My sister opened her mouth to speak.

'Exactly,' I pre-empted her, 'I *know*. The math is not the hard part. The problem is the fucking gate!'

'Mar, are you sure you should do this?'

I met her eyes and dared her. 'Having calories beats not having calories. Don't you think? So, yes, what I am doing is morally defensible, in a situation that is not.'

Neither of us could bring ourselves to say the G-word out loud.

After their weekends out, UNRWA staff met at a café near the Ashkelon train station on Sunday mornings, to drive back into Gaza. I watched the implacable concrete walls of Gaza fill the windscreen of the van that Sunday morning, as we approached the Erez Crossing. My colleagues slurped the last of their Israeli take-out coffees in the seats around me. As we piled out for the first passport check, they tossed their paper cups into rubbish bins and their talk turned to the coming work week.

My mind was still with my sister, and our generational shuddering at the G-word.

In the opening pages of my journal, I had rejected the shorthand so often used to describe Gaza, 'the world's largest open-air prison'. Gaza had never felt like an atomized, predatory prison. It was a whole, trapped, audaciously human society of mutual assistance and resistance and domesticity and dreams. The metaphor bothered me especially at these walls, which were indeed prison-like. 'Prison' saw these walls and missed everything within them.

'Prison' folded Gaza into the morality of law and order. Consenting democratic societies sentenced individuals to prison after due process. They paid for prisoners' electricity, food and water; allowed families to visit, and released the prisoners at the ends of their sentences. They accepted prisons as permanent institutions, and prisoners remained rights-bearing members of society.

Gaza was none of those things. Prisons did not hold a million children.

At the exit from Israel, armed soldiers counted our passports against the number of bodies in the van. They returned our passports and raised the traffic barrier arm. The van passed between the thick concrete walls of the Erez Crossing. No civil analogy described our entry into Gaza, because those gates were an act of war.

I took a deep breath – the Gaza side always felt hotter – and I said it to myself: *ghetto.*

An enduring, locked, ethnic community was properly called a ghetto. Ghetto walls judged an entire ethnicity to be dangerous, and condemned its children and its babies to live in open-ended confinement. The people behind ghetto walls could be deprived of their human rights, because someone considered them to be less than human.

Israelis had devalued Gazan Palestinians that way. As they prepared for war in the spring of 2014, Israelis were again goading their army to 'finish the job', 'mow the lawn', 'cut the grass' and 'clean it out'. Those things were not said of humans. Those were precursors, code for a zone of human and ecological sacrifice.

The word 'ghetto' offended me, because Jewish ghettoes had been the way-stations to concentration camps and genocide. For exactly that reason, the Jewish ghettoes and the campaigns of Jewish dehumanization were supposed to be the last. No matter who built the next ghetto wall, we were all compelled to oppose it.

I tried that. *I oppose the building of ghetto walls, even when the builders are Jews.*

The final, massive gate was powering shut behind our van. When I looked back at the steel and jumbles of concertina wire that completed Gaza's horizon, it became simpler. The algebra of the Gaza side made it simple.

It doesn't matter who built it. I oppose this wall because *I am a Jew.*

Just like that, my politics joined my religion after their long estrangement. My pieces fit.

I wrote to Bob and asked to remain in Gaza through the coming war, to work on the emergency response. He replied that I would be welcome, but he pointed out that (thanks to my disinterest in UNRWA staff jobs), I did not have United Nations privileges and immunities to protect me if something went wrong. I volunteered to stay and work without them.

Chapter 17

In the middle of March 2014, the IDF killed three Islamic Jihad fighters. Islamic Jihad fired 55 retaliatory rockets. Israel responded with seven air raids, 22 missiles, tank shells and border fire. The evening felt like a rehearsal: speeding pulse, eyes crossing the ceiling, estimating neighbourhoods. Fatalism welled up as a momentary relief, an end to the waiting. Then a storm rose. Thunder crashed between the explosions like a sustained, night-long bombardment.

In the morning, I opened the workroom door to greet a subdued project team. We forgot our divisions and pretended to work.

I was speaking when we heard a rocket launch at mid-morning. No one moved until my phone beeped. I snatched it from the desk to read the security text. Militants were firing salvoes of rockets at Israel, from three of Gaza's five governorates. As I looked up from the text, we heard more launches. A circle of gloomy faces tried to read my expression, pleading for any news other than the news I had read.

A plane flew low overhead before I could speak, and every eye tracked it across the ceiling. Then the room erupted in cellphone sound effects. Each person reached for their phone, to read and relay messages, to verify the locations of each of their family members.

Rasha banged through the door, white-faced in her big, belted parka. She left the door to bounce shut, and sat next to me without a word.

'Take your time,' I rasped through my dry mouth at the texting project team. I sat down hard, trying to take them all in with my eyes.

Until that morning, I had imagined that a gulf of time and

action still separated us from war. War would not happen yet, not to this room full of insufferably stubborn, undefended young parents. There would be forks in the road ahead of us, moments at which to turn aside. Those texts ripped at the membrane that held normal things in place.

More planes rumbled overhead.

They had babies. They had done nothing wrong.

We made disjointed conversation.

I had time to reflect that I knew how to wait for good things. Births, travel, a lover's return. I ticked off time like an optimist. The Gazans in this room were steeling themselves to be attacked with unaccountable force, in a closed space. They ticked off the agony of waiting for something that would be immeasurably worse than the wait.

Then I rose, nodding in a conclusive way. 'That's an hour. It'll be okay, it's been an hour,' I said, as if the rockets had been a time-limited offer. As if rules forbade the declaration of war after sixty-one minutes.

From that morning, the days were reduced to sheer, bullish endurance. My ears strained to hear the first stirring of jet engines overhead. I had given up my hopeful way of waiting, and I listened only for the sound of a trigger.

One of the group began to arrive late, and to work erratically. She came upstairs to talk, and she acknowledged that her concentration was slipping as the war approached. Rasha watched her leave my office. Then she summoned me with one hand, and pointed silently to the woman's name on a list. She waited for it to sink in. When it did, I gasped and slapped my forehead, and ran after the woman to have a different conversation.

Israel had bombed a family home in the last war, killing eleven members of the Aldalou family. I employed this member of the surviving family, supervised another relative on a separate project, and I knew their neighbour. In tiny Gaza, one bomb reverberated that way.

***

Ultima Thule, the wee headland beyond the port, felt unconquerably distant; the vanishing point beyond which no further decisions needed to be made. Late one April night, we stared glumly at it.

'Have you ever been all the way out there?' I asked.

Bob shook his head. 'No, never. You?'

'No.'

We both followed the headlights of a solitary car, all the way out to the end of the breakwater. There, one after-hours escapee parked and left the lights shining out to sea.

I said, 'I hope there's a pair of teenagers in that car.'

'If there is,' Bob sighed, 'it'll be a pair of boys.'

The car reversed into a tight three-point turn. We picked up the glasses and the empty tub of hummus.

***

We worked underwater, propelled by all the things we wanted to finish, and then stranded in the backwash of futility. Shortly before Rasha's thirtieth birthday, and six weeks after Laila's wedding, both women received permits to leave Gaza for a few days of work in the West Bank. I booked myself out for the weekend, and arranged to meet them for a carefree afternoon in the sunshine of Jaffa, the Palestinian town adjoining Tel Aviv.

They picked their way over the cobblestones toward me, frowning, squinting, sizing up their surroundings. The withdrawal of stress had somehow made the physical world untrustworthy. Laila wore a flowered blouse. Perhaps it was new; the flowers took her aback, as if they had grown since she last looked down.

'She sleeps twelve hours!' Rasha exclaimed. 'Every night! Not like sleeping, like a rock. I keep getting up to see if she is breathing.'

I wondered what to make of the day. We were so rarely together on foot. The outdoors felt unfamiliar, but sun always felt good on skin. I suggested, 'Let's just walk up the beach.'

I measured the steps from the clock tower plaza down to the curb before I placed my feet.

At the base of the boardwalk, we stepped into an alien, fleshy, Hebrew world. We ambled, and we hardly spoke. I watched them watch everything. Laila walked with her mouth open, nearly gasping the sea air. The salty breeze ushered in clouds, unsettling the sunlight and the temperature. They let each variation flow over them. In unison, they tilted their faces up to the sun's appearance, and turned their heads into the wind. Laila's eyes lost their daze and began to shine.

I fell in behind them, scanning the oncoming Israelis. One mutter, one glance at their long sleeves or Rasha's hijab might shatter their light. Thankfully, Tel Aviv took no notice of us. I stayed behind them, enjoying the way that the shifting water framed them as a single shape, until I found that I was sobbing. I cried behind them for a long stretch, because a walk on the beach should never mean as much as those minutes meant.

We strolled all the way to the port. By then, a stiffening wind was piling up more businesslike clouds. I hailed a taxi to find a restaurant for a late lunch. Rasha and Laila got into the back seat.

At the first traffic light, the taxi driver lowered my window from the controls on his armrest. Levering himself against the steering wheel, he leaned halfway across me and let loose a cigarette-voiced screed at the driver in the next lane. The other driver rolled up his window in haughty offense. He peeled away as soon as his light turned green. Our driver took his time about sitting back, straightening his shirt collar and stroking his stubbled neck.

At the next light he did it again, to a different driver.

Between intersections, our driver apologized for his poor English, and then used it to curse anyone who came to mind. He hated everyone who came to mind, and menaced everyone who caught his eye.

'Ya-fugha-fugha-fugher . . .'

I counted off the passing hotels and tried to gauge the likelihood that he would use the car as an offensive weapon within the remaining kilometres.

Wiping his lips after another mouthful of invective, he growled at me, 'Whar ya from.'

'New Zealand,' I admitted.

'Unh.' New Zealand may have been too remote to muster a meaningful grudge.

I glanced back at Laila and Rasha, who were holding hands in alarm. This gave the driver an idea, and he twisted in his seat to bring them in to view. I felt as if I'd shown Little Red Riding Hood to the big bad wolf.

'Whar ya from,' he growled.

Laila cleared her throat and whispered, 'We're Palestinian.'

'Yeah?' The driver wrenched himself around further, to see them more fully. 'You? Really? An' you – yes?' He took a deep breath, filling his gravelly lungs, and he bellowed, '*Ahlan*! Welcome l'Yisroel! *Ahlan w'sahlan*!!' He thumped one hand over his combustible heart. Transformed, he spent the remainder of the drive begging us to understand how well he liked Palestinians – unlike all of the other damnable people around him – and how wholeheartedly he meant his welcome.

We stumbled out of the car, laughing in relief on the sidewalk. Rasha fanned herself and recovered a squeaky voice. 'I think we are the only people in the world that he does not hate!'

We had lunch on a café terrace, putting up with the wind in order to watch the scudding waves. I saw them off in a taxi as the rain began to fall. I held my hands out and watched the drops land on my arms.

They returned to Gaza on schedule, but Erez mysteriously closed to foreigners. I worked from the hotel room and bought a pair of consolation shoes in the evening, because the only confinement worse than being locked into the cauldron of Gaza was being locked out.

The following day, I bought another pair.

And then a third, each day's heels higher than the last.

On the third day, barely noticed, a Fatah delegation from the West Bank slipped into Gaza. A new National Consensus Government announced itself on the fourth day, uniting Hamas and Fatah in a technocratic government.

I jammed my weekend bag full of shoes, and returned to Gaza.

***

The Palestinian factions had never united to represent the interests of all Palestinians. Their visceral rivalry superseded any national vision. Fatah, through its domination of various institutions, was Palestine's international interlocutor. Hamas – and therefore Gaza – was excluded from conversation.

Since 2010, Israel had openly maintained a 'separation' policy to divide the West Bank (which it contested) from the Gaza Strip (which it disavowed).[24] More specifically, Israel wanted to exclude Gaza's population from the territory under its control. If Israel acknowledged its responsibility for Gaza, then the majority of people under Israel's control would soon be non-Jews. Israel's claim to be both Jewish and democratic could be maintained a little longer, if Gaza could be forgotten. Gaza's numbers threatened Israel far more strategically than its rockets.

Israel's separation policy deprived Palestinians of their rights as humans, and as a people living under occupation. It divided families and hobbled Palestine's political and economic life. The separation policy disfigured the State of Palestine, while Palestinians' lived experience of occupation diverged. Blended national statistics resembled neither place, nor the occupied city of East Jerusalem. The Gaza Strip was one-fifteenth the size of the West Bank, with a population density nine times higher. The West Bank was fragmented by the growth of illegal settlements, which housed hundreds of thousands of Israelis. Countless checkpoints obstructed movement and community life in the West Bank, while Gazans were locked together.

Despite those differences, Palestinians' own aspirations and political rights, international law and the prospects of the State of Palestine all required the nation to be understood as one unit. Anything less would help to erase their nationhood.

Sadly, the rivalry between Hamas and Fatah made a single Palestine even harder to envision. To the dismay of many Palestinians, the factions furthered the separation agenda in their rush to fortify their own turf. They established separate ministries and legal codes for the West Bank and Gaza. They paid rival public sectors and security forces. They took evident pleasure in their rival's failures. The donor states funded the separation policy and chose its winners in neoliberal configurations. Both they and the Palestinian factions excluded – and the factions sharply suppressed – other prospective leadership.

Given this history, no one viewed the Government of National

24 For more on the separation policy, see https://gisha.org/UserFiles/File/publications/separating-land-separating-people/separating-land-separating-people-web-en.pdf or this fact page: https://gisha.org/publication/1662. (accessed April 2, 2019)

Consensus optimistically. By May 2014, many observers thought that Hamas was eager to be rid of its administrative responsibility for Gaza, but I knew no one who believed that it would relinquish control. Rather, if it could persuade someone else to govern, Hamas would wield power from the shadows, and fight unencumbered.

The new Government of National Consensus was sworn in on June 2, 2014. Heretofore, Israel had protested the absence of a unified Palestinian leadership with whom to negotiate. Following the formation of the unity government, Israel refused to negotiate with any entity that fully represented Palestinians by including Hamas. It urged other states not to recognize Palestine's government.[25]

The 2014 Government of National Consensus never came to life. Hamas let go of the gears of government, and no one stepped into the void. All of a sudden, Gaza had no government. Diminished by bankruptcy and relieved of its burdens, Hamas had no incentive to refrain from fighting.

***

The dry, crackling time of listening gave way to a clammy certainty. One Gazan man told a colleague that he felt like a child, locked naked in a dark room, waiting to be beaten.

The trigger was pulled on June 12.[26] Three teenaged Israeli boys disappeared while they were hitch-hiking in the West Bank. From the first moments, Israel's Prime Minister Netanyahu blamed the kidnapping on Hamas. On the third day, Israel's Deputy Minister of Defence threatened, then launched air strikes on Gaza, although no one ever suggested that the boys were in Gaza. Through the month, in the absence of information about the boys, the Israeli government reported on its punishment of Gaza. They found the boys' bodies on June 30 in the West Bank. The IDF blew up the homes of two West Bank suspects before the sun set.

25 For a summary of the immediate questions raised by the Government of National Consensus, see https://www.aljazeera.com/indepth/opinion/2014/06/palestine-unity-deal-201465958139661O5.html

26 For a snapshot of those confusing June weeks, see Nathan Thrall, 'Whose Palestine?' New York Review of Books (June 19, 2014). https://www.nybooks.com/daily/2014/06/19/whose-palestine/

Israeli forces had killed nine Palestinians, raided 1300 buildings and arrested 800 people without charge or trial.[27] Subsequent reports indicated that the Israeli government would have known that the boys were almost certainly dead, from shortly after the time of their disappearance.

The Israeli families buried their sons on July 1. UNRWA sent many of its international staff out of Gaza, and all my Tiaba 2 friends departed. Emails stopped. Everything stopped. Gaza was scared stiff, laid bare beneath a sky of hard, metallic blue.

I watched footage from the burials without sound. The families' faces looked so stoic. I hoped also to see some demand that the funerals should end. Instead, I thought I saw resignation, even on the faces of children. I wondered if the risks of war would come to feel more normal to my niece than the risks of peace.

Netanyahu whipped Israel into a paroxysm of righteous, blind, misdirected rage. Ayelet Shaked, a rising member of Israel's governing coalition soon to become Israel's Minister of Justice, posted on Facebook that 'the entire Palestinian people is the enemy'. She urged soldiers to kill the elderly and the women who gave birth to 'little snakes', and destroy the infrastructure and homes where the 'little snakes' would be raised.[28]

The next day, a slight Palestinian teenager was abducted in East Jerusalem. His assailants beat him, and set him on fire while he was still alive. Rioting spread through Palestinian neighbourhoods.

Watching the news, I reeled at the savagery. What monster could burn a living child?

For long minutes, I feared that we had entered a purely criminal time, a war of attrition by child murder. I didn't know how to face it. I wanted to run away. I wasn't made for that kind of emergency response. I jumped up from the news to wash my hair, anchoring myself in the mundane world.

27 https://en.wikipedia.org/wiki/2014_kidnapping_and_murder_of_Israeli_teenagers#Suspects_killings (accessed April 1, 2019).

28 A full translation of Ayelet Shaked's July 2014 Facebook post appears at: https://electronicintifada.net/blogs/ali-abunimahisraeli-lawmakers-call-genocide-palestinians-gets-thousands-facebook-likes

Later that evening, I sipped whiskey on the terrace with my neighbour, Mike. He was a trim, blond man in his forties. We went to the gym together early Saturday mornings, and he drove the weekday high-intensity circuits at maximum volume, in the clipped tones of the British military. He was no less tenacious outside the gym, and we sparred as often as we agreed.

I offered to bet that the endless excavations of Beach Road concealed the construction of a command bunker, directly below Bob's and our apartments.

'You laugh now,' I warned. 'But you'll get in that elevator one morning, and it'll open two floors below the street.'

Mike snorted. 'If I were invading Gaza, I'd come in from the sea. While everyone is looking the other way. Amphibious landing. Frogmen.'

'Frogmen, there?' I scoffed and pointed at the very spot where Hamas would later erect a monument to its frogmen. 'Don't be silly.'

Phantasmagorical ceasefires and goading volleys flew around us for one further week. Israeli forces massed openly at the border. Israeli police were filmed beating a cousin of the murdered Palestinian boy so badly that his face swelled into one undifferentiated sphere. The IDF killed seven Hamas fighters, and Gazan fighters began to send rockets into areas of Israel that were unaccustomed to them. July 7 was payday for Fatah's Gazan staff. That morning, Hamas's unpaid fighters detoured to destroy some of Gaza City's ATMs. The banks closed. No one got paid.

Everyone provoked everyone else. Hamas had begun to fire alongside the other militants, signalling the onset of war.

I sat with the ashen project team one last time on July 7. No one said much. Festooned with charger cables, the workroom looked like a zombie slumber party. For the past week, we had invited the group to bring pillows and nap at their desks whenever it was quiet. Gaza Gateway coffee mugs – 'Outsourcing In Gaza, This Is Where It All Began' – were glommed onto the tabletops by rings of dried coffee. They brimmed with chocolate bar wrappers. Yasmin's chair was empty. She was home with her one-day-old baby in Shuja'iyya. The night terrors of a toddler's first war had reduced Mama's eyes to little dashes across her face. Two residents of Rafah, where the bombing had been heaviest thus far, dozed against their pillows while the Aldalou family relative sat bolt upright and preternaturally alert, scanning, scanning.

I found Laila and Rasha transferring files upstairs. They stopped when they saw me.

Laila began, 'If we have to run from the house, these laptops will be too bulky.'

Rasha interrupted to list the files they were copying onto external drives, but her voice trailed off and she toed the floor.

Laila finished fast, 'In case they blow up this building.'

'Nobody's bombing UNRWA,' I declared, slapping their office wall to prove its permanence.

They mumbled agreement, as if we were not standing a hundred metres from the New Warehouse, which had replaced the one that the IDF blew up in 2009.[29]

Rasha and I Skyped with the New Zealand company that had won the poverty survey tender. Two bangs, two rocket launches interrupted us. Rasha flinched at the sound and I felt it obliquely, like a movie reflected on a familiar face. We held hands under the desk and finished the call.

When I left Rasha, I stopped in the hall to examine my steady hands. I felt no fear. Foreigners enjoyed so much unearned power in the countries where we worked, but we had none when it counted. The bombs repudiated my care, and left me feeling numb and distant. I rubbed my palms briskly, and went to my office.

29 https://www.aljazeera.com/news/middleeast/2009/01/200911608972875 9.html

Chapter 18

I ate dinner on Bob's terrace. We raised our voices over the steady rumble and crump and bang, and spoke about other things. In the morning, I bought a jar of chocolate chips. I planted them on the front edge of my desk, asserting that there was still time to bake my niece's chocolate chip cookie recipe for the whole third floor, before the war.

But there wasn't.

Bob formally declared the emergency across Gaza, and UNRWA suspended all of its non-emergency activities.[30]

I unscrewed the jar's lid and poured chocolate chips into my mouth, sifting them against my palette for one last rich, familiar sensation before everything familiar fell away. Then I went downstairs to wave as the Gateway project team carried their pillows onto the last staff buses. They went home to sit and wait beneath the bombs, and I went to hug Rasha and Laila.

Laila had purple gouges beneath her eyes. 'They fired a rocket from my street, so Ahmad and I spent the night on the ground floor of the apartment, in case . . .'

I shook my head, fearing the effects so early in her first pregnancy.

We were slow to let go of each other. They lingered in the doorway and we said, 'I love you – *Allah yatik el afiah*' one more time. Through my windows, I watched them scurry past the workroom, and leave the compound by the back gate. Ten minutes later, supremely organized Rasha phoned to say that she had left her tablet behind. I retrieved it, smoothed my hand over the

30 The attack of 2014 is variously dated. This refers to UNRWA's operational declaration on July 8, 2014.

cover – the pink of her running shoes – and tucked it into my desk drawer for safekeeping.

I sat down to write to others from Mercy Corps. I sent the first group emails – the first of my platitudes – as the noon count arrived in my inbox: 46 rockets had been launched out, and 49 missiles had been fired in during the morning. UNRWA fell silent as it emptied. Colleagues slipped home to comfort their children. I spoke with Gazan friends by phone.

165 rockets and 92 missiles.

At some hour already past, war had begun. I tried to remember what had felt important a month ago, before the world shrank to the size of Gaza, and I wondered if anything would ever be harmless again.

Then I followed the scraping sounds downstairs to the room which took up the whole first floor of the Front Office building. A logistics team was converting it into the Central Operations Room, or COR; boxing up the existing files and shunting the desks into T-shaped groups. COR had a tiny kitchenette and two showers at one end. Foreigners could eat lunch in the anteroom at the other end, while Palestinians continued to fast through Ramadan.

I logged into COR's new emergency database. Gaza's history of brief wars suggested that 30,000, or even as many as 50,000 people might seek brief shelter in UNRWA schools. However, having distributed emergency supplies after the December storm, we had supplies for a maximum of 35,000 people. I had been assigned responsibility for the distribution of non-food items – including bedding, personal consumables, small equipment, cleaning and hygiene supplies – to the flagged United Nations schools that we would press into action as designated emergency shelters. COR's 'Central' label distinguished our Gaza City room from UNRWA's tier of governorate-level emergency structures, and I would also centralize their reporting and the counts of people displaced in the shelters.

At the end of the afternoon, we gathered around a long table in the centre of the COR room. We briefed between five artillery explosions. A few of the ex-military men parsed each detonation, identifying the armaments and guessing at their targets. Jenn caught my eye, the only other woman among seventeen international men. She had recently arrived to lead UNRWA's communications department, and I knew her only as a positive, frank Australian.

'Iraq was way louder,' one man was boasting. 'This is nothing – nothing.'

We rolled our eyes in irritation. Jenn shook out her long hair and I found something important to read on the far wall.

The night sky over Bob's terrace was congested and futuristic. Lights streamed around us at a dozen speeds. Rockets arced over our heads, missiles sliced down and inward to erupt as fireballs in the streets around us, jets discharged their chaff, the Israeli navy bombed to the north, trackless drones zipped and zagged, and one unidentifiable projectile slid in on a frisbee's low, flat trajectory. I texted intermittently with a woman who I supervised on another project. How would she ever sleep, alone with four frightened pre-schoolers while her husband worked at the hospital?

Around 1.00 am, an explosion threw my heart against my ribs and woke all the fears that had gone numb. The bedroom curtains flapped inward from the open glass doors of my terrace. I cursed and hurried outside as fire engulfed the fire station across Beach Road. Dark figures sprinted up the beach and across the boulevard, running straight at the fire in case anyone was still alive. Where they converged, I could just make out their firelit silhouettes, throwing up their arms to fend off the heat while they peered in. I would see them again and again. In the vacuum of sound that followed the bombs, I would see my neighbours racing heedlessly toward that fire, willing to dig with only their bare hands, to haul forth survivors or carry what they found for burial.

Standing on my terrace, pressing my hands onto the railing to keep them from shaking, I wept with dread for everything that was about to happen. I drifted in circles through my apartment, missing my Tiaba 2 friends. We would have texted. We would have been sensible enough to say that we were afraid.

A few hours later, the IDF struck the Hamas training facility next to my old apartment building. A fellow gym-goer lunged from her bed there, out of the path of her falling window frame. Jenn, too new to know where the foreigners would gather, spent the pre-dawn in her bathtub, wearing her UN helmet and Kevlar vest.

All of the international staff left our apartments in the morning. Mike and I swept the contents of our hibernation shelves into his long kit bag; cans of vegetables and boxes of apple-cinnamon oatmeal and freeze-dried packs of every instant noodle flavour. We trotted down to the truck, each carrying one bag handle, and moved into the UNRWA compound.

I found Jenn in the compound, and told her that I thought her overnight judgement had been superb.

'Thank you,' she breathed. She set her jaw and made her round face rounder with resolve. 'I've never had to do that before. But I decided, I'm okay with being afraid. I mean, it's a bomb. You're supposed to be afraid, and I'm okay with that.'

'Yes – exactly,' I agreed heartily. '"Iraq was louder," my ass. Listen, you're very welcome to share the floor in my office, if you'd like company in being afraid of bombs.'

We collected our thin foam squabs and too-warm fuzzy blankets from the stock room, and wrestled them up the stairs. Laila and Rasha's office was larger than mine, long and narrow. By swinging their desks around, we cleared enough space to lay out the two squabs diagonally, each pointing protectively into the kneehole of a desk. The CPs spread themselves out in the rooms around us, favouring the shelter of the director's massive wooden conference table. Scott took the office at the entrance to the hallway.

We all put our things down and went to work.

In the Central Ops Room, I sat at a T of desks opposite Damien, a slender French man who had recently become a father. I knew him primarily by the statistics he teased forth from vast pools of economic data. Broad-shouldered Mohammed sat at the head of the T. I enjoyed his upbeat, exacting way of working. They would manage the supply of food to the shelters. We all began by doing the things that were evident to us, while we speculated about the things we could not yet see.

Israel fought from the air, a bombardment with no epicentre. From the emergency stocks in the big northern warehouse, I began to reposition supplies to smaller warehouses across the five governorates. I handed each distribution spreadsheet to the logistics team at the next cluster of desks. They converted plans to action by assigning trucks, shepherding their movements and scheduling the deliveries in the streets around us. Thousands of UNRWA's Palestinian staff continued to collect rubbish, deliver water, operate health clinics and distribute food in those streets. They worked beneath the bombs, protected only by their reflective UN vests and the blue logos on their white vehicles. Each time I handed off a sheet, each time another driver had to take his chances in the streets, I worked my neck in sympathy with his nerves.

Explosions interrupted from time to time but they were not very close. I gauged the size and proximity of bombs by the angle of the blinds that flapped inward from our windows. Beyond the windows, a concrete baffle limited our vision and made COR feel timeless, isolated and inbred. I immersed myself in the logic of assumptions that I would use to order shelter supplies through the Jerusalem procurement department. I wrote formulae until summer's late sundown surprised me.

The Gazans went home to break their Ramadan fasts, and the internationals scattered around the garden to Skype home in a dozen languages. We watched the prying drones manoeuvre for the best angle to watch us. Someone found a croquet set that Bob had brought in during the previous war.

I sat in the darkening, dusty enterprise workroom, picturing the graduates whose neighbourhoods had already been hit. I thought back to the opening days of our business course, when they had explained global supply chains as traversing one vast neighbourhood. Now they were protecting their families and rescuing their neighbours. In that contrast, I glimpsed a way to salvage our dreadful dynamic.

Then I went upstairs to my office. I wrote group emails to the project team, to friends, and I added to a running email with my sisters and niece. We had maintained a more substantive dialogue since I had arrived in Gaza. I was proud of that. We disagreed, but I knew that the legacy of our family's dinner table would be our continuing willingness to speak and listen. That felt vital, and optimistic.

Chapter 19

July 11, 2014

The IDF struck 320 targets during the night.

Like a caterpillar, I rolled away from the windows with each blast nearby. Noise that loud was physical, thumping into my ribs or my back. I clenched my teeth and scrunched beneath my heavy blanket against the impact of the sound. Then I flattened out to reset my heart. Jenn and I said 'phew' or 'that was loud,' exchanging little markers of relief. Between 4.30 and 6.00 am, they hit a nearby police station more than a dozen times: the whistle of the bombs angling in, the juddering explosion, 'phew', screams, sirens, screams. First, I steeled myself against the fear, and then against the awful knowledge that people were maimed and bleeding, and I was listening without helping them. I could not run from, and I did not run toward. I had to learn stillness. As the bombs kept falling on the same site, I worried for all the neighbours who would have come to help.

I went downstairs at dawn to shower and step outside before work. Anonymous pillars of smoke rose along the horizon of the compound wall. Whose homes were burning – who lived at that point on the compass? Was Hani running to his cousins, was one of our graduates staring into wreckage? Radio stations broadcast the names of people killed and buildings struck, but I would not hear until one of my team told me. I peered into the smoke for news, but it gave nothing away.

Around 8.00 am, I turned to speak to the man at the desk behind me and found him transfixed, open-mouthed, pen sliding out of one hand as the other hand clutched his phone. He was around my age, eyes puffy with lack of sleep, collar askew, frozen. I leaned closer.

He lifted his phone an inch and breathed as if he didn't want to disturb it. 'My brother-in-law. A knock on the roof.'

We sat for long seconds before his phone rang again. His family had gotten out before their house was destroyed behind them. My colleague worked the stiff hinges of his jaw, and spoke as if I might need reassurance.

'They're alive. Nothing else matters. My sister is alive.'

He gulped hard. Then he rose on unsteady feet, walked around the building a few times, returned to his desk and resumed cajoling warehouse managers and shouting at truck drivers to move.

Those stories proliferated. A knock on the roof – a missile through the roof that turned the knees to water, fired in warning of worse to come. A minute or two to grab children, purses, photographs before the house, or the house next door, was blown apart. Some families and some neighbours used those moments to race into the threatened houses and onto their roofs, to make the largest number of civilians visible to the Israeli pilots and computer screens. Palestinians wagered their bodies against the military benefit of blowing up a family home.[31]

Families were dying wholesale. Seventy-six Gazans had been killed already, and more than 500 were injured.

The IDF warned residents of Beit Lahiya and East Khan Younis to leave their homes within twelve hours.

'All of them?' I whispered at my screen, incredulous. 'You can't mean all of them.'

Israeli news websites claimed 780 strikes by the end of the day. I no longer heard the smaller ones, and I had mastered the rhythm of the heavy, proximate explosions. After the boom, I measured the angle of the flapping window blinds. I, like the faces around me, turned with trepidation toward the neighbourhoods of co-workers and friends. That made a void of silence. Then the noise rushed back in and returned us to the fact of our Central Ops Room. We rarely bothered to comment on the bombs. What could anyone say, 780 times?

---

31 See B'Tselem, *Black Flag: The Legal and Moral Implications of the Policy of Attacking Residential Buildings in the Gaza Strip, Summer 2014* (January 2015). https://www.btselem.org/download/201501_black_flag_eng.pdf

July 12

When I stepped out at dawn, I saw that trauma bags had distributed themselves around the buildings overnight. The head of security appointed me warden of our building, and I laughed.

'Me? In other words, everyone else has a more urgent assignment in a mass casualty event, yes?'

'Something like that,' he agreed.

Damien and I both arrived early to our T of desks, to boil water for apple-cinnamon oatmeal and coffee. He opened iTunes and we sang 'Every Little Thing Gonna Be Alright' once through, as if singing softly could make it so. Our humming lasted only until we turned to the news.

The IDF struck a colleague's home, killing six members of his family. And then three more. *But I just saw him*, I objected, because a loss that staggering should not happen without some portent. A phone rang, and I looked up apprehensively, in case it had happened to someone else.

I began to assemble lists of the flagged UNRWA schools that could be designated as emergency shelters. UNRWA's emergency shelters were crowded, minimally provisioned places of last resort. They were hardly desirable, but they were legally protected places for Gazans who did not have more amenable, or more private alternatives. UNRWA would notify the IDF of each building that it opened as a shelter. These notifications did not create new obligations for the IDF. The buildings were already marked 'UN' on every rooftop and military map. Israel was already bound by international law to refrain from attacking UN buildings, and it was required to distinguish between civilian and military targets each time it fired – and Israel fired at will, with plenty of time to meet its obligations. UNRWA's notifications added one more, cautionary layer of protection to Israel's existing obligations. The list of designated emergency shelters would be sent frequently, usually twice a day.

While I worked on the list, Hamas fired a number of rockets toward Tel Aviv. Even as that news reached us, the sky over our heads swarmed with waves of engines. Then came volleys of missiles, artillery and naval fire.

Unlike the jets overhead, Israel's ground and naval forces fired horizontally, without sighting their targets. They fire… weapons, so called because they measured the statistica… hood of killing anyone within a given radius. The artillery s… being fired most frequently into Gaza weighed 40 kilograms, and spewed out nearly 2000 metal fragments when it detonated. Those shells were statistically very likely to kill anyone within 50–150 metres, and to injure people up to 300 metres away. Therefore, in order to be considered 'a hit', those shells had to be aimed only accurately enough to place the intended targets within their kill radius.[32] Statistical weapons posed a blind, generalized threat to every person who also happened to live within their kill radius.

Not meant for cities, I punctuated the explosions under my breath. *Not meant for cities.*

The firing built through the evening, while I sat in the Gateway project team's echoing workroom. The sound of artillery invoked Gazans' dense social capital. Their neighbours were integral. They rescued and perhaps they were the pretext of threat, they made and enforced solidarity in resistance, they competed and they carried water up the stairs to bathe children. Those layers had to be the Gateway's starting point. We had to work and train from that life experience, not from anyone else's.

I wrote to the enterprise project team, ducking into my T-shirt each time the monitor rocked with the blasts. The graduate who argued most staunchly with me, invited me to join his family after work. He swore that the noise was never as loud among relatives. Another wrote in shock, having witnessed the killing of a neighbouring family in their home.

From 3.30 am till sunrise, the *musaharati* should have been walking through the streets, banging drums to wake their neighbourhoods to another Ramadan day. Instead the bombing grew incessant then, just as Gazan families gathered for their *suhoor* meals before the day's fast began. Twenty times, they bombed

32 See this excellent longitudinal study of Israel's weapons selection and targeting policies in Gaza, *Under Fire: Israel's Artillery Policies Scrutinised* (December 2014), by Action on Armed Violence. https://aoav.org.uk/wp-content/uploads/2015/03/AOAV-Under-Fire-Israels-artillery-policies-scrutinised.pdf

near enough and powerfully enough to shake my building. Pages of the poverty survey process flow shook loose from the office walls and fluttered down.

I tossed and I listened to Jenn toss while the desks jiggled around us. I remembered my parents' indignation, when Israel had been attacked on the Jewish holy day of Yom Kippur, in 1973. The choice to bomb so heavily during *suhoor* showed an equal disrespect.

July 13

I staggered into COR, sandy-eyed and dumb. Gazans, veterans of the sleep deprivation of war and Ramadan, arrived fresher or at least more polite.

COR voices rose and outdid each other. To COR's original dozen inhabitants, specialists were being added: engineers, medical, technology, water, mapping. The volume mounted. We shouted to be heard. Deprived of sleep and placed under stress, a few of the international men became aggressive to each other and insulting to women. Jenn arrived, and lasted just thirty minutes before she unplugged her laptop, stalked out and flatly refused to return to the room.

I tried to consolidate the daily situation report of overnight damage, casualties, services operating or suspended, and neighbourhood news; but the 'sitrep' disobeyed my formatting. Numbers swam in their columns, and formula brackets neglected to close. I closed the first version of the sitrep without saving it, and swore under my breath.

Two men had risen to their feet to swear at each other across my desk. My morning phone callers wanted to know who was threatening whom in the background. I took my laptop outside to finish the sitrep that normally required half an hour. The bombs were louder than my colleagues, so I went back indoors. I finished the sitrep at mid-morning, and circulated the email without the attachment.

My inbox filled with 'No attachment!' replies.

'Oh, for fuck sakes. Scott,' I pleaded as he walked past, cupping my ears.

'Sound baffles,' he agreed.

Although it was a throwaway line, I still appreciated it.

The overnight pounding had driven people from their homes

in the Gaza and North governorates. I streamed a few minutes of TV news. Distraught families searched for people they loved in hospital halls, and neighbours scavenged for recognizable body parts to bury. Children clung to each other with their teeth chattering uncontrollably. I felt my eyes sting.

Damien enquired across the desks.

'News from the North governorate,' I began. 'Children—'

Damien held up one hand to stop me, and said kindly, 'I'm sorry, I can't.' He turned to pictures of his baby.

By the end of the afternoon, 15,990 people had taken shelter in twenty UN schools. I completed and sent the evening shelter notification list with a sense of foreboding. A single day's displacement had consumed nearly half of our supplies, and most of our mattresses.

July 14

Governorate and shelter-school staff phoned steadily, urging me to position more supplies near the next, likely, shelter-schools. I explained that I had raised the orders for mattresses and diapers and pallets of cleaning supplies from thousands to tens of thousands. Several thousand additional reflective UN vests were being manufactured for the safety of staff in the streets – but my recitation was of no help to frontline staff.

'The storm – December?' I reminded them. I didn't need to add that the organization was broke and overwhelmed by competing, urgent claims on its funds. Everyone knew that already. Donors and diplomats went on holiday in the summer, so funds were not flowing to Gaza yet.

Resentment crept into my own voice as the phone continued to ring, and I continued to repeat my apologies. Our low stocks made me feel dishonourable. Through the day, each mattress acquired the moral weight of welcome, and the symbolic value of one safe bed for one person in danger.

Scott and I went to four of the first shelters in Gaza and North. Four neighbourhood schools now held their four neighbourhoods.

A claptrap red truck pulled up as we arrived at the first. Its flatbed jounced beneath three generations of an extended family.

They unloaded themselves and their bundles, one toy for the children, and one mattress for their paterfamilias. Then the truck turned around to fetch the next family group.

The building felt taken-over and repurposed. Classroom rubbish bins, of the size needed to hold paper and pencil shavings, overflowed. Adults stooped as they reached for something at a child's height, or scrunched into a child's desk. Whole families stood in lines before the bathrooms. I walked into one, and although it had been scrubbed, the smell of its overworked plumbing mingled with the Dettol. Women and girls hunched over industrial hand sinks to wash their hands and their babies. Seeing me, one older woman mimed washing her own hands, pointed at an empty soap container and shook her head. I nodded my acknowledgement, apologized and tried to recall how few cartons of liquid soap remained in our warehouses. Outside, mothers propped their infants on desks and yawned through the scorching hours of their fast. Only the children fit their space. A pack of boys charged across their usual schoolyard, past one listless boy who had isolated himself in a corner.

The school principal-cum-shelter manager arrived, and followed my eyes. She gestured to individual shelter residents while she spoke. 'He is sometimes violent when he's afraid. They have a disabled child who cannot line up for food. That one, that one will collect food for others, and give it to his own family instead. This little boy? He needs counselling for what he has seen. And I am running out of bleach and toilet paper.'

I nodded, 'And liquid soap, I'm sorry.'

These neighbours, she was implying, had sheltered together before. UNRWA was Gaza's primary emergency responder, because UNRWA responded from within each neighbourhood.

The northern school buildings were very large and rigorously organized. Rows of working donkeys were tethered to the outside walls, as close as they could be kept to safety.

I found the UNRWA colleague who had lost nine of his family. He had continued to work while his hair turned grey. I gave him my condolences and he shrugged, not dismissive but hollowed. He steered our conversation to soft and hard brooms, and the proper public health ratios of disinfectant and rubbish bags to shelter population. I told him how sorry I felt about that, too.

Al Fakhoura school had been bombed in 2009.[33] Those Gazans who remembered the chemical burns of white phosphorous had no choice but to gather at the same site for shelter once more. The school was packed full, and people were arriving so rapidly that registration teams were working in two shifts. We found children's spaces neatly marked off, and stocked with toys. Cleaning crews moved between doorways, and the smell of just-washed floors reached us outdoors. Shelter residents pressed in on Scott as we crossed the courtyard, explaining their dilemma through a translator.

'Israel warns us we must leave our homes. Hamas orders us not to move. The others, Islamic Jihad and the others, they threaten to block our supplies to make us go home – but Israel is bombing the homes!'

Newcomers interrupted and repeated, and added their complaints about the insufficient supplies. Scott kept listening and reaching for their hands. He made eye contact with an unfeigned smile and kept listening. He squatted down to extend his finger for a cheerful toddler. Dressed all in green, one broken arm in a cast, the boy gripped Scott's finger with his uninjured hand.

'Listen, I apologize,' Scott spoke up to the crowd while the boy latched onto his finger and began to haul himself upright. 'I hear you. We're not getting it right yet. You need stuff, and we're too slow. I'm sorry. We need to do better. And you, whose is this?' He looked up to locate the boy's parents and move on from the apology. 'This little fellow is not what you think of when you hear "casualty", is he? How's he doing at night? Does he sleep?'

As we began to move across the school playground again, two bombs exploded very nearby. Everyone ducked by instinct, and turned to measure the distance – except Scott. He didn't flinch. People resumed speaking more swiftly, because he had made it feel less dangerous.

On the way back to COR, I said to him, 'You were born for emergency. You know that?'

He grinned. 'Thank you. It does bring out something.'

33 https://electronicintifada.net/content/photostory-israel-attacks-un-school-gaza/9740

'It sure does. Me, lose a few nights' sleep and I'm ready to bite.'

'Mm-hmm,' Scott began. He led the Central Ops Room and we talked about its tensions.

That afternoon, an email arrived from my sisters. The Red Cross was evacuating Gazans who held foreign passports. The news had inspired them to tell my mother that the Red Cross had evacuated me to Israel. I shrivelled onto my desk and piled both arms over my head.

'What's the matter?' someone asked.

'My sisters have sort of reported my evacuation by the Red Cross. I'm in Israel!'

Guffaws all around.

'Couldn't take the pressure?'

'Enjoy the beach!'

The laughter subsided and left me drumming on my keyboard. I planned to go to my mother's 95th birthday party at the end of August. We hadn't had a rich relationship, but I treasured the moments when my mother recognized, maybe even shared some of what drove me. *'If I'd been born in a freer generation, I would have travelled the way you travel, to the Arctic and the jungle . . . I don't know if Israel was a good idea. So many people have died, and there doesn't seem to be a solution.'*

They had told her I was spending the summer as someone else, and that hurt with the half-submerged pain of exile.

July 15

We heard of the first Israeli casualty: 195 Gazans had been killed, and COR voices mulled over the disproportion. I turned off my computer and stared at my own sepia, too-wide eyes. I tried to swallow, and I tasted ash. The Israeli had died at Erez, where my niece had gone to deliver care packages to foreign IDF volunteers. Forcing my eyebrows back down to their normal height, I took my phone outside. She didn't answer.

Time hung, as it had been suspended for so many of the Palestinians around me. She was my turn. She was one – I glanced back at the COR – but she felt like more. For an unbearable time, she felt like the whole world.

I made mental lists of the logistics that would be needed to get me out. After all my subterfuge, it was so easy to compose an email identifying myself not simply as a Jew but as the aunt of an IDF reservist. I was wondering who to copy when my niece confirmed that she had left Erez before the building was hit.

I became aware of motion as someone hurried down the path behind me. Heat, as the sun beat down on my head. I heaved one shuddering breath, shoved my niece out of my mind, and went back to work with a pulpy stomach and stale adrenaline compressing my voice. Somehow, it was still the same day.

July 16

The IDF fired missiles at four small, skinny boys, killing them on the beach north of my apartment. Journalists took pictures from the Al Deira Hotel as the boys tried to run away, and the IDF fired at them again. Everyone in Gaza felt those boys flop onto the sand, dead, inexplicable.

My colleagues turned to each other with certitude. I tried to reason through the shock. Little boys – Israel had fired repeatedly at children who were playing in an open, recreational space, in daylight. The IDF boasted about their detailed vision technologies. Either they saw and fired repeatedly at children, or they fired repeatedly into an open, recreational space without caring who they killed.

My mind was still on the beach when my neighbour, Mike, sent me the shelter notification list. He held the sheet as the head of the legal office.

'It's been changed,' I called across the room.

'Reformatted,' he called back.

I compared the old and new versions, shaking my head. Someone had made cosmetic changes. They had copied the data, rather than transferring the references for the data. The spreadsheet monster within me erupted.

'No-no-no, Mike, someone *changed* it.'

'Don't get emotional,' he warned, seeing that I was being territorial but not seeing the reason.

I grabbed the sheets I had printed, and started across the room. 'Listen to me. The changes have altered the information. We're going to report the wrong co-ordinates!'

We began to shout, and spun sourly away to our own desks.

'Emoootional,' he crooned to his computer.

'Oh, for fuck sakes,' I replied with venom. I hunched with the spreadsheet for some minutes, then I snatched my laptop and papers, and marched across the room. I felt the all heads turn to follow me. 'Look! Look at this!'

'Lower your voice.'

'Fuck my voice, *look*. This school has moved since this morning. And this one, longitude and latitude, both changed. Do you understand – someone copied numbers, without moving the formulae or the links that generate those numbers. Now the numbers are wrong.'

He studied the sheet and swore in a voice that was far more controlled than mine.

While he read, I lectured myself that my neighbour was a reasonable man. I imagined my car breaking down. Mike would hear the changes in its idle. I would not, and I respected him for that. I flattened all the inflection from my voice. 'Someone has to be responsible for the continuity of this information. This sheet has to be owned.'

We apologized to each other and started checking the information together.

From the moment of my outburst, I held that notification spreadsheet as protectively as the buildings it listed. Beyond the walls of those designated buildings anything might happen, but within them, 22,385 Gazans were safeguarded by law. In the absence of the decency that would have let civilians move to a safe place, law was all the protection those human beings had. As I fixed my heart on the mattresses, I placed my trust in that sheet and in the flimsy, limited, civilizing law that stood behind it.

Talk of a ceasefire gave way to a terrible, long night of explosions and sirens and screaming. The earth shuddered and the building swayed. In the first blue light of dawn, I padded barefoot down the hall to wash. Soft rustlings came through doorways, as everyone sighed and rolled over to try for just one hour of uninterrupted sleep.

I slumped at my desk, still with the towel over my shoulder.

I tried to recall how long I had lived in the COR building; how few nights it had taken to scrape away any veneer of manners and patience and make the violence seem eternal. When had they rearranged the desks? I tried to unroll my notebook to check the dates, but it had gone lumpy from a wet table and it would not flatten. I started the oatmeal. Mike arrived, rubbing his face briskly, and we exchanged another apology.

July 17

The IDF killed three more children while they were playing on their roof. Rasha called, fretting softly so that her own girls would not hear. 'I'm afraid they are trying to break our will by killing the children.'

'No, I'm sure they're not. I'm sure they're not,' I repeated.

'Why? What have you heard?'

'Nothing. It just . . . can't be. I can't believe it,' I amended, more apologetic than certain.

I paced in circles in front of the building, talking first with Rasha and then through a staticky connection to a colleague in the Middle governorate. Although I nodded sympathetically, I had to yell to be heard, and I doubted that I was conveying much sympathy at that volume.

'I know, I do! I understand! Cleanliness and public health, you're right! Bleach and disinfectant, they're on a truck, but the truck is stuck at Kerem Shalom! Brooms, yes. I said brooms! Broom handles, toilet paper – everything on your list, mattresses – I completely understand but we *do not have* stand-by inventory to send you! Every single thing we receive is going straight out again, and I will . . . are you there? Can you hear me—'

Something exploded near enough to make me stumble. I gritted my teeth and kept nodding in robotic sympathy. Above me, the Front Office vestibule window opened. The laconic Close Protection team leader leaned out and observed, 'Be good to get under cover now.'

I stepped under the eave as something clanged onto a roof. I glanced up at the interruption and kept repeating that there were brooms on the trucks.

An enormous boom cut through our late afternoon briefing,

near enough to hear the approaching whistle of the bomb before it exploded. The sound thumped into my chest, the floor trembled, and the blinds sailed inward beyond 45 degrees. I looked uncertainly at Jenn. Others half-rose and craned their necks toward the windows, to see which building in our compound had been hit.

Imperturbable, Scott resumed his briefing. We all shrank away from the windows in unison with the next detonation, which was just as near. Monitors shuffled on desks and plaster chips pattered down onto our heads.

'Thousand pounds, maybe the mosque on the corner?' someone guessed.

'Jesus Christ!' Scott yelled at the ceiling. He shot upright, slapped his phone from the table and jogged out of the room. He said later that he demanded of his military liaison, 'Do you fucking people know where we fucking are?'

I sat in my office upstairs as the night's bombardment gathered force, and built, and built. I scrolled through the Israeli news, trying to find the perspective that eluded me during the workday: why? It used to be that Israel fought to survive, but no one even tried to pretend that Gaza posed an existential threat. Netanyahu had said that the war aimed to restore calm to southern Israel, and his Defence Minister gave the goal as 'zero rockets'. More than 100 rockets had been fired each day since then, while the IDF struck as many as 300 different targets daily, hitting many of them repeatedly. The war consisted of endless explosions, an undiminished flow of rockets, and one report that someone had popped out of a tunnel to fire on IDF troops.

I hunted across websites for a military objective against which to measure progress. As I read without discerning any strategy, I felt the dread that accompanied the onset of food poisoning: an inversion of order and the certain, sickening knowledge that it was going to get worse.[34]

I wrote an email to the general COR address, offering to do a white wash for everyone in our communal washing machine, turned off the computer, and went to bed.

34 A subsequent report by Israel's State Comptroller confirmed the lack of a consistent military objective for the war. See https://www.haaretz.com/israel-news/

The head of security came down the hall some minutes later. He spoke softly into each doorway. 'Boots on the ground.'

Israel had invaded the Gaza Strip.

Sometime in that night, my pattern changed. Previously I had scrunched away from the sound of the explosions, and woken up facing the hallway. That night, I began to wake, huddled in my caterpillar ball within the kneehole of Laila's desk. My sleeping brain was distinguishing new sounds before my waking brain comprehended them. Outside was not only the slicing whistle of angling missiles but the whoosh of explosives raining straight down. And more often, the sound of shrapnel clattering down roofs and falling onto the compound's paved walkways. I gave up on sleep and listened in thoughtless, limp exhaustion and waited for the time to pass, or to end. They bombed all around us, and they could not possibly fire around us that many times without hitting us.

I understood why Randa always called around before sundown. Formerly a quiet respite from Gaza's crowds, night had become a slow-moving enemy.

Dawn came as a tremendous relief. Jenn and I blinked wordlessly at each other before we untangled ourselves from our sweaty blankets and stood up. There was no brain function to formulate speech. I turned to the windows. Beyond the wire grilles, black was giving way to blue. Air reached further into my lungs as buildings took on some definition around me. For a moment, I felt less alone among those buildings. Then, a minute later, the morning grew pale enough to reveal the many, many plumes of smoke that were rising from the city.

I staggered into COR. I rubbed the stretched-taut skin of my forehead, and pressed at the sleepless pockets that were puffing over my cheekbones. Hypnotized by the swirl of oatmeal around the teaspoon, I rested my cheek on the desk to nap and drool until the next arrival woke me up.

LIVE-gaza-war-11-key-headlines-from-report-rattling-israel-s-politicians-and-military-1.5443050

Chapter 20

July 18–19

Each shelter reported its overnight population for the morning situation reports. Late each afternoon, they updated their numbers with that day's arrivals. The evening count, recorded on a white-board behind my desk, determined the priorities for the following day's food and water trucks.

On the eve of the ground invasion, UNRWA sheltered 23,329 displaced people. A single day of the invasion doubled the displacement of civilians to equal the outer limit of UNRWA's forecasts. UNRWA's planning had been based on Gaza's history of brief civilian displacements. This already looked different, and we threw away the forecasts. Having scoured the region for 90,000 mattresses, the procurement team in Jerusalem began to hunt for rolled mats, which took up less floor space. In the classrooms, some displaced Gazan civilians began to sleep in shifts.

I saw what I had been unable to see on the first day: information systems that had sufficed for fleeting displacement. I had a list of schools, but not the numbers of rooms or toilets or the storage capacity of water tanks. When I hunted for those, I found multiple and inconsistent descriptions of the buildings themselves. Some longitudes and latitudes pointed to Cyprus. Each time a shelter opened, I found the UNRWA colleague who lived nearest, or else the oldest Gazan in the room, and I took a history of the building in order to describe it more accurately. Marjean, the boyish South African Close Protection officer known universally for his kindness, sighted each building on a series of military and satellite maps, and assigned meticulous co-ordinates to the twenty-six buildings then in use.

The following day, Marjean came back to locate the 22 new shelters that had opened overnight. If they felt we were slow about opening a shelter, neighbours scaled the walls of their school and opened the gate themselves. Two more whiteboards were affixed to the wall behind me. One thousand people were surging into UNRWA's shelters every hour, and many more were being taken into Palestinian homes and buildings throughout the Gaza Strip.

Across the T of desks, Damien and Mohammed formulated algebraic supply chains of tuna and bread. Jumping up to pace in tight circles, Damien's voice lowered and Mohammed's boomed as they steered food to each shelter in time for each *iftar* evening meal, at the end of each day's fast. Their circadian slog began anew with each evening count.

I stood before the whiteboards, rocking from side to side to compose a consistent response to the waves of new arrivals and demands from shelter managers. Should the next truckload of blankets go to the shelter whose early arrivals had been waiting longest, or the one most overcrowded, or the largest, or perhaps we could reach two shelters near the warehouse in the same time it took to reach the furthest one.

The invasion swiftly imposed its own logic. The Israeli army stranded 40 per cent of Gaza's land and shelter-schools on the far side of its column. Access overruled fairness. Shelters in the militarized east had to be supplied whenever passage could be negotiated for the trucks, because no one knew when passage would next be offered. Then the numbers outstripped the supplies we had received, and no priorities mattered. I went back to making apologies until more goods could be yanked through the blockade.

An emergency airlift was taking shape, landing supplies at the airport in Amman, Jordan, two countries away from Gaza. Each truck would have to be loaded in Amman. Then it would drive to the border, and cross into Israel via the Allenby Bridge, which had to be repurposed as a goods crossing. After traversing Israel, the trucks would line up to enter Gaza through the blockade's sole functioning entry point for goods, the Kerem Shalom crossing in Rafah. Within Kerem Shalom, each truck would be required to unload and transfer its goods to a Gazan truck, because Israel's blockade did not permit delivery trucks to enter Gaza proper. Each big Gazan truck would drive to an UNRWA warehouse, where goods had to be offloaded again, and loaded onto trucks that were small enough to pass through Gaza's side streets and alleys. Those trucks would distribute supplies to the shelters and their residents. Shipments of bottled water, medicines and food took precedence. After that, I filled the remaining space with diapers, bleach, disinfectants, buckets, brooms, soap, toilet paper, rubbish bags, torches, family hygiene packs, sanitary napkins, blankets and mattresses.

Emotionally, mattresses meant safety and hospitality to me; one narrow, personal space within the crowded rooms. I couldn't have adopted a worse talisman. Mattresses were not a life-saving priority. They were also bulky: a fully loaded truck carried 1106 mattresses, barely one hour's supply. I dispatched blankets for people to fold beneath them, but I could not talk myself out of wanting mattresses. At any given moment, refreshed a dozen times a day as information changed, I knew the number of shelter residents who did and didn't have mattresses, and the number of mattresses that were – and were not yet – en route.

In the first week, Israel had bombed more than one hundred family homes. The bombardment was ongoing, compounded now by the ground invasion. With the invasion, we entered a war of numbers and the grinding hardship of crowds. Images circulated of the demoralizing conditions in the schools, and we were falling further behind each minute. Kerem Shalom did not work nights.

July 20–22[35]

The IDF's invading column halved Gaza into east and west along the spinal Salah al-Din Road, one of the oldest roads in the world. Fighting dislodged a human wave from the east, and because Gaza remained locked, those people could only flee west across Salah al-Din Road. They left neighbourhoods that had been made uninhabitable, and they inundated neighbourhoods whose infrastructure was already staggering. They squeezed into homes and yards and office buildings, and by the end of the day, 84,843 had been shoehorned into UNRWA shelters.

35 My journal dates are confused for July 19–22.

The logistics team ripped a fourth and a fifth whiteboard from other office walls, and mounted them on the walls of the Central Ops Room. Colleagues began to turn and solemnly acknowledge the wall of runaway numbers, conditioning themselves before they properly entered COR. So many people were in motion. My eyes flitted from the numbers on my computer to my phone, as I waited to hear from acquaintances who were somewhere within that wave. Multitudes, one, multitudes, one.

A woman called. We had been exchanging messages since the first night of the war. English was her first language, but exhaustion had disordered her vocabulary. She found and spoke her words one by one. Alarmed by her voice, I took the phone outside. She was spending her ninth day in an interior room of her house, alone with four pre-school children. Her husband, a doctor, could not leave the hospital. The hail of shells around her had not stopped for twelve hours.

'I can't,' she whispered. 'There. Is. No. Time. When. Someone. Is. Not Screaming. I think . . .' Her voice trailed away.

'What can I do for you?'

'Breakdown. I think. Last. Night. I can't do this. No more.'

'Okay. It's okay. Think about who I can call. Who is near you? Can you give me your husband's phone number?'

'Get. Me. Out. Out.' She took a deeper breath to compose. 'I have to get out. Of Shuja'iyya.'

'I will. Hang on, I will get you out.'

I raced up the stairs to Front Office. I had heard that six Israeli soldiers had been killed, and I feared that the shelling was retaliation. I grabbed Scott's door jamb, swung myself in, and told him who had called. 'In Shuja'iyya. She sounds desperate, she has to get out. Have you heard anything about a pause for people to get out?'

The phone was in his hand. 'Let you know,' he mumbled.

I called her back. 'You hold on. There must be a pause coming. Charge your phone, and hold on. *Allah yatik el afiah.*'

Then they hit a ceramic factory across the road from a man on the Gateway project team, ripping away the upper half of his house.

I worked and I texted, but there was no pause.

Every child's scream sounded louder that night. I got up early, intending to mark the passage of time by seeing the sky grow light. Instead, I saw news that 7000 people had overwhelmed a Beit Hanoun shelter. I sank into my chair and read. Unknown numbers of people were gathering at the UNRWA health clinic nearby. Still more frightened people were piling into any building that had a UN flag. The buildings, not designed for such numbers, had already run out of potable water. Generators were failing.

UNRWA was sheltering 102,788 displaced Gazans, 6 per cent of the population. I had no brooms and no bleach for these new concentrations of people; nothing that would enable them to keep their surroundings clean. My inbox and phone messages were litanies.

'I asked you for 100 brooms and you sent one!'

'You sent the torches but where are my mattresses! I bet you have a mattress to sleep on!!'

'Do you understand the connection between cleanliness and public health??'

They pleaded with me and I yelled at the procurement people in Jerusalem, and none of it loosened the blockade around us.

Yet my anger at UNRWA evaporated with that morning's report. No credible stock levels would have lasted through the first ninety-six hours of Israel's invasion. Cassandra herself could have hoarded one hundred truckloads of mattresses (if she had the money and the trucks and a way to get them through the blockade), and they would not have sufficed. UNRWA's planning was not the problem. The problem was Israel's catastrophic war strategy. In just four days, Israel had forced twice as many Gazans from their homes as had ever been unhoused before. And still it would not let them move to safety.

A shell damaged a school in Maghazi. I glanced up only long enough to hear that no one was injured, before I returned to the task of locating our proliferating shelters on military co-ordination maps. The lists of school names rarely matched the maps, because UNRWA's schools went by multiple names. The morning school often had one name and the afternoon school another. Schools had a formal name and another in common usage, and some had an honorary pseudonym or two for donors. One compound might hold several buildings that went by more than a dozen names in total. Which building held displaced people?

While I tried to make sense of one particularly convoluted school history, damage reports began to arrive from Shuja'iyya. They mounted so improbably that I told myself the same information was being repeated and compounded.

COR hushed voice by voice. I threw up my hands and listed the shelter as Unnamed School. When I looked up, everyone around me was staring at their phones. They exchanged locations and names in stage whispers. I reached heavily for my own phone.

Tens of thousands of Shuja'iyyans were in the streets amidst the bombing. The war shrank from the size of the Strip to the size of a few blocks, to the shade beneath the awnings where petrified families caught their breath as they ran.

Shuja'iyya was a dense, high-rise neighbourhood of 92,000 people, just six square kilometres in size. Invading soldiers had taken heavy fire there on the previous day. Thirteen Israelis died, six in a single vehicle. Israel bombed the city to cover the extraction of the remaining troops. The soldiers had been withdrawn. The fight was over, yet the IDF was continuing to bomb in a lawless, pointless fury.

Laila lived near Shuja'iyya. Yasmin and her newborn. The exhausted woman, trapped with four pre-schoolers.

Scott entered at a run and slapped my desk to get my attention as he passed. 'Pause – get 'em out! Move now!' He circled COR once, and ran on to give the same message to those in the security building opposite. 'Without fail!' he yelled back as he yanked the door open and lunged through it.

I called the woman with the time of the pause. Everyone made the same calls around me, and then we held our breath and lived through our screens as civilians fled through the streets. A city bolted in terror with children in hand, leaving everything else behind.

But Yasmin – how could she run?

Some of our phones beeped with messages, other news got lost in the bedlam. My exhausted colleague texted from a safer part of Gaza City. I heard no word of the others I knew in the area before Israeli forces eradicated the neighbourhood as a site of human settlement.[36]

The earth trembled with the obliteration of Shuja'iyya.

In the evening, I cried uncontrollably in the garden in front of my old office.

What have we done? I asked myself.

The words of a Holocaust survivor and writer, Primo Levi, rang in my ears. 'Meditate that this happened.'

Israel's overwhelming force suggested that they fought a battle whose outcome they doubted for one blink of time. But there was no doubt. The fighting had ended, leaving only the spite. Israel assaulted a trapped community by wiping out their homes.

How many Palestinians were homeless, who had had homes when the sun rose; and how many hadn't gotten out? Who was still bleeding in the rubble?

What have we done?

I felt a fabric tearing as Israel left me.

They. What they did was monstrous.

Where was Laila? Where was Yasmin?

I could smell it in the morning. Atrocity hung in the air like the smells after a fire.

An UNRWA colleague had died with his family. A Mercy Corps colleague was the sole survivor of hers. Yasmin and Laila were fine.

Morning reports counted 65 trucks backed up at Jordan's Allenby Bridge, waiting to cross into Israel with supplies that we had ordered when UNRWA sheltered 23,000 displaced people.

---

36 An Al Jazeera investigation (see: http://america.aljazeera.com/articles/2014/8/26/israel-bombing-stunsusofficers.html) found that '11 Israeli artillery battalions — a minimum of 258 artillery pieces... — pumped at least 7,000 high explosive shells into the Gaza neighborhood'. The AOAV report counted 100 one-ton bombs. A UN commission found 'strong indications that the IDF's Shuja'iya operation on 19 and 20 July was conducted in violation of the prohibition of indiscriminate attacks and may amount to a war crime'. Report of the detailed findings of the Commission of Inquiry on the 2014 Gaza Conflict, ohchr.org (United Nations A/HRC/29/CRP.4), paragraphs 251–299.

117,468 people waited for that cargo now. By the time the trucks arrived, how many would there be?

We could have cleaned out Gaza's neighbourhood shops to provide for our shelters. However, more displaced people were sheltering privately with their relatives and neighbours. They needed everything that was on the shop shelves, so we waited for our airlifted supplies.

I picked up my phone yet again at mid-morning. My callers were angry, distressed. They had 30,000 new arrivals and no cleaning supplies. When I replied, the same vocal effort produced less sound. I felt a kind of vertigo drawing me back to Shuja'iyya, but I was required to be present because the violence had not abated around us. Gaza had no day's grace to gather its news.

For the second time, rockets were found to have been stored in an unused UNRWA building. This was a violation of law, and of the neutrality of United Nations' facilities. I added a section to the notifications list, specifying the buildings that we could no longer reach to assure their neutrality. I begrudged each building. If we could have reached them, they might have been shelters.

July 23

UNRWA staff were rotating out. I waved at the departing van: for the second time, my own replacement had been diverted. I would have to wait for my turn to sleep soundly for a weekend. In the meantime, every third or fourth night, regardless of the noise, I slept some hours in a blackout so impervious that I knew I'd never really understood the meaning of sleep before.

Twenty minutes later, the others were back, shrugging off their Kevlar and shaking their heads. We could no longer reach Erez.

Israel bombed Gaza's power plant. COR voices listed the implications: light, refrigeration, internet communications, sewage treatment, hospitals. Phone chargers.

'Bodies,' someone said mournfully. 'Where they can't get to the cemetery. Now they'll have no ice.'

'Water pumps,' another added. The water infrastructure had been hit so often that UNRWA was broadcasting requests for Gazans to bring what bottled water they could to the nearest shelter.

'They hit a shelter,' someone shouted. 'Deir el Balah!'

I scrolled. An IDF drone had fired a missile at the Deir el Balah Prep Girls C School. Schools had been damaged before. Militants and the IDF both fired very near all kinds of buildings. This time, though, a drone appeared to have fired *at* a shelter. That couldn't be, unless the notification list contained an error. For a moment, I was stricken. Had my typo protected the wrong building in a compound? Had I moved a wall ten metres to the south?

Marjean arrived, unruffled but unsmiling. He pulled up a chair and the satellite map book. I back-checked the notification lists, balling my hands into fists and pecking at the command keys with my forefingers. We repeated co-ordinates to each other, halting to listen to each update from the school and dreading news of casualties.

I wondered how long Bob had been standing at the end of the desk. 'Was it us?' he asked heavily.

We shook our heads: there was no error.

I exhaled with a sigh of relief as Marjean closed the map book, and then I felt dizzy.

'This is what we do,' I said to Marjean. My voice sounded plaintive as I confirmed the facts. 'We protect people in flagged shelters and they fired at a shelter. Now what?'

'Palestinians won't trust us if they aren't safe,' he replied.

'Where else should they go?'

A man called from across the room, pointing at his monitor as he read from an Israeli news site. 'This says they might close a beach in Tel Aviv. Shrapnel. Hey Marilyn, you still on that beach?'

I grunted at Marjean, 'Oh, please, MJ, shoot me now.'

The situation of one shelter in Beit Hanoun was especially precarious. The IDF was bombing the surrounding neighbourhood heavily, and desperation made the streets more dangerous. Supply trucks were waylaid. We dispatched them with concern and followed their progress minutely. Shelter and neighbourhood committees struggled to maintain order in and around overcrowded buildings during the distribution of supplies. After days of wrangling, all parties agreed at last to evacuate the shelter. We heard the news with great relief.

Some hours had passed without news of new arrivals to the

other shelters, and a consensus formed and solidified through the room: the worst was over. The displacement had peaked.

Scott stepped into COR with a bitten, wry grin. 'It's off,' he said, flapping his arms because it made no sense to him, either. 'They do not agree to leave the shelter.'

A chorus of voices shouted at Scott, 'What – why not?'

'Because they do not agree! It's their neighbourhood, and they do not wish to leave. It's – are there any Beit Hanounis here?'

No one admitted to living in the stubborn environs of Beit Hanoun.

Everyone gathered to watch the recording of the evening shelter count. Scott postponed the briefing until we had the confirmation we all needed. Five people wrote out the details of 83 shelter populations on the whiteboards, while I tabulated.

'Fu-u-uck,' I breathed, and checked my formulae. Scott walked around the desk, to read over my shoulder. I added again, in a fresh column, and twisted to look up at him.

Impossibly, 23,000 new people had walked through the gates of the shelter nearest them. We had been too beset to notice. UNRWA was sheltering 141,338 displaced Gazans.

Everyone stared up at the bastard boards.

Scott turned back to me and opened his mouth, but I reported without waiting for him to ask. 'Not enough. Ninety thousand mattresses, fifty thousand rolled mats. I don't think there are any more.'

He shook his head. 'Not in the Middle East.'

July 24

At its peak, the shelter in Beit Hanoun had held over 4000 people. It was frequently unreachable, and plainly it sat near, or on top of, an IDF target. Everyone but the Beit Hanounis wanted it closed, because it could not be made safe. Finally, finally, all the parties agreed to a last-ditch evacuation, and shelter residents began to leave.

'We leave today,' Scott told the morning briefing. 'We, UNRWA, we will leave that building today. Understand – tell anyone you know there. Once that school is empty, we *will* withdraw our staff, supply line, and protection. We will not endanger our staff by remaining.'

Buses mustered.

Bob and the CPs bolted from the building at mid-afternoon. They passed me shouting into my phone in the courtyard. Even at a run, I could see that Bob's skin had turned an unhealthy white.

Someone had shelled the school while its residents were gathering to evacuate. Someone fired at least two mortar shells into a group of wholly undefended civilians, in a school playground, beneath the United Nations flag. They killed 16 people. Hospitals were trying to cope with at least ninety injured people.

UNRWA staff gathered around screens and sobbed. We asked each other where a Gazan could go to be safe. The question was literal and immediate, up and down the Gaza Strip. Where could displaced Palestinians go before darkness fell in a few hours, to be safe from the bombs behind a blockade?

And who did it? Who had fired at civilians when those civilians were known, by agreement, to be getting out of the way?

A team with military and legal experience went to investigate, measure, photograph and collect physical evidence from the school. They stayed until someone fired at them, and they departed so hastily that someone left the school keys in what remained of the gate.

In the evening, I went to the building across from the Central Ops Room, and I asked the head of security to see the shell fragments they had retrieved. Fragments had been carefully laid out around the conference table, neatly spaced, each standing on its own white paper. The papers mapped the location and details of each find. One shell looked intact, and several other tail fins and disks were easy to recognize. Some pieces held partial serial numbers or other identifying markings. The rest of the parts meant nothing to me until I read their placemats.

We knelt among the collected pieces that had been laid out on white sheets on the floor. Surrounded by these hunks of high-explosive ammunition, I hugged my arms around my waist. I had chosen not to see this collection before, and when the head of security handed me a curved chunk, I took it with misgivings. It was an ugly mud-green, jagged, dense and unexpectedly heavy.

My imagination made too much of details like that. Each time I heard a blast outside, I had not wanted my hands to remember the weight of the thousands of sharp metal shards that would be hurtling through the air and tearing through flesh. But the time had come to know. I weighed it in my hands and committed this tangible proof to my memory. Catalogued and drawn on maps, these pieces of metal were evidence. They would assign responsibility for the murders in that school in Beit Hanoun.

July 26

A brief ceasefire cleared the skies overhead. Gazans filled the streets and found each other. I ran to colleagues in the aisles of the supermarket, gripping their hands in what would elsewhere have been hugs. The handshakes rumpled my list of every COR colleague's preferred breakfast cereal, bread and instant noodles. Next door, others were buying armloads of fruits and vegetables.

I called Rasha from the garden, beneath an empty, quiet sky. One of her daughters asked if the calm meant that all the pilots had gone home to their mothers.

Rasha translated for me with regret, 'I told her yes, those pilots went home. But there are other pilots who will come to work later. They have to do the jobs they are told to do. This is really too long, too bad for the children. They just want to play outside again. How will they be healthy after this?'

Laila came to visit, alabaster-pale and shadowy around her eyes. Without electricity, she could no longer refrigerate the medication she needed during her pregnancy. She listed all the news I might not have heard. Yasmin was recovering from her escape. After witnessing the bombing of his neighbours' house, another man had formed a group to conduct play activities for children in shelters. Ibrahim, having sheltered dozens of people in his home, had taken his family to Egypt after an ambulance was blown up in front of his house.

Laila fell quiet with her face on an angle as if she were listening hard. I waited while she fidgeted with her hair, her summer cardigan, her cuffs, as if nothing fit properly.

'There's this dust,' she confided, rubbing her thumb and fingers as if to sift the dust, 'this white dust. Everyone is afraid of poison, or the dim. Do you know about the dim?'

'Dim,' I repeated. I thought. 'DIME. Dense Inert Metal Explosives, yes, I've read about the DIME weapons.'[37]

'Everyone is afraid of poison, and this dust keeps floating into my apartment. It's making us all sick. Have you heard anything?'

We both glanced at her stomach. 'No, I haven't heard. Maybe it's . . .' I sighed, and cleared my throat. 'Maybe the dust is the concrete from Shuja'iyya. All those buildings.'

Laila nodded, not agreeing but agreeing that we had no answer. 'This has to end. It's too long.'

'It sure is.'

I saw her off and went to run in the staff gym. I stepped over the baskets of laundry that were lined up before our communal washing machine, and I stepped over the rowing machine that Olivier, the largest of the Close Protection team, had broken in half at the onset of war. I worked the elastic out of my shoulder-length hair. A filigree of hair came away with the elastic. My hair was falling out, from stress and a compromised diet. I held it in my palm – such a shabby little thing. I turned my hand over and watched it drift into the rubbish. Disgraced by my faint-hearted hair, I wrapped the elastic around the hair that remained, and slunk back out of the gym. I napped under Laila's desk, and dreamed that I was going bald. Scott was chasing me with a camera.

'C'mon, everyone needs a laugh! Don't be such a poor sport,' he chided while I climbed over the COR clutter with one hand on the crown of my head.

The first big detonation ended the ceasefire at 9.45 pm, and I listened to the drones multiply overhead.

July 27–28

Everything seemed to teeter and diminish around us, except the falling bombs and the flow of rockets.

A Gazan man dropped heavily onto his chair at the next desk. He rattled a shopping bag at whoever was watching. 'Four hours I waited. For bread.' Fewer bakeries remained intact. Those that functioned had to skew their production days, in order to fill the

37 On the accusation that Israel used DIME weapons in Gaza, see https://www.youtube.com/watch?v=LyBS6j5WR-c

trucks that delivered bread to 182,604 people – 10 per cent of the population – in ninety UNRWA shelters.

The calls to prayer were quieter because mosques had been blown up.

The IDF bombed medical facilities, so the wounded had fewer places to go. Families now arrived at shelters carrying their wounded. In a corner of the Central Ops Room, a team of doctors was outfitting instant clinics within the shelters.

Wandering groups of the displaced assailed Gazan colleagues as they came through the streets to work each morning, asking where they might find shelter and safety. Those were the real shortages.

Notwithstanding predatory incidents, Gaza remained overwhelmingly civil and solicitous.

The Commissioner-General of UNRWA warned publicly that the organization was reaching the limit of its shelter capacity. Every accessible building had been pressed into service. Conditions were dire in our shelters and ours were not the only shelters. We also sent what supplies we could to the many, many Gazans who slept in other classrooms, in mosques, offices, or apartments; in tents or on mats spread beneath tarpaulins, or on any patch of bare land they could find. Neighbours collected and distributed food, water, clothing and bedding to the people who were displaced along their streets, along with anything that might shade them. Water, sewage, transport, electricity, sanitation, healthcare and telecoms infrastructure had all been battered.

Yet the IDF escalated. As I sat with Bob to push out the procurement and shelter assumptions one more time, the IDF warned all residents of Jabalia to leave.

I frowned at the new shelter projection on my laptop, and informed it, 'They won't fit.'

That many people could not be wedged into a building. It would burst. Bob knew that. I looked sideways at him, wondering what kept him going. The lines at the corners of his forehead curled like Charlie Brown's sixes and nines as he read from my laptop. He scratched absently, furiously, at his hairline. Catching himself, he grinned an apology. I pulled a few strands of my hair free in reply, and let them float down.

'They'll fit,' I decided, and closed the laptop.

As I left Front Office, Scott beckoned me into his office and said, 'Tell your ladies to stay indoors.'

I made call after call from the courtyard. Laila had errands to do, and I tried to talk her out of it without sounding alarmed. 'Mm-hmm, I know they're talking about a pause. We're also hearing something different . . . I don't know more. Just stay in for a while, just wait and see. Maybe it's nothing, but wait a little.'

Feeling watched, I looked up to the director's vestibule window, where Close Protection sat. It was open, and Olivier filled it. He nodded down and spooled one hand, encouraging me to continue: he had heard something, too. When I returned to my desk, the IDF was warning all residents to evacuate Zeitoun.

Jabalia and Zeitoun were cities. Jabalia had shown me Gaza's density on my first morning. It could not be emptied. Where would hundreds of thousands of civilians go? Gaza had already been cut in half. Shuja'iyya had been destroyed and its population had been crushed into every cranny and crevice that remained. I didn't know what to call this, this stirring of civilians in ever-tightening circles with no way out. I found that I was shivering, and I shook my head, refusing it. Damien walked past and raised his eyebrows enquiringly. Still shaking my head, I stirred the air with one finger: around and around. What did it mean?

Chapter 21

July 29

The most terrifying night closed in, a night of unremitting noise and smoke and great gobs of flame. Explosions shook the ground, and fireballs lit the horizon. Screaming. Unlike other nights, there were no sirens. They didn't dare. Jenn was away. I knelt on my mattress and peeked over Laila's desk as the horizon glowed and burnt through a smoky film. The desk and I shook with each ear-splitting blast. The thump of sound rattled my ribcage. The whole world churned.

Flares wafted down, trailing smoke. Through the grilles over my windows, the sinking flares wove little squares of light that snaked across my floor and up my walls.

I tried to console myself by deciding that someone in East Khan Younis was catching up on their sleep right now, because tonight was Gaza City's turn. Then my optimism deserted me, and I knew we would be hit. Knowing was unlike fearing, and I knew. Dense metal, packed with high explosives, would land with mortal coincidence. One room in our hallway would be within the kill radius and another just beyond it. You could draw all of Gaza in the same arbitrary luck.

Chiaroscuro, I thought for no particular reason, pleased to be visited by a word I hadn't heard in a very long time. Shades of light and darkness. You could paint the Gaza Strip in chiaroscuro that night, in overlapping radii of grey and black. Dead and maybe-soon-dead. Curled beneath my desk, I understood how people lost their minds. When there was nothing left to grip, they pushed thought away. They dispensed with their minds when a mind was of no conceivable use.

Then I uncurled myself, lay back and watched the flickering shadows of Gaza's fires trim the top of my walls. I watched the little woven grilles slide across the floor and I listened to the jet engines and the blasts and the clatters. I tried to guess how many people were dying around me, and how many were trapped with only their bare-handed neighbours to find them, because no one sent rescue teams into Gaza. I hypnotized myself by counting slowly.

Israel bombed incessantly, all night, without pause or mercy. The number of explosions did not blunt each one. Every single bomb tore through sound and added one more wall to the heaps of rubble, and thickened the smoke that would slide like hooks into the throats of neighbours, and choke the young men who ran to help when they dared.

At dawn, my sleepless hands shook and splattered coffee across my desk. The bellows of my lungs would not draw more than shallow breaths. The morning report counted more than one explosion per minute through the night: 132 air strikes, 840 tank shells in addition to the 435 that had been counted before midnight, and 430 naval shells.

I opened news websites, and I thought at each page, *What would your headline say, if someone bombed Tel Aviv this way?*

The top floor of Front Office was declared unsafe. I towed my mattress down the stairs and across the courtyard, and I helped myself to the floor beneath Jenn's desk.

July 30

I woke up eye to eye with the cockroach husks on Jenn's floor, and trudged into COR. I found my neighbour Mike there already, jowly from lack of sleep, hair askew.

'What,' I said, on guard because Mike's hair was never askew.

The IDF had shelled Jabalia Elementary A & B Girls School, shortly before dawn. The school sheltered 3000 people, many of whom had been forced out of Shuja'iyya and Beit Hanoun. They had left their homes as they were warned to do, and they had moved in the direction they were ordered to take. The IDF had fired four artillery shells into a protected United Nations building with no advance warning. They killed sixteen people while they slept or prepared for prayers, and they injured ninety-nine.

I sank slowly down onto my chair, hearing the screaming, and the scramble of three thousand thrown-awake people groping for their children's hands, grappling and herding each other through darkness and clouds of cement dust. And then another shattering boom in the pandemonium, and then another, and then another.

Mechanically I opened the shelter notification lists, and found the map book. Then my dread fell away, and I moved a little faster. If I could find an error, then the principle of protection might still be intact. The other shelters would be safer if this could all have been a mistake. I checked again and again and again, to no avail. The Israeli army knew the school was packed to the rafters with civilians. They knew because we had told them more than two dozen times. They fired into it anyway.

I flapped the map book closed, and I shook my head when someone came to ask if the error had been ours. I felt too sick to speak. My skin crawled. Had there been a fire? The hallways must have been pitch-dark. Was there panic, were the stairs intact, were they all out now? And where would 3000 more people go under fire?

Still they bombed and the world let them. Everyone saw civilian protections attenuate. Deep fears bubbled up and Gaza's civil order began at last to fray. A Red Crescent office was sacked and burned. A UN driver was struck while driving a marked vehicle in his reflective vest. More supply and water trucks were hijacked, their drivers beaten and their cargo diverted. More food deliveries degenerated into violence. Shelter committees and family notables managed to quell most of the conflicts among neighbours. If people felt they had to fight for food and water, these clashes warned that they would likely divide along clan lines. For the first time, I feared that Gaza was being driven to some kind of dystopic break.

In forty-eight hours, 43,000 more displaced people walked through school gates. UNRWA was sheltering 225,178 increasingly distressed people. They had nowhere safer to go.

War and blockade notwithstanding, Gaza's militants continued to fire scores of rockets each day.

I still wrote to the teams in the evenings, but as more of them lived in darkness, I wrote more often into a void.

July 31

With no electricity and little sleep for four nights, I could not hear what remained of Rasha's voice inside COR. I took the phone away from the building, although we were no longer supposed to linger in the compound's exposed spaces.

'We are living in minutes now. I hold both of my daughters all night and we count each minute that we do not die. "That bomb didn't hit us." "That bomb didn't kill us."'

'Rasha, every minute must also be one minute closer to the end of this. One minute closer – one minute closer.' Even as I chanted it, I doubted it. Violence had been detached from purpose some time ago, and the minutes led nowhere.

One colleague insisted that Gaza would hold on forever because 1500 deaths must not be meaningless. Another despaired that the world was ready to let Gaza die and Israel was willing to kill it. Some of the families who had spread themselves out in 2012 began to gather, preferring to die together.

USAID contributed hygiene kits, while the US government said that it understood Israel's need to do whatever it deemed suitable.

News reports claimed that some Israelis, in communities near Gaza, had perched on their hillsides to watch the bombing like sport, complete with popcorn.

The UN Under-Secretary-General for Humanitarian Affairs said that the world 'watched in horror'. I fumed at that: what good was doe-eyed horror? I raged at everyone who had ever protested the low quality of a battery hen's life, while they settled for watching the lives and deaths of human beings in Gaza.

August 1

COR's morning briefing began with updates on the five UN buildings that had been damaged during the previous day, two by direct strikes. Damien described a supply line that might import ten metric tons of bread from the West Bank each day, to relieve the pressure on Gaza's bakeries.

'Could we get it in here, still edible?' Scott doubted, and they debated. The complication lay, of course, in the line of trucks that were forever backed up, waiting at an insurable distance to pass through the Kerem Shalom bottleneck.

'The thing is,' Damien said, 'If we do it? If we get ten tons of bread baked, packed, loaded, transported across Israel and through Kerem Shalom, every single day, without fail and without too much mould, that would only cover 15 per cent of our daily requirements.'

The briefing fell silent on the line between awe and paralysis.

We discussed drilling wells for water because the existing infrastructure had been hit so many times, but Gaza's aquifer was too polluted to offer a solution.

Scott shook his head. 'And, the big finish – Marilyn – any breakthrough?'

I held out my empty hands and avoided the eyes of the doctors at the table. 'No, still nothing. No one, no army, no manufacturer keeps 60,000 bottles of lice shampoo on their shelf. Procurement is rounding up every small supply they can find. It's arriving in boxes, rather than pallets. We may have to have it manufactured. No one knows how long that takes.'

We had reports of viral meningitis. We were racing against contagion.

After the briefing, I visited Uta in her office. It was so quiet that I could hear my ears ring. Bob stuck his head in the door and said peremptorily, 'It's going to get worse.'

He walked past. He tipped himself back into the doorway from the other side a moment later, angular as Dick Van Dyke, and said, 'Sorry. I've been asking people if they are willing to stay, because it's going to get worse. I just assumed . . .'

He cleared his throat, planted himself upright in the doorway to slow himself down, and composed a third time. 'It's going to get worse. Are you willing to stay?'

We laughed at him, normally so erudite.

'Yes,' I said. I was expecting more, but he set off without another word.

Uta flung herself across her desk. 'Don't just tell me that – worse how?' she called, but he was gone.

By email, we were instructed to wear our heavy Kevlar vests and helmets each time we walked between the buildings.

I started across the courtyard to find my blue vest. The white-hot glare drove me back, blinking, into the gloom of the entrance. I kept forgetting that it was summer. Squinting, I shaded my eyes and darted across the open space. I dragged my vest and helmet back to COR and kicked them into a corner before I got the news from the next desk.

One Israeli soldier had been captured in Rafah, Gaza's southernmost governorate. In retaliation, Israel had begun to bombard the city. Thousands of Rafahites were running, unprotected, through chaotic streets. Ten days after Israel had obliterated Shuja'iyya in the north, it threatened to happen again in the south.

As the bombing grew more furious, groups of exhausted, terrorized people roamed through the cities of Gaza and banged on gates, wanting only to be safe. On the confounding wall of whiteboards, though, a quarter of a million Gazans already filled the schools. Fifteen thousand more had joined them during the day.

I wrote in my office on the top floor of the building that night, listening to the voices crying out for safety in the street. They pleaded from the very limit of human tolerance, their desperation more piercing than the sound of the bombs. The hairs jumped up along my arms, alert, answering to something primal.

This is how the world will end. This is how the deluge will feel. We are one microbe away from the collapse.

August 2

The bombing of Islamic University across the street woke me up and dusted my hair with plaster chips from the ceiling. I lifted my head slightly from the floor and shook the dust away. Explosions had become the environment through which I moved. My body conformed like a fish to the currents of noise, twisting under the desk, ducking into a collar. Unthinking motions.

I washed in the hand sink upstairs and wandered back, trailing my towel. Marjean waved me into the garden to show me a rosebush. Freshly scrubbed with his own towel over his shoulder, he looked twenty years younger than the rest of us.

'This one's new,' he said, cupping a bud. 'Come and see, it's really beautiful.'

I inhaled, and smelled a heady pink. 'Mm,' I sighed, remembering flowers.

'When're you out?' he asked.

'Three days. I've tried to hand over three times, but people keep getting called away. This time for real. It's my mother's 95th birthday party.'

'Ninety-five?'

'Yes. Her parties are special, they tell me; lots of music. I've never been. Last year, I sat for twenty-four hours in the airport, but my flight didn't take off. It just never works out. At ninety-five, though, you can't take too many more parties for granted.'

'Good for you. And have you straightened out that little story about spending the summer on the beach in Tel Aviv?'

'It's, ah, still up in the air.'

I went to drape my towel over Jenn's office chair, wondering why I hadn't finished the story.

If I went to my mother's birthday party, my sisters wanted me to pretend that I had spent the summer in Israel, watching the planes fly south to bomb Gaza. My mother was declining, and fixating on her worry. And they thought that the mention of Gaza might politicize the party for others.

The Deputy Speaker of Israel's parliament was calling for the 'annihilation' of Gaza's fighters and all of their supporters.[38] My mother had been the humanitarian at our dinner table, and prior to her decline, I believe that she would have shared my disgust. I had tried for days to talk myself into lying to my mother as they thought best, at what might be our final visit. I couldn't do that, while Israel was doing this.

A short time later, half of COR clustered at the end of the conference table, holding a large street map flat with books and hands. People peered quietly over others' shoulders while several Gazans made phone calls, speaking fast and low.

'Are the soldiers to the left or the right of the door?' Mike asked an engineer. The edge of Mike's hand hovered over a city block on the map, ready to slice it into portions. 'Right? Is he sure – no, god, don't ask him that. I don't want anyone going into the street to check.'

---

38 https://electronicintifada.net/blogs/ali-abunimah/concentrate-and-exterminate-israel-parliament-deputy-speakers-gaza-genocide-plan

I tapped an arm, and a colleague whispered, 'No one knows where the IDF is.'

Mike pointed to a block on the map. 'Anyone here – anyone?'

The Gazans scrolled through their address books, seeking anyone who lived on that block.

Information addicts, we were blind. Phones and radios told us that Rafahites were running through their streets as shells fell around them. We heard that sixty-two Palestinians were confirmed dead, and that Israeli soldiers were going door to door.

Bob made notes in his palm-sized book. 'Massively stupid fucking thing,' he informed the map table, and he left to negotiate for access to a border entry point, a warehouse and a route between them. A quarter million people needed water, food and safety but the attack on Rafah had cut us off from Kerem Shalom. We had no way through the blockade, and no access to our three largest warehouses.

At the logistics team's desks, someone was making call after call, looking for forklifts to equip a makeshift warehouse.

I went with Bob and the CPs to Jabalia. Without people to colour it, Jabalia Camp was the monochrome shade of concrete dust. Every block was studded with vacancies, craters and spills of rubble. A thin, desultory trickle of people walked through the streets. We inched past a gathering of Jabalians, arms akimbo, shaking their heads at a bus that blocked the street. It was suspended on two wheels, at a gravity-defying angle. A concrete slab had rolled and pierced the bus, and held it in place like a stick-up.

There were no children playing in the streets, and their absence felt as eerie as all the shattered buildings.

The head of UNRWA's Jabalia organization was an older man whose jowls and hands quivered from lack of sleep. Way beyond sleep, he had been mediating local politics, haranguing COR, listening and resolving disputes, intervening when delivery trucks were held up, remaining present and visible to the 80,000 people who resided in Jabalia shelters; nonstop, day after day and night after night. He could not hold off the damage from the sky, but he, personally, was going to stamp order over chaos on his patch of ground. Around him a number of younger men had gathered.

One famously sharp-tongued man angled away to avoid being seen ministering to his elder like a son.

I pointed back as we drove through the gate. 'That man is going to have a heart attack. He's going to keel over. Like, any minute.'

'Mm hmm. You want to try to stop him?' Bob smiled, wider, and laughed out loud in appreciation. He lifted his feet from the floor of the car and slapped his legs, and I couldn't think of the last time I'd heard anyone laugh. 'Unbelievable. He is utterly, indispensably, in his element. *He* is holding that together.'

Gaza's character was most evident in the fact that such structures held as well as they did. I tried to imagine a quarter-million other people, squeezed into shelters like the UNRWA schools for this long; being bombed without defence, losing family members and friends, uninsured homes and streets; deprived of privacy and light, fasting and minimally fed, heat-boggled and parched, forever frightened and sleepless. Incidents did not surprise me. I was astonished that the shelters functioned at all.

We passed a bakery, where a dozen people queued for bread. I craned my neck out of habit, trying to see into the building.

Bob said, 'So, remember that livelihoods job that you don't want?'

'Nah – don't want. That job description is just bloody UN business as usual.'

'We could resource it properly, as part of a post-war recovery plan. Establish a real business and livelihoods program.'

'Nah?' I said less convincingly. The CPs smirked at each other in the front seat.

Then, without explanation, the websites signalled a unilateral Israeli pullback. The bombardment ended; yesterday's obsession with a single soldier forgotten. The IDF reported the soldier's probable death, and added that kidnapped soldiers were not Israel's soft underbelly.

'Kidnapped,' I mused, and I turned to Mike. 'Can you be kidnapped in uniform, on duty, on a battlefield? Aren't you captured?'

'Anywhere else,' he agreed.

August 3

Fifteen per cent of the population, 269,793 Gazans, waited in the shelters for news of the withdrawal.

I told myself that it was over, because everyone needed it to end. A unilateral suspension of bombing would not suffice. The IDF was killing 100 Gazans a day and it had to end, so I told myself that it was ending. *Yalla*, done.

I turned resolutely to my flight bookings. An absence of noise, that mausoleum hush, made me look up. 'What?' I said to the room around me.

'Rafah Prep Boys A,' came a reply. 'They fired a missile by the school gate.'

Reports arrived: fifteen people had been killed. I picked through the reports for some exculpating detail. I searched afresh each time, because each attack was a violation of the protections those schools had promised. Then I stopped myself, because no one else had drones with missiles overhead.

August 4

Israel unilaterally drew its forces back to the buffer zone.

Mike and I went to check the damage to our apartments. I wore thick-soled shoes to step between the splintered window frames. The suitcase scraped against the glass on my bed, and I didn't bother to shake it out because the whole world was an inch deep in glass. I opened a drawer, but what season would it be – which month was it? All I knew was that I hadn't slept forever and ever.

Mike came from next door to hand me his phone. He placed it in my hand before he said, 'Procurement, for you.'

He strode away before I could give the phone back. The head of the procurement department had received the preponderance of Bob's shrugs for the past year, as he made policy exceptions for the Gateway enterprise. Our relations had been further strained in the frantic rush to supply the shelters. I sighed before I brought the phone close enough to be heard.

'Hi,' I said sadly. 'I don't care. No, I didn't mean that I don't *care*. I mean that I have no preference. Handles or no handles, either way. You must have some record of the rubbish bags you procure for the schools . . .'

I listened, more to crackle than words.

'Rubbish,' I said, relishing the word. 'They're rubbish bags, right? They hold rubbish. That *is* a complete description of their function . . . Really, 50,000 . . . I know it's a lot. It's a quarter of a million people in ninety schools with an average of thirty classrooms, so you've got a hundred people sharing one little classroom-sized rubbish bin and it's going to need to be emptied often . . . the rubbish bins your department procures for the schools – that size . . . You must have a preferred supplier . . .'

My brain throbbed, and the watery, sleepless pouches over my cheekbones reverberated with each pulse. My whole head was beating and soon my cranium would explode. I wondered what Mike would do if I threw his phone into the sea.

'Listen, stop, please. I'm very sorry – my bad on the size, okay? – because I didn't want to give you a measurement that turned out to be hard to find. Any size – or sizes – that you can get right now, in very large quantities . . . would you just, just buy bags, lots of bags . . . No, I do not know how long they will be living in schools. Do you? . . . Listen, this list is signed off and I'm leaving now. I am turning off the phone and I'm going to Canada, goodbye!'

I heard myself panting, wrestling with rage that had only the most glancing connection with the person I'd been shouting at. I was one big bundle of aerated nerve ends. I was root canal.

I crunched next door, and handed Mike his phone with poor grace.

Chapter 22

In the middle of the block, I forgot to walk. I leaned back to ogle the smooth, white, straight, narcotizing walls of Tel Aviv. None of Gaza's lines were straight any longer. I let the beachgoers stream past me on the boardwalk, seeking among them the face of the malevolence that was loose in Gaza. Tanned leathery or fishy-pale, they wore expressions as untroubled as their walls. I drank on the hotel roof, staring down the coast and counting off a few of Gaza's minutes. Just down that coast, war was happening, but it did not appear to be happening to the faces around me.

I slept fretfully despite the safety. I feared losing rather than dying, and I could lose anywhere. All around me, precious things had been lost with nothing more than a thud. Maybe I had already lost, and I didn't yet know.

Joan met me in New York for a day. The sight of her promised that there could again be first-world rules and grammar and seasonal colour palettes. They still existed somewhere. Ten minutes after we sat down for breakfast at a Manhattan hotel, Joan declared that we would not discuss the war.

'How?' I wanted to know. I saw the war behind my eyelids and I smelled its charred residue. The war had stiffened all of my clothes into hessian. What else was there to talk about?

'Mar, you're my sister and I'm so, so sorry for what you've been through. You deserve all the support we can give you, but we cannot talk about the war.'

I was speechless. I watched her face, an approximation of mine, saying words that we had been raised to speak. I had been so sure that we would be the ones to keep listening across the gulf.

I turned my attention to the perfect sphere of the restaurant's wrought iron table, with its delicately scumbled surface. Twee, too small to hold much. I disliked the table.

The unspoken war dogged us until I saw her off in a cab for the airport.

I spent a few days in New York, walking with my feet in Manhattan and my mind in Gaza. I sat for hours at the window tables of cafés, losing myself in books of Jewish ethics. I asked the pavement and the pages, *What am I going to believe, everything I have always been told, or the world in front of my eyes?*

I visited my mother and left before the party. It was the only concession I could make.

I returned to Jerusalem in the third week of August, as the war's final, gratuitous violence erupted. The IDF bombed Gaza City apartment towers, twelve and fourteen storeys tall. UNRWA was sheltering 292,959 people when the bombing stopped.[39]

Israel had killed 2251 Gazans, of whom 1462 were civilians, and 551 were children. Sixty-six Israeli soldiers and six civilians were killed, including one child.[40]

Palestinian militants had fired 4881 rockets and 1753 mortars toward Israel. The IDF reported that it had supplied 5000 tons of munitions, fired 14,500 tank shells and around 35,000 artillery shells. Israel had sent forth one ton of munitions for every homemade rocket, and Israel had carried out more than 6000 air strikes on the Gaza Strip – an occupied community, in a locked space the length of a marathon.

There was nothing to show for it. No one was deterred. The ceasefire of August 26 did not touch the causes of the violence. The bombing and the rockets were simply suspended, pending further discussions that would never follow.

I found Bob in a corridor of UNRWA's Jerusalem office, and we

39 Including non-UNRWA shelters, half a million Gazans were displaced during the fighting.

40 Immediate casualty and damage reports would change. These figures are taken from OCHA reporting dated June 23, 2015. https://www.ochaopt.org/content/key-figures-2014-hostilities (accessed April 2, 2019).

stepped into an unlocked room.

'If it's okay, I'd love to do the recovery and livelihoods work, as long as I can do it as a consultant.'

'Done,' he said quickly, and a little quizzically. 'You have something against UN staff benefits?'

'Sort of. It was Kirstin's idea. Do the work, just don't take the job.'

'Done – write yourself some better terms of reference. And, Marilyn? Could you possibly stop calling us "you people"? You work for UNRWA. Handle it.'

'Sorry. I'll try. It worked through the war.'

Chapter 23

On my first weekend back, I swept up the glass splinters and the desiccated leaves of my plants. I restocked the kitchen shelves, minus the apple-cinnamon oatmeal because my cheekbones ached at the thought of lumpy blond mud trailing after a spoon. Through the new glass doors in the bedroom, the war underscored the sea. There were concave depressions in the sand and a burned-out fishermen's storage unit. To the right, beyond the blackened ribs of the fire station, lay that disgraced stretch of beach where four boys had been killed while playing hide and seek.

I stared into the port until my eyes lost their focus, to reacquaint myself with its qualities of light. The sun dazzled one corner of the lagoon. As its reflection lengthened, it drew the white wavelets into its trail. I took off my glasses that decoupled light from motion, and all the white feathers swam together in one sparkling train. Everything was quiet; sound had not yet resumed.

I froze in the doorway of the Gateway's project workroom, unprepared for the empty seats. Rasha bumped into my back, and I reached for the door frame.

'No, don't worry,' she assured me, nudging me into the room.

Loss ringed the room. A dozen or so members of the project team had made it to work. One woman sat with both arms clenched around her core, as if she still held the twelve dead members of her family in place there. Next to her, a man shared the remains of his ground floor with ten relatives, whose homes had even fewer walls. The empty spaces had been left by those who were packing to try their luck on the new refugee trail that crossed the Mediterranean Sea. A few had already left.

People swerved to greet each other each time they crossed the UNRWA compound. They propped each other up with long, rocking hugs, relieved yet maladroit, wearing thousand-yard gazes. Conversation was studded with false starts. Women nodded at my shorter hair and pointed to their own headscarves to commiserate.

I stopped to greet one vibrant young woman. I had never before seen her dress in black. 'I don't feel whole anymore,' she fluttered, shaking her head with the tiny motions of a tic.

I settled into the visitor's seat between Rasha's and Laila's desks. The room looked empty without its foam squabs. 'So, I would sit in the Gateway room in the evenings for a bit, before I wrote emails, and I thought . . . We can turn this around, if we start with what they do know. Employers want teamwork? Gazans know all about teamwork. Teamwork is neighbours, relying on each other for their lives. Time management?'

Rasha and Laila nodded, intent and blank, while I babbled. Not a word registered, and I had no idea what I'd said, either.

'I'll explain it better another time,' I decided, and I stumbled away as if my arms and legs were all different lengths.

In my office, I turned to a task I had been promising myself. I planted copies of the painstaking master shelter list in every emergency-related location that I could think of. Wherever they turned, future emergency responders would find each building's number of classrooms and toilets and water storage capacity, prevailing name, co-ordination map references and more.

Bob arrived in my doorway. The treads came back to me, familiar as fresh bread: Bob plus two booted CPs equalled six feet. 'We need a contingency plan. Can you pull a first draft together? To restart COR if the ceasefire fails.'

I gulped, and wrote down his parameters. 'Okay, okay. And a timeframe, say, six months? Three?'

'Weeks,' he spoke past my shoulder.

I laid my pen down. Weeks were out of the question. Bob left before he had to hear it. I didn't write the weeks down, in case Laila or Rasha happened across the notes on my desk.

UNRWA enjoyed no respite. It had 118 damaged buildings, among them 83 schools. The school year was upon us, and the shelter-schools all needed maintenance before they could resume teaching in double shifts. However, the schools were still operating as shelters. The IDF had damaged 100,000 homes, and destroyed 18,000. Of the hundreds of thousands of Gazans made homeless by the bombs, 60,000 still lived in UNRWA schools.

The internationals who had worked through the war began to leave Gaza within weeks. Their replacements were inexperienced but keen to break into UN careers. Short-term emergency specialists arrived. Grinding its post-adrenal gears, UNRWA diverged into furious motion and stunned, trackless drift.

Gazans resumed demonstrating at UNRWA's gate, less than two weeks into the ceasefire. The protestors demanded faster reconstruction. One leaflet read, 'The Israeli aggression is over, the UNRWA aggression continues.'

Bob and Scott struggled to make one coherent whole from the pieces.

In the second week, I left the workroom and paused in the breezeway to read my texts. Then I looked up at the Front Office window. Twice during the war, as we had sat in the evenings, I had assured Bob that I would understand if the Gateway social enterprise appeared to be an unaffordable luxury after the war. Its start had not been stellar.

On my way up the stairs to his office, I anticipated the ways he might ask. Is the Gateway still feasible? Is there any reason to think that its prospects have improved? I was ready to concede to those questions, and I sat down at the rattan table with a genuine smile of thanks for having tried.

Instead, Bob asked, 'Is it still relevant?'

'Relevant?' I repeated, a little miffed. 'Of course it is.'

'How, then? How do we make it work?'

We closed the original, parlous project in favour of three wiser pilot projects, and we accelerated the work of the poverty survey.

Randa left Mercy Corps and joined UNRWA to build a business and livelihoods unit. She began with Sulafa, UNRWA's sixty-year-old embroidery programme. Three hundred women embroidered for Sulafa, and that number would grow with business development and marketing.

For the unit's first new work, UNRWA did what the donors could not: Scott negotiated the approvals to send recyclable plastic bottles and waste paper out of Gaza. Plastic drinking water bottles lined every alley and filled every trash heap. The local housewares factories could not process them. Those bottles could be collected for sale, much like the plastic that Beit Lahiya families sold – but export involved much larger quantities. The owners of recycling companies had hollowed out underground storage beneath their houses for tons of stockpiled paper. They lived in fear of fire while they waited for a way to get their inventory through the blockade, to their partners in Israel or the West Bank. UNRWA unlocked that gate. We wrote these and all of our plans into the post-war recovery strategy, and waited for funds for the unit to start work.

Ibrahim returned from Cairo to join the Gateway enterprise management team. They all piled into the office next door. Passing their doorway, I often leaned in and counted them with relief. And then I would turn away before they saw my face cloud over. The bombing had only been suspended, and contingency plans were circulating.

Beyond our hallway, the pieces of the place where I had lived for three years had been blown apart and draped in a pall of dusty grey shock. Buildings sagged over their broken concrete slabs, and every sidewalk winked with the shards of a million fallen windows. The land itself had been altered by so many bombs. Landmarks and alleys had vanished into two million tons of crumble. People crawled, dwarfed, across the brittle plains. Gaza was drawn in zones of grief, pockets of disbelief, and vacuums.

Barter and subsistence prevailed in some non-refugee areas, where there was no government to order and meet people's needs. Gazans began to surround UN vehicles and diplomatic convoys, to plead for help.

Sombre young men waved outsized Palestinian flags from atop the remnants of buildings, to reclaim Shuja'iyya. We drove through canyons of incalculable violence. All the apartment buildings had been hammered into a new floor, one or two storeys above the land. I looked for the edges of the shattered city blocks, because the rubble itself was just too raw, too intrusive into private lives. I had always peered down Gaza's alleys to spy on its life, but the alleys of Shuja'iyya were occluded by the avalanches of fallen houses. Shuja'iyya had fused into one mass.

Boys and old men sat on concrete blocks in front of the mass, dusty specks against a dreary landscape. Behind them, the face of the rubble already bore scores of phone numbers as people reached for each other and for help. Sticks of furniture, frames and rebar broke the surfaces of the mass. People scrambled over its hillsides, salvaging for something of their own, or some memento to give to their children. Higher up, at the outer fringes of the dead zone, men were preparing to live on tilting slabs of concrete. They swept out the floors of apartments that still had three, or even two walls. A few had already strung quilts or plastic tarpaulins across their missing walls. Higher still, someone had planted Palestinian flags upon the summits. A seeping danger pervaded the air – the lingering malice that had wrecked the city, and the threat that now emanated from the landscape itself, every element of it unstable and sharp as shale.

Rasha and I had gone to find the edges of a neighbourhood economy, the torn flaps that might be knitted back together. With each such foray, it was becoming clearer that the bombardment had not left enough to call an economy.

Our driver kept restarting his monologue. 'And here . . . and here . . .' His free hand hung out the window as it tried to take in the rubble. 'And here . . .'

'It's enough,' I whispered to the driver after we had circled a few times. We drove back without another word. All I recalled of economic activity was a bakery.

I returned to a stack of red HR files on my desk, awaiting sixty signatures to hire the next project team. I read my expanded title: Early Recovery, Business and Livelihoods. I picked up my pen and could not remember how to sign my name. I made myself coffee and straightened my desk, busily touching things to remember myself, but when I tried again to spell my name, the date palms beckoned. Outside my window grille, brown threads fluttered at the edges of their leaves.

Reeling myself back, I traced my 'M', but I did not know how to attach the letters which followed it. Odd that the date palm leaves should be frayed and creaking this early in the season. The file said it was September. If that were so, where had the summer gone? The war had breezes that stirred the curtains and bombs that flapped them inward, but I recalled no glare, nor the heat that would have parched the leaves of the palm trees.

I said goodbye as Randa and Laila led Rasha home early. I tried signing my name on a bit of paper, but my hand had lost its muscle memory. Two hours passed before the shock of Shuja'iyya receded sufficiently for me to write to the end of my name.

One evening, I thought I might burst. I felt saturated and useless. I needed urgently to know the final count of the dead, the wounded, the homes and livelihoods lost. I wanted it defined, capped so that I could grieve within boundaries that would not expand further. I wanted more work to immerse myself and obviate thought. I felt something rising in me like a blurt, like bile, like revelation just out of reach. I didn't know whether to hold it down or open my eyes to it. I didn't know anything.

Bob called. I went upstairs, and we spent much of the night drunk and profane. The worst prospect, we agreed, was the prospect of falling from the headlines once more, of cleaning up and having to do it all over again. As Gazans were saying, worst was the possibility that it might mean nothing at all.

UNRWA's mental health unit served its Palestinian staff, and UNRWA's international counsellor arrived from Jerusalem to assess the fitness of the international staff who had worked through the war. He moved and spoke at a tweedy, deliberate pace. I liked him and I thought he should smoke cigars. But what constituted fitness now? If anyone had not been changed by seeing 5000 tons of explosives dropped on a trapped populace, they must have been unwell before.

I closed the door to my office when my turn came, and I reclined on an angle that matched his. 'How are *you*?' I asked, curious because he looked as wrung out as the rest of us, and the rest of us looked recently deceased.

'Me? Thank you. I'm okay. It's always draining here. When I leave Gaza, I sleep and sleep from the vicarious stress. And how are you?'

'I guess I'm okay – I mean, to the degree that anyone can be okay after what was done here.'

He asked what I had found most difficult while carrying out my own responsibilities.

'The conditions in the shelters,' I said without hesitation. 'I was standing in front of that. I think I will tow those mattresses to my grave, you know? That was my symbol of our inadequacy. We were there, but we could not be enough. That was the worst fact of my own job, confronting the failure – the futility – of law and protection behind a wall.'

'And, mm, who were you angry at?'

'At us! We didn't have enough; we couldn't do enough to protect people. We couldn't keep them safe.'

He nodded too long, until I wanted to ask him what he saw that I did not. Finally, he said, 'Mm hmm, mm hmm,' and he rose to leave the room.

I emailed him later in the week, to thank him for leaving me to think that through. I was angry at UNRWA for the same reason that Gazans were resuming their protests at the compound gates. UNRWA was the accessible, reactive face of the blockade regime. The real object of anger was that impassive, blank wall and the unaccountable choices that had been made beyond it. I was angry at us, because it did no good to beat my little fists against that wall.

Chapter 24

The violinist, Itzhak Perlman, is said to have broken a string onstage. Rather than pausing to replace the string, he performed the remainder of his concerto on three, and then explained to his astonished audience, 'Our task is to make music with what remains.'

In that spirit, Gazans draped festive red and green pennants across intersections and over the blackened entry points of missiles into their buildings. UNRWA got the school year underway.

Industry assessments and priorities piled themselves upon my desk. At least 360 factories and 4000 businesses had been damaged or destroyed. One thousand smaller workshops were gone. The Food and Agriculture Organization estimated that 30 per cent of all cultivated land had been damaged, along with greenhouses, irrigation, fishing boats, and 40 per cent of the livestock. Donors pledged a theoretical $5.4 billion, around half of it for reconstruction.

Fertilized by a month of vitamins and exercise, a thick new crop of hair plumped out my old hair like a mushroom cap. We called it my peace dividend. But we were not ourselves. We floated alone like wreckage. Laila turned a ghostly white in her flowered maternity blouses, after her surviving sister lost twin foetuses at seven months. Rasha wore a SpongeBob SquarePants muff to hide her hands, which clenched and unclenched beyond her control. Randa had always written notes on scraps of paper, but the papers had begun to pile themselves up on her desk. I bought her a notebook and begged her to use it for my sake. Returning from Egypt with something to prove, Ibrahim's gentle surface turned sandpapery. I spoke over the ends of other people's sentences, unless I folded my hands on the desk and gripped them tightly to earth my impatience and frustration because, donor pledges notwithstanding, I had no funds with which to work.

By night, I read about military accountability. What violence was judged to be disproportionate elsewhere? How far did other states go to protect their forces, at the foreseeable expense of civilian lives? I read a page, a paragraph, and put the Kindle down. Sometimes it sat for days or weeks before I could resume reading. For three years, I had been content to say that things just exploded, letting the blockade wall shield me from reckoning with the individuals who made choices beyond it. Military accountability assigned responsibility to individuals, not walls.

Military accountability judged this assault by normal standards. If Gazan lives were not different from other lives, then the bombs that killed them were not different from other bombs. There were no exceptions.

Half a kilometre from the Israeli fence, Khuza'a was a town of around 10,000. The town had been cut off and held by Israeli soldiers for days. Some of the war's darkest accusations concerned the treatment and killing of Khuza'a residents during those days.[41]

Approaching Khuza'a, we passed swathes of field where each building had been smashed, with scarcely a crater between them. Someone had precisely destroyed each possibility of returning home. Rubble spilled indiscriminately from the houses along Khuza'a's main road. We threaded through the lane that remained. It was quiet in a way that Gaza was never quiet: Khuza'a was still. It felt remote, although nothing in Gaza could be remote.

But not empty. People moved slowly, minimally, exposed to us and soon to the winter rains in their two- and three-walled rooms. Young and old men slumped on salvaged couches the colour of the road. Our car stirred the next layer of dust that would settle on their upholstery and their hair. Children with serious faces clambered over the concrete. I leaned nearer the window to see how many of them had shoes fit for their brittle ground. Few did.

41 See *This Is How We Fought in Gaza*, the testimonies of Israeli soldiers: https://www.breakingthesilence.org.il/pdf/ProtectiveEdge.pdf

'Jesus,' I breathed, 'how do you raise a child in this? What happens to a child who sees this every day?'

Randa didn't answer. Instead she clucked from driver to passenger windows and back. I followed her gaze.

Grey people were drifting toward us, drawn to the truck's UN logo. An angular man stepped through his wall like a bone poking through skin, hailing the truck as he stumbled down from the rubble to the road. Another rose from his plastic table in a room with two walls. One young man raised his thumbs in approval from a couch by the road, while his companions grew sullen on either side. A few strode angrily toward us; angry with their legs, faces expressionless. I wanted to squeeze my eyes shut against the sight of people so reduced, to leave them some privacy and blot out their abject loss. I could only wonder what had left them this limp, and who was not sitting with them. Khuza'a felt intensely private, surviving within the kind of moat that could not be crossed by anyone who didn't already know.

On the way back from Khuza'a, Randa began to murmur, 'When it's like this, raising a child is like having an animal. What's the word – a pet. You feed them, you take them to the bathroom. There is no emotion left. You just do what they need.'

In a monotone, she talked about parents so mad with fear from a knock on the roof, in moments so disordered, that they fled their homes with their children, only to realize in the street that one was missing. A baby was clutched in neither parent's arms. The child who hid from the noise, and gave her parents only seconds to decide whether to save the visible children or die hunting for the missing one.

We passed a mosque near Randa's apartment. The streetside half of the mosque had been ripped away, its interior wrecked. Parts of the back walls still stood. Randa became agitated as the car drew alongside. With a low moan, she jabbed her finger at a windowless building across the street.

'There – I was there. It's a mosque, I thought we would be safe near a mosque, so I hid with my boys there. I was in that basement while they—' She shook out her hands as if drying them in the air. 'They hit it so many times! So you never know when it's over. So you don't know when you might be safe. So you just stop feeling safe.'

***

Scott leaned on my doorframe. Greyer than before the war, he fingered the quilted pouches beneath his eyes and neglected his necktie. I listened, and although my heart sunk, I tried to think of some approving thing to say.

'I wish you the best, Scott, I really do. If anyone deserves some sleep, it'd be you.'

'I gave him long notice,' he said again.

'I'm sure he appreciates that. And, um . . .' I folded my hands and inspected the white knuckles between my fingernails.

'I'll let you know, as soon as I know who'll be replacing me,' he promised.

The enterprise and the nascent livelihoods unit were his dependents.

Scott shifted, and jutted his chin past me. He came into the room and inspected my disconnected phone cord.

I was mortified. 'Would you look at that.'

'How long as your phone been . . . out of order?'

'Ooh, a while. It's quieter this way. You know that I answer all my emails.'

He considered me, and shook his head. 'You are really not cut out for the United Nations, are you?'

I let my head fall forward over my hands. 'What will I do when you go?'

'Long notice,' he reassured me as he handed me my phone cord and opened my door. 'Months to go before I sleep.'

I left Tiaba for groceries on a Saturday morning in November. Swedish Jenny was parking her car, and I walked over to chat. She must have been running, because she was wearing long sweatpants and a modestly high-necked T-shirt. Instead of her usual runner's glow, Jenny's complexion was sallow. I ran my fingers over my own cheeks as I walked toward her, wondering if I looked as wintery. She drew on a cardigan, and ground the heels of her palms into her eyes as if she were holding off sleep.

Even in running shoes, Jenny towered over me. 'I had a coffee with one of my team yesterday. I couldn't believe it, one of her children was watching a cartoon on her tablet. She showed me.

It was a scene from the war, made into a cartoon but violent, awful. My colleague,' she repeated, pointing at her own chest and clutching her sweater more tightly around her. 'They would never have let that stuff in their home before, but they're just too tired to pay attention now.'

'I know. How can it be, we survived the war and *now* turns out to be the hard part. Week by week, I'm deleting lines from the early recovery plan because it's not early anymore. Where's the recovery money? Just sweeping the plans off the desk, line by line.'

'I kind of asked them, my colleagues, how they could . . . you know, let their child . . . and she said the lesson of that war is that there are no more civilians in Gaza. In the IDF's eyes, there is no more civilian protection. So they might as well prepare to die fast, because they are just dying slowly now. Here,' she added, pulling bunches of cut flowers out of her car. She always remembered to buy extras.

On her wrist, Jenny wore the green wristband of a conflict protection program: *Civilians are not targets!* I thanked her, and reached for the flowers. I was wearing my green bracelet, too.

I rummaged through the supermarket aisle for a credible sponge. In Gaza, housecleaning pitted a sponge against glass threads, the fine yellow sand that drifted into corners, the black mould and bright aquamarine nodules that crusted over water pipes. Palm-sized sponges didn't stand a chance.

'Bigger – and thick?' I explained to one of the young fellows.

He shook his head. 'Maybe next month.'

A drawstring tugged at my neck muscles, and I walked quickly away. I picked a package of the good wholegrain crackers from the shelf in passing, and then went back for a second and a third in case those ran out again. I thought about going to more stores in search of a sponge, but the prospect drained me. It was so much simpler to let a little sand gather in the corners.

Kirstin wrote from her new address in Geneva. In the aftermath of blockaded life, it had taken her some moments to decide whether or not to board a bus.

***

A fresh project team of graduates prepared for the first visit of the Gaza Gateway's first donor delegation. The Gateway start-up would be South Korea's first programmatic investment in Gaza, and the presentation would be the first by this group of graduates. Rasha, Laila and Ibrahim had asked for volunteers to speak on behalf of the group.

'Coach them,' I cautioned. 'That's a lot of firsts in one room, with a journalist.'

In its second iteration, the Gaza Gateway social enterprise was making sense. We had learned the difference between a privileged English workplace and a truly multilingual one.[42] Bilingual team leaders (including Mama from the original group) encouraged the use of English in an Arabic-speaking milieu. Rasha had Skyped with trainers on several continents, learning to derive employability from local, lived experience. Then she and Laila and Ibrahim wrapped study around every single task of project work. Work became the raw material of every study hour. Learning-practice-learning-practice; we drew it as a helix. We were learning slowly, yet we were racing to launch independently of UNRWA. UNRWA had embarked on a different phase. Bob and Scott had held a space open for the Gateway while they could, but the cacophony of post-war imperatives was closing that space.

On a bright, balmy December afternoon, I sat at a table in the garden to hear the individual presentations. One bold woman had always stood out from the group. Her demure coats could not contain her crackling energy. I gauged the rainfalls by the depth of mud that clumped around her ankles as she hiked out of Khuza'a to find transport each morning.

She spoke about the opportunity that IT offered women. Her two male colleagues recalled graduating into the world's highest unemployment rate. They were natural speakers but, not wanting to promote themselves at the expense of their group, they were forfeiting the power of specifics.

I listened for a theme. When I heard it, I swung my finger

---

42 I have expanded on this concept in 'Language that works: creating a multilingual learning culture in social enterprise' in *English Across the Fracture Lines*, edited by Elizabeth J. Erling. (London: British Council, 2017).

around the plastic garden table, taking them in collectively. 'Khuza'a, Shuja'iyya, Toufah?'

They nodded. They came from three of the most battered neighbourhoods of the Gaza Strip. I waited for any sign that they knew why I was asking, but they were only expectant.

I made myself swallow hard and I gripped one knee with my hand beneath the table, so that I could speak with no tremor. 'I want you to tell the donors where you come from.'

My own team was getting it now. Ibrahim shook his head. 'We didn't—'

'I know,' I said brusquely, because I wanted it said positively. 'It's so important – look what you did! You applied for your jobs before the war. You got through that war, and you still have your ambitions. The donors may have heard the names of your neighbourhoods during the war. They may not associate those names with education and achievement, so you must take the time to explain it to them. Okay? You correct their impressions. That is a part of your story. You let them know that you come from neighbourhoods full of talent.'

They looked purposeful, and equal to the task.

I congratulated my team afterward. 'You did it. In the middle of all this, you created a merit-driven workplace. The enterprise is right there, in those faces that didn't know why their neighbourhoods were part of the story.'

I took Uta and Jenn aside before they went to receive the donor delegation.

'We've got a fallback plan, okay? Because no one knows how these young folks are going to handle questions, especially from the journalist. Laila's due in a few weeks, but she's already so big and beautiful that she calls herself Laila Squared. So, in the event of . . . unscripted-ness, Rasha's going to throw a glass of water on the floor, and Laila will scream. We're all going to hustle her out the door and leave the whole clean-up to you. I told them, that's how Front Office works, too.'

The individual presentations went well. Then the journalist chose a graduate at random, and asked him what he knew about South Korea's government. The fellow's eyes searched for Ibrahim while he declared himself very interested in South Korea.

When the journalist pressed for details, I latched onto Uta's sleeve and whispered, 'Oh-oh. Oh-oh-oh-oh.'

'In Arabic?' he requested of Ibrahim.

The young man beamed with relief at the arrival of the delegation's translator, and he outlined the form of South Korea's government. Flourishing his Samsung phone, he went on to describe the country's emergence from conflict to economic powerhouse.

Coach Ibrahim was grinning slyly at me from a side wall.

Chapter 25

The donors had made lavish post-war pledges. In the four months after the war, they sent to UNRWA less than one-seventh of the funds needed to shelter the Gazans who remained homeless. At the end of 2014, a scant two weeks of shelter funding remained. Not one home had been rebuilt, and winter had arrived. Tens of thousands of Gazans shivered in remnant housing.

I tried to capture the speed of Gaza's decline. Of our projects that had worked in 2011, how many would still work in the post-war conditions? Of the class that had entered university as I arrived, how many would study for their graduating exams without four walls around them?

Thirty-five years after the Western states had embargoed Cambodia's survivors, they forgot Gaza. I felt old to see these as my bookends, and disillusioned to know how little had changed.

Laila gave birth to a healthy, black-haired baby girl with a perfectly pink pout. After naming the baby for her late sister, Laila reportedly took charge of the maternity ward in a memorable temper.

Scott arrived in my doorway moments after the first pictures.

'Look, Scott, come and see what Laila did!'

He leaned over the computer and agreed that the baby was a wee replica of Laila. Then he closed my door and fidgeted with his purple necktie. Suspicious, I shifted him to the periphery of my vision while he outlined the new reporting structure of Front Office. Midway through the description, I scowled. He poured words over my rage, and backed himself out the door.

I slapped files around my desk, swearing and paging through

the junk to find the original, lacklustre job description that I had turned down. Its author was about to take Scott's place.

Scott sighed audibly as he tipped himself around the doorframe for a second time. Reluctant but stalwart, he closed himself into my office and sat down again.

'I get that you're not happy.'

I turned the job description around, and held it in front of my face to remind him. 'UN business as usual? Shovelling plankton. I have no aptitude for it.'

Scott left Gaza and a compressed, helium edge snuck into my voice.

I lived in the staff gym. The Close Protection team had bolted a stack of car tires around a heavy punching bag to harden it, and Olivier showed me how to box. Standing still, Olivier had the physique of a patched tank. He threw punches the way a sea lion slid into water and became one liquid, muscle-clad motion.

I did not throw punches that way. Bruises bloomed across my knuckles and swelling encased my fingers, until I learned how to damage the tires more than my fists. I had no need of footwork because I had no intention of punching anything that was remotely capable of punching me back. I bashed away at those car tires flat-footed, until I could hardly lift my arms.

Limp with fatigue, I was more able to drive through the elegiac streets of Gaza. As its mutual assistance mechanisms were depleted, I heard more often of abandonment, begging, migration, barter, and suicide. Pre-war Gaza was wrecked, and I wondered what the Children of Oslo would make of their new, infinitely harsher environment.

The war of 2014 was conspicuously absent from Israel's election in March 2015. Avigdor Lieberman promised that, if elected, he would propose a death penalty for Palestinians as his first act. On the afternoon of voting, Prime Minister Netanyahu galvanized his supporters by warning them that the Arabs were 'voting in droves'. He won handily.

***

I waited with avid dread for the UN Secretary-General's Board of Inquiry to report on the bombing of the shelter-schools. An earthquake struck Nepal shortly before the report was released in April 2015, shunting the report and everything else out of the headlines. I printed the summary report and brought it to the gym to batter the car tires until my nervous energy was spent. I read at home on my couch, gulping chardonnay.[43]

Weapons had been found in three UNRWA schools which had been closed for the summer. None of those schools operated as shelters. No shelter was found to contain weapons, and no one had been firing from any of the shelters that were attacked. Contrary to the disinformation that was circulating, the IDF had not been firing *back* at UNRWA schools.

The IDF had fired on seven notified, designated United Nations emergency shelters, which it knew to be packed full of displaced people. Those seven strikes had killed 44 shelter residents and wounded 227. Most of the casualties were people who had sought shelter in response to the IDF's own warnings.

From the playground in northern Beit Hanoun, to the southern school gate in Rafah, responsibility had been assigned. The IDF knew, and they fired anyway.

'You. Should. Have. Been. Safe.' I pronounced, in case any corner of my apartment had not heard it a thousand times. I told it again. I flitted through the phrases, recombining them because they still held something I needed. I hadn't said it right yet. 'We could not keep you safe. I am so sorry. We told them, and I thought it would matter if they knew. I told them, because I thought it would matter. *Them. Them.* Who are they, anyway?'

The army was accountable to law, and the report indicted them. Them – what about the rest of them? 'They' who had recoiled in horror or in credulity; how could their knowing not matter?

My head lolled back against the couch, as heavy as my arms. Then it bounced forward again, wide awake. I had been one of them, for half a century, complicit and willing not to know. I'd had to be shown.

---

43 Full text of the report https://unispal.un.org/DPA/DPR/unispal.nsf/0/554E1CC298B3BFEF85257E44005ABD18

***

While writing comments on a draft of UNRWA's new emergency response guidelines, I could not summon the name of the office to which I had sent the shelter notifications list every 0800 and 1800 hours. I hadn't forgotten it. It had been buried beneath an absurd number of newer acronyms. I rattled off the acronyms that drifted around my head like the thought bubbles of a comic book. Like pink soap bubbles, like dish-detergent-pink bubbles with dayglo patches, luminous, iridescent, incandescent, phosphorescent, opalescent, pearlescent . . .

It required superhuman discipline to heave myself away from my list of soap bubble adjectives, and climb the steep few metres to the team's office next door. I fell into their spare chair, and no one seemed to mind. We opened a new bag of their seasonal favourite, Israeli honey cookies. Ibrahim called them the taste of his childhood. I squinted at the Hebrew label, trying to picture Israeli settlers snacking on Gazan shawarma in their hilltop outpost, purely because Gazan shawarma tasted so good. I shook my head, failing to muster the image.

Rasha assured me, 'It's just a cookie. It's not political.'

'What *hasn't* changed?' I asked them over the cellophane. 'Eight months on, what feels better and what still doesn't work?'

Laila, steadily losing her baby weight, gestured at her lunch of fruit salad and spoke through a mouthful. 'Salad fruit. I know it's called fruit salad, but what comes out of my mouth when I order is "salad fruit".' She pursed her lips as though she were grappling with something particularly weighty just then. That pinched expression had become her norm.

'I want to put my car in reverse,' Ibrahim offered, holding his ribs with one arm and stroking his chin with the other hand. 'Every minute. I must be ready to get out of any street.' I waited for more. Did he know that the war had left him dissatisfied, or did he see only that others disregarded him? I had begun to intervene when their disagreements escalated to shouting.

Laila pointed her spoon at Ibrahim. 'My husband can't hear the engine revving anymore. To change gears? He used to hear it but now he says he can't.'

Rasha held up her SpongeBob SquarePants muff in silence.

With the poverty survey one month from its pressured rollout, she overworked and spoke in unpunctuated torrents once she began.

They waited for me.

'I don't know what's happened to the seasons! I keep expecting it to be summer, because I don't remember that we had a summer. And I can't finish things. I can't—' I cast about for some explanation but Laila jumped in.

'Me too, me too! I really am sorry, Marilyn, I know that it causes all kinds of complications when my work is so late but I just, just I *can't* finish.'

'Oh, Laila, is that why?'

'Yes, yes, and me,' Rasha blurted. 'It's so much harder and you know that I am really very organized but I cannot finish what I start and I get almost all of the way through but then I somehow just *can't* no matter what I do—'

Laila cut in when Rasha drew a breath. 'It just sits there, and I know that you need it, but I refuse to finish it.'

I glanced at Ibrahim, who nodded sadly. I slapped my thigh with resolve, and went to search for failures of the finishing brain. I reported back a few hours later on my discovery of the anterior midcingulate cortex. Study of war veterans' brain function showed changes in its perseverance function.

'Apathy.' I spelled it for Rasha to google, and waited while she read out the definition. 'Apathy-ville, that's where we live now.'

Randa had returned from the embroidery project office. We caught her up, and she waved one hand over her desk. Randa had begun to work in the director's conference room opposite, abandoning her desk to its piles of papers.

'It's neurological,' I continued, tapping one temple. 'It's in our brains. With our natures, we have each been blaming ourselves, and trying to fix it by pushing ourselves harder. We would be smarter to rethink some of the deadlines that we set for ourselves, don't you think?'

Laila looked amenable and Randa downright relieved, but Rasha turned to her computer screen. She found the tab where she habitually converted my management timelines into project burndown charts with coloured sprint blocks.

Rasha enumerated the implications of slowing down. 'Should I redo all of these?'

I shook my head. 'No. Rasha? You should not. You should go home early.'

'But the—'

'Someone, take her home. Everyone, go home.'

***

'Can we unfuck this? Please?' I asked Bob through clenched teeth in his kitchen.

'I did.' He smacked a package of popcorn on the microwave turntable and rat-tatted at a button. Our microwaves had been procured with Hebrew instructions. Someone had located a button that accumulated cooking time in 30-second increments, so we all microwaved like the Pavlovian pigeons that pecked at grain dispensers until they made themselves sick or broke their beaks.

Consultants had not been issued passwords to UNRWA's new software. I was a consultant, staffing up to employ thirty-eight other consultants on the Gateway's projects, and I had been rendered dependent on a Front Office executive to make every single one of my transactions. 'No, I don't think so.'

'I already fixed it.'

'*No,*' I huffed.

'*Yes,*' he insisted, peeling butter into a bowl with a tablespoon. He handed me the inflated bag of popcorn and pecked again at the microwave. 'I signed a . . . an exception, a thing with your name on it. I made an exception to give you a password.'

'Didn't change.' I tipped popcorn into a bowl.

'Change order, that's it. I signed a change order to give you a pass – fucking mother of – fuck. Too much butter?'

'Doesn't matter,' I shrugged at the pool of melted butter, but Bob thought I was dismissing his change order.

'I signed a thing, and it had your name on it. And that's what you get for being a consultant. And I will come up there and melt your phone cord into the wall. So there.'

'Oh, you heard about that.'

Bob glared, and picked up the wet popcorn. I picked up the glasses, and we went outside.

'What're you reading these days?' I asked him neutrally.

'Outside of work? I can't read anymore. Can you?'

'Sort of.' I tossed popcorn into my mouth. We ate in silence for a while. I inspected my shirt for drips of melted butter and admitted, 'Can't remember much of it.'

Bob's reply was lost in the clamour of car horns ten storeys below us. He sprang from his chair and leaned over the terrace railing.

'It's a *roundabout*! This isn't difficult – you go *around* it!' He stirred the air with his forefinger. Seating himself, he shrugged his shirt straight and combed his fingers through his hair. 'That's better. I feel much better now. You were saying?'

Drawing down the corners of my mouth, I reached across the table and filled his glass.

***

The Gateway enterprise had its start-up funds, and its management team, and its helix. I was burning out, disenfranchised and approaching the maximum duration for UNRWA consulting contracts. I gave Bob and my team long notice. Outside of Israel, I bought a cheap netbook for cash. I disconnected it from the internet before I left the store. Back in Gaza, I began to transcribe my journals.

May 2015 was a month of accounting. The World Bank reported that Israel's forces had inflicted $4.4 billion of damage and losses upon Gaza, including $400 million caused by bombing public infrastructure.[44] The International Crisis Group calculated that, of the $5.4 billion pledged publicly after the war, donors actually sent only $340 million to rebuild in that first, critical post-war year.[45]

The United States approved the sale of $1.9 billion of weapons to Israel.

UNRWA announced a budget shortfall of $101 million for the year of 2015.

---

44 http://documents.worldbank.org/curated/en/563181468182960504/Economic-monitoring-report-to-the-ad-hoc-liaison-committee

45 https://www.refworld.org/pdfid/55dd8c284.pdf

The new poverty survey and assessment system rolled out. 868,000 Gazans needed relief food.[46]

Bob resigned. He left Gaza in the week of the war's anniversary.

46 https://www.unrwa.org/sites/default/files/pas_fact_sheet_english.pdf

Chapter 26

We ate breakfasts together every Saturday in August and September. From the spacious terrace of the Al Deira Hotel, Gaza looked like one more Algarve fishing village. I always went early, straight from the gym, to recline in a wicker chair at a table for six. Until the others arrived, I sipped coffee and wrote, or I gazed out over the sea and the place where the four little boys had been killed.

'Little' mattered. If anyone else had seen four little figures on any other beach, in a disproportionately young community, they would have seen four children at play. In Gaza, an Israeli had been primed to see four skinny enemies running across the beach on July 16, 2014. Although they posed no threat to him whatsoever, he fired repeatedly at them until he killed them.

An Israeli investigation had found nothing criminal in the killing, because the soldier had not gotten out of bed that morning intending to kill children. The investigators had chosen to hunt for a phantom child-killer, rather than querying a structure which precluded the innocence of children.

That structure was part of me, too. Rather than securing my next contract in the next country, I knew that it was time for me to stop, digest what I had seen, and show others what I'd had to be shown.

On the first Saturday morning of September, a couple lay facing each other on the sand beneath the Al Deira terrace. They luxuriated in clean morning air that the sun had not yet fried. His T-shirt and shorts were already wet from swimming; she was draped from head to toe in fabric the brassy green of the Statue of Liberty.

Balanced on their elbows in the sand while the surf cooled their toes, she spooned shells into a bottle. Each time she spoke, he lifted his head responsively to listen. They inhabited an intimate beach bubble, in public.

I was rapt, and transported by a breeze to Mazar-i-Sharif. An Afghan girl had once clung to the handrail of a flatbed truck there, while the wind unspooled her hair. A dozen children swayed at the handrail, but this girl stood a bit taller, anchoring an endless river of jet-black hair.

My colleagues and I were all struck dumb in the car behind that truck: *hair*!

On the terrace of Al Deira, I was riveted the same way: *love*!

When I returned from my reverie, the couple was wading toward three children, who were playing catch in the waves with a yellow beach ball. Their father joined in their game, while their mother sidestroked in billowing, blousy rings around them.

Rasha arrived, and I pointed with my chin. We watched the parents rent a rowboat. The husband helped his wife climb over the side, because her clothing would have weighed her down. The oarsman stood in the stern like a Venetian gondolier, steering with an elongated kayak paddle as was the fad in Gaza that summer. The couple faced each other on two benches in the bow, leaning in, drawn together.

'They are sooo romantic,' Rasha breathed. 'You can see how much they love each other.'

As the boat rowed away, Rasha traced its motion with her hand. 'Bopping?'

I thought a minute and enunciated. 'Bobbing. Bobbing on the waves.'

'Like Pop?'

'Bob – yes, like Bob. Bobbing like Bob.'

Rasha pulled out her pink tablet to search 'bob'. We had interchangeably referred to Bob Turner as Bob, Bop and Pop for 28 months, but it was never too late to sort these things out.

Watching her spindly fingers scroll, I asked, 'Do you know how you changed me?'

'We changed you? No! How?'

'Fifty years,' I began. I turned to the beach and back again.

'For fifty years, I measured life by what you build. I always tried to build something that would last, in the places where I've lived and worked. Gaza showed me that it's not the right measurement, because so much can be beyond your control. Someone can withhold the building materials, you know? You showed me that life should be valued by what you give. Really, Rasha, I cannot see things the same way, after seeing what you give to each other.'

***

On my last full day, I stepped onto my terrace and spread my notebook open against the concrete to write:

> Four years ago, I agreed to come here, thinking I understood about Gaza ('pity about Gaza'), knowing that Gazans were not my enemy, knowing they were conflict-affected but having no sense of the ways in which they and their conflict would affect me. They tore apart things that I thought I knew, because, well, I had always known them . . . I knew them as surely as I knew that day is light and night is dark . . . except in the Arctic. Except when it is not.
>
> I came for the most secular reasons . . . But then Gaza threw open its arms and insisted, '*Ahlan*, you are welcome in Gaza', and what could I do? What is an activist – someone who cannot unlearn what they know.

I called for a car, and asked the UNRWA driver to drop me at the hotel where the team would meet for what turned out to be my surprise farewell lunch. I arrived an hour early, opened the glass doors of the hotel lobby and hastily spun away. Being Gaza, of course I knew one of the reception staff, and I didn't want to be seen. I dawdled at the gatepost instead, pretending to check my phone until Jenny's car pulled up. She and another friend sat in the front. I slunk into the back seat, violating the security rules that forbade UNRWA staff to ride in non-UN vehicles.

When I sat up, we were driving onto the forbidden breakwater that hugged Gaza's seaport. At last, I breathed out the stew of concrete smells and breathed in Gaza's own sea air. I had always counted fishing boat lights as a proxy for good and bad times. At last, I saw how the banks of lights had been fitted beneath the boats' awnings. Along the breakwater, UNICEF had painted some of its heavy blocks in carnival colours. I saw that rebar still sprouted crazily through the jumble of reclaimed rubble.

We parked where the road ended, and scrambled up the rubble. Revolving slowly, I could see what the strollers saw when they turned back to the city for their late evening dinners. Vertical walls leapt straight up from the flat Mediterranean horizon.

Three Hamas soldiers appeared over the seawall. They said 'peace be upon you' and walked on.

Once they had blurred into the heat-wobbled air, we had Ultima Thule to ourselves. I flung my arms wide to stake out an epitaph – *I was here* – and I heard myself begin to place Gaza in the past tense.

***

I took my usual 6.30 am car to the office, dropped off my apartment keys for Jenn to move in, and propped my feet on my desk. I looked at my book, put it down and stroked the gold tag they had engraved for me with the distance from Gaza to New Zealand: 16,339 kilometres. I drummed my fingers on my upturned book.

I had waited four years to tell them, and when they filed in an hour later, I still had no idea how I would say it.

The war had burrowed into each of us. It sat on Ibrahim's shoulder and whispered resentments into his ear. It lingered in Rasha's fingertips. They now worked beneath the vivid, whirling dancers of Sonia Delaunay's *Le Bal Bullier*. I had brought the abstract poster back from Paris in 2012, when I craved colour. Since the bombing of 2014, I could tolerate only the palest palette of whites and washed-clean seafoam greens. The poster's colours stung my eyes, and I'd had to take it down.

I studied their faces in case they refused to look at me later, and then I began. 'You know that I didn't apply to come and work here. Remember? I was excited to be here, but I want you to remember that I did not seek Gaza out. I didn't come here to play politics. Israel and Palestine matter to me because I am a Jew. But that's not why—'

At their flabbergasted faces, my words failed and I clutched the arms of my chair. I don't know how long we stared at each other.

Randa threw her head back and stamped her feet and roared

in exasperation, 'Aargh! Is that . . . it doesn't *matter*! Don't you know that we love you? It doesn't change anything – how could you not know that?'

They spoke over each other as I wept in my office chair. They counted their Jewish Facebook friends, their university friends, all the ways they had shown that Jews were not their enemies. By the time the outburst subsided, we were all crying freely.

'Wait,' I said at length, sniffling and composing myself one more time. 'Wait. I couldn't tell you that because there's another . . . There's this other thing. Oh, it was so hard not to tell you! I wanted you to find out. All the conversations we didn't have.'

I told them about my sister's offices. 'Do you understand? I don't care who knows that I'm a Jew. I would never have denied it if anyone asked, and I would have told you once we knew each other. It's not that I don't trust you. But my sister; I was afraid that someone would search Garson-Zionism. They would have seen my sister, and they might have drawn the wrong conclusions about me. That's also why I refused your invitations so often. What if I got into trouble? What if Hamas decided that you and your children were spending your weekends with a Zionist spy?'

Rasha clapped her hands over her hijab. 'Of course! And we were so angry at you! How many times – oh, we felt so disappointed.'

'I know. I hurt you, and I'm sorry. Now that you understand, please accept my apology. You did not have the information to agree to the risk of me, so I made excuses because I thought it might keep you and your children safe.'

'No,' Laila declared. Angry pink patches flared on her cheeks. 'It would have been fine!'

Randa flicked her eyes at her friend for only a moment. 'No, it wouldn't – that's exactly what people would think. And you know what they do to people who work for the other side. She's right. This is the way it had to be.'

I nodded. 'I think that many Jews will believe I worked for the other side, too.'

Laila sidestepped. 'Okay, okay, maybe you're right. Maybe it had to be like that but we don't care. We could keep the secret now. That's no reason to go!'

'That's not why I'm leaving. But I am going to tell this story, as a Jew who came to Gaza and saw it with my own eyes. I'm going to add some adjectives to the way that people understand this place, and once I speak, you know they won't let me come back.'

Ibrahim said angrily, 'You tell the story with my real name. I am not ashamed to work with a Jew, and I'm not afraid of anyone here.'

Rasha had lit up with a beatific smile. 'You came here, knowing what your own people would think. And still you stayed with us in the war.'

'Oh, Rasha, that was the easiest choice. That was my privilege. We're in a tug of war. A million hands are pulling toward war, and a thousand are pulling toward justice. I can be the thousand-and-first.'

Randa asked, 'What do they think about Gaza, the Jews you know?'

'Many of them think that what happened here is sad, but they believe the people who tell them that it was necessary.'

Laila made a strangled sound, but Randa's eyes flashed. 'What do they think we are?' she demanded.

I knew I had heard the question before, but now I was sure of my answer. 'The enemy. That's all they see. Gaza needs its better stories told. I've been telling you: if people like you spoke, this would change.'

Laila asked, 'Do you think you can make a difference?'

I measured a tiny space between my thumb and forefinger.

She began to cry again. 'Then it's not worth you leaving.'

Walking to the parking lot, hugging them and climbing into the car, I agreed with her.

I emerged from Erez as if I were tumbling off a rush hour train. On the train, you conform to the crowd. You sway en masse and blend your voices into one buzz. Others' speed on the platform determines yours. At the exit, the singular crowd dissipates into strangers, who scatter for their cars.

I liked to pause at the exit. The view from Erez was forbidding. Walls to the left, with big dog kennels. On the right, a field ran all the way to the horizon. Nothing in Gaza ran all the way to the horizon. Even the sea flowed only as far as the gunboats.

As the door of the Erez terminal swung shut behind me, I expected to hear the sound of a switch that would turn one of them off, Israel or Gaza. It had always been hard to believe that they existed at the same time, in so very nearly the same space.

But they did. Instead of a switch, I heard a latch click. The gates of Gaza locked me out.

Chapter 27

Jerusalem

A few hours later, I inadvertently slammed the taxi door in front of my Jerusalem hotel. I'd grown accustomed to the weighted doors of armoured cars.

'Sorry,' I said to the taxi driver. 'Eid Mubarak.'

For four years, each time I left Israel through the Erez wormhole, I entered someone else's country: Palestine. Israel was the occupying power there, and I opposed it. I held Israel itself at a distance, but I could hold it only as far away as my own hand. I was ready to reckon with Israel *qua* Israel. I arrived on the eve of the Jewish High Holidays, which happened to coincide with the Muslim holiday of Eid Al Adha. I felt lucky to find a room on the line between the Palestinian neighbourhood of Abu Tor and the Jewish German Colony, a few blocks from the Old City of Jerusalem. Most hotels were overbooked and overpriced around the holidays.

The taxi pulled away, and I reached down for my bag. A *Mad Max* convoy hurtled toward me. The original surfaces of each vehicle were lost beneath imposing grilles. New, mismatched plates had been welded over old. I jumped back from the curb without my bag, dodging the gravel that spat out from armoured wheel wells. The vehicles raced into the Palestinian neighbourhood behind me. Watching them go, I understood why this particular hotel had last-minute rooms.

I dreamed liquid Gaza in the morning. A hotel room solidified around me, and I checked the time that remained before the 6.45 am UNRWA car left for Erez. The time came and went while

I imagined the second-guessing that would soon be taking place in the office next to mine. Around 7.00, I opened my eyes in Jerusalem.

I loved to walk in Jerusalem, whose fractal neighbourhoods would never be unwound. I went straight to the Old City. Sirens wailed without, and surly police lined the cobblestone alleys within. Dozens of police, exoskeletal in black leather and shields. Violent protest was radiating outward from the Temple Mount. The air crackled as I made my way out, walking faster as the shopfronts clanged shut around me. It was no better the next day.

Or the next. I backed away from the Old City for a third time. I walked instead through the Sultan's Pool, a leafy defile cut beneath the Old City walls. Footsteps ran at me, and I whirled around with my heart pounding. A stocky Palestinian man charged straight at me. He ran like the wind, legs pumping, head thrown back to suck the air. He passed me in seconds, not exercising but fleeing for his life. I turned to find the object of his fear. Six shaven-headed men powered after him like a single machine with tattooed pistons. They blew past me without a glance.

I slapped my pockets until I remembered that I had turned in my UNRWA SIM card. I ran after them, feeling all the obsolescence of my 54 years. They sprinted, I scampered until I saw that they had left the park and reached the busy road into Abu Tor. I presumed that six Israeli skinheads would go no further.

My niece showed me a hint of tender, country-mouse pity when I asked her to check the news. 'Oh Auntie Mar, those things aren't news anymore.'

***

I read newspapers in an outdoor café, in Israeli West Jerusalem. Netanyahu was requesting authorization for city police snipers to fire at the protestors who threw stones. The military already did so. Rifles for stones. Those had been the proportions of the First Intifada, a generation ago.

Israel's Public Security Minister was urging Palestinian Jerusalemites to 'live together, calm things down – nothing has changed in the status quo'.

Indeed, I thought.

I put my tablet away to listen to the city around me. I turned to smile at an older couple, seated nearby. I wanted to see the woman's face, because she spoke with an inflection that reminded me of one of my more unusual aunts. They smiled back. Buskers were singing a Hebrew folk song on the far side of the square. I recalled the chorus from summer camp. Half a dozen teenagers were dancing, revelling in their summer rite of being openly Jewish in Israel. I remembered that, too.

In Gaza, I listened and I tried to learn. In Israel, I remembered. They knew me and I recognized them. Even as I opposed its politics, I felt the relief, the anonymity of being Israel's normal – a visiting Jew who knew the tune. For a moment, I wanted to print my disclosure on a T-shirt: *I do not agree with you*. I knew, though, that even wearing my shirt, I would still be able to hail a taxi or walk past a group of youths without danger, or enter a restaurant without suspicion. I would still enjoy the benefits of membership. I could neither discern nor disavow the outlines of majoritarian power by walking around within it. It still contained me.

I had one last breakfast with my niece, outside the city. She was about to marry an Israeli and fully become one. As she drove me back, she reminded me, 'You used to say that you'd spend a season here, after Gaza, working on your Hebrew.'

'I did. I wanted to. I want to study and explore being a Jew after all the secrecy. Being hidden was so much harder than I expected. But this, I can't pick and choose the parts I enjoy and the parts I reject. It doesn't work. I guess I'll have to go study somewhere else. In the end, Israel is a country with ethnically determined rights and life prospects, and I can't be at ease here.'

'For now. Not "in the end", but for now.'

From the side, my niece had the obstinate Garson jaw. 'Good luck with that,' I bade her.

***

On the day I left Israel, the next wave of violent resistance lapped onto its shore. Two Palestinians – one of them a 19-year-old woman – stabbed Israelis. Israeli police shot and killed the Palestinians.

Young Gazan men and women accompanied the Jerusalem

violence by protesting at the walls of Gaza. They went to confront the real source of unaccountable power, protesting frontally at the Erez Border Crossing itself. In order to reach it, they walked past the checkpoint of Hamas's bankrupt authority. They passed the scorching sand dunes where Islamic Jihad trained. They carried on past the checkpoint where the Palestinian Authority co-ordinated permits with the Israeli government. The Children of Oslo dismissed their elders, and went to set their own flesh against concrete, and demand their lives.

From emplacements behind the soaring concrete walls, Israeli soldiers shot seventeen protestors dead in the first month.

Emmanuel Levinas wrote, at the moment when all is lost, everything is possible.

Chapter 28

New Zealand

I set off from Canada in 1986, with a backpack and a curious disregard for consequences. I nudged closer to the world's tripwires, without expecting anything to blow up. Then I went to Cambodia, where one man's face showed me the universe of our unmet obligations.

As Afghanistan's war became more debased, there were days when the killers drove truck bombs into gatherings of undefended civilians.[47] Windows shattered into multitudes of new glasses, while a crowd of identities puddled together in the street. The explosions deafened me to everything but my own breathing, rhythmic as waves on a white sand beach; the sound of all the time in the world. The *wheep-wheep-tinkle* of swept-up glass was always the first sound to reach me. Then my Afghan friend would go out to learn the names of the street cleaners who had been killed. That was our corner of it, our coping with it. Street cleaners always died, and we ransomed a little specificity back with gestures to their families.

Then I went to Gaza, with its contact-cement social capital. Lock two million other people behind a wall, deprive and demonize and bombard them. See if they respond with half a dozen universities, 96 per cent literacy and a flourishing start-up scene. See if they cheer the power cuts, making and requiring resistance in its many forms.

In Gaza's miniature world, I rediscovered my Jewish sources,

47 I believe that Hamas must be held accountable for its choice to use suicidal violence against Israeli civilians. The suicide bombing of soft targets will always, only, ever be an inexcusable crime in my eyes.

while I experienced Israel through its project of military force. Eventually, I saw my corner of that incongruity. I could tell what I saw. Human beings live in great danger behind a blockade wall. Half of them are children and most of them are civilians. They are being confined and brutalized as if they were something less than fully human.

I could add some adjectives to our blinkered picture of Gaza. I could help restore it to our moral universe – from which it has become such a shameful exception.

In late 2015, I came home to New Zealand and settled in Wellington. After working with such intensely bonded communities, New Zealand's new structures of work, wealth and community were hard to recognize. I spoke and wrote about Gaza in stages, as my former team members there agreed. Each time we Skyped, they told me how conditions were deteriorating, and how the hardship and the stresses were mounting.

I joined a synagogue. When I left Gaza, I had resolved to learn a language and a music. I found both when I joined the choir and studied the Torah for my Bat Mitzvah. My synagogue made me welcome, and each morning of social prayer elevated me.

For a time, I sifted the Zionist content out of the prayers and social calendar. Then Israel openly allied itself with the ultra-nationalist right and embraced Donald Trump. Mainstream, Zionist Jewish institutions acquiesced. The Israel exception – that cognitive dissonance by which otherwise-principled people enable actions that they would oppose anywhere else – stretched wider and wider. The institution was moving rapidly away and I could not go with it.

My mother died, a few weeks short of her ninety-seventh birthday. Six weeks later, the dearest friend in my new life also died. I fell flat.

My Hokianga house needed twenty years of maintenance. Lonely, burnt out and spiritually starved, I needed repair no less than my house. I came home to work on both of us.

I declared 2018 to be my Year of Primary Sources. Halfway through a Biblical Hebrew primer, I began to sound out the syllables of the books of the prophets. At last, I had dug down to the raw, spiritual content of the Judaism that stands with the oppressed. After the prophets, I began at the beginning, with Genesis. I lived in my dictionary.

Hokianga being what it is, I also discovered a neighbour with a doctorate in scriptural languages. We read Torah together one afternoon per week. I studied at home in the blackness before each blue dawn. I brought all my rage at the waste I have seen, my impatience at the injustice, my exasperation at the indifference, my old search for some grounded source of dignity and decency in this world, and my wonder at the elemental mysteries I have been shown.

***

For eighteen months I studied and wrote, re-cladded and re-roofed, and painted my house in whites and the palest, washed-new sea-foam greens. I began again. While I wrote, some of the Gazans who are named in this book joined the brain drain of professionals leaving the Gaza Strip. It was difficult for each of them to choose their children's safety over their own sense of home, belonging and responsibility to Gaza.

The GGateway evolved and outgrew its first vision. It is now being handed on to its second generation of Gazan management. The new management team includes Mama from the original project group, and the fellow who invited me to spend war evenings with his family. The handover will allow Rasha and Laila to move to New Zealand. We have imagined standing up together, telling our story and working for justice.

On March 30, 2018, Gazans began to protest weekly in the Great March of Return. Although they are standing on their own land, Israeli snipers shoot, kill and maim protestors each Friday.[48] Gaza's blockaded medical system cannot keep up with the thousands of protestors who need surgery on complex gunshot

48 The UN Commission of Inquiry into the protest found no justification for shooting protestors with live ammunition. https://www.ohchr.org/EN/HRBodies/HRC/CoIOPT/Pages/Report2018OPT.aspx

wounds and 'pulverized' bones.[49]

I feel desperate when I hear news of them. My voice catches and the hairs rise along my arms. My body remembers the sensations of being so exposed to Israel's staggering violence.

As of April 30, 2019, Israeli forces had killed 202 Gazan Palestinians and wounded 31,249 in the protests.[50] One Israeli had died and six were wounded.

In those fields, Gazan Palestinians have refused to accept their intolerable life prospects. They were not born wanting to die. Their willingness is the measure of their plight. They are standing up for justice.

I stand with them.

Marilyn Garson,
Hokianga, New Zealand,
May 2019

49 Read Medecins Sans Frontiers' reporting on the pattern of these gunshot wounds here https://www.doctorswithoutborders.org/what-we-do/news-stories/news/gaza-thousands-people-shot-during-protests-require-urgent-treatment Or https://www.middleeastmonitor.com/20190125-msf-doctors-struggle-with-bones-pulverised-by-israel-bullets-in-gaza/

50 https://reliefweb.int/report/occupied-palestinian-territory/humanitarian-snapshot-casualties-context-demonstrations-and-10

Bibliography

Ongoing sources of information:

- https://gisha.org and https://www.btselem.org – Gisha and B'Tselem, two dedicated Israeli organizations
- https://al-shabaka.org/en/ – Al Shabaka, The Palestinian Policy Network
- http://jps.ucpress.edu/ – *Journal of Palestine Studies*
- https://www.ohchr.org/EN/Countries/MENARegion/Pages/PSSpecialProceduresReports.aspx – six-monthly reports of the UN Special Rapporteur on the Situation of Human Rights in the Palestinian Territory Occupied since 1967, S. Michael Lynk
- https://www.ochaopt.org/content/coordination-structure – Gaza aid agency clusters, located on the OCHA Coordination page
- https://www.crisisgroup.org/ – International Crisis Group

To understand the assault on Gaza in July and August 2014:

- Read IDF soldiers' own testimony. *This Is How We Fought in Gaza – Soldiers' Testimonies and Photographs from Operation 'Protective Edge' (2014)* – https://www.breakingthesilence.org.il/pdf/ProtectiveEdge.pdf
- *Under Fire: Israel's Artillery Policies Scrutinised.* London: Action on Armed Violence, December 2014 – https://aoav.org.uk/wp-content/uploads/2015/03/AOAV-Under-Fire-Israels-artillery-policies-scrutinised.pdf
- Regarding the seven attacks upon UN shelters, read the Board of Inquiry's report – https://unispal.un.org/unispal.nsf/22f431edb91c6f548525678a0051be1d/554e1cc298b3bfef85257e44005abd18?OpenDocument

- Finkelstein, Norman G. *Gaza: An Inquest into Its Martyrdom*. Oakland: University of California Press, 2018.

What's happening in Gaza?

- https://wearenotnumbers.org/
- https://www.buildpalestine.com/organizations/gaza-poets-society
- http://www.eltiqa.com/
- https://ggateway.tech/

Further Reading

Baconi, Tareq. *Hamas Contained: The Rise and Pacification of Palestinian Resistance*. Stanford: Stanford University Press, 2018.

Chamayou, Grégoire. *A Theory of the Drone*. Translated by Janet Lloyd. Paris: The New Press, 2015.

Cohn, Marjorie, ed. *Drones and Targeted Killing: Legal, Moral, and Geopolitical Issues*. Northampton: Olive Branch Press, 2015.

Eisen, Robert. *The Peace and Violence of Judaism: From the Bible to Modern Zionism*. New York: Oxford University Press, 2011.

Ellis, Marc H. *Judaism does not Equal Israel: The Rebirth of the Jewish Prophetic*. New York: The New Press, 2009.

Erakat, Noura. *Justice for Some: Law and the Question of Palestine*. Stanford: Stanford University Press, 2019.

Falk, Richard. *Palestine's Horizons: Toward a Just Peace*. London: Pluto Press, 2017.

Gross, Aeyal. *The Writing on the Wall: Rethinking the International Law of Occupation*. Cambridge: Cambridge University Press, 2017.

Haddad, Toufic. *Palestine Ltd.: Neoliberalism and Nationalism in the Occupied Territory*. London: IB Tauris, 2016.

Halper, Jeff. *War Against the People: Israel, the Palestinians and Global Pacification*. London: Pluto Press, 2015.

Hever, Shir. *The Political Economy of Israel's Occupation: Repression Beyond Exploitation*. London: Pluto Press, 2010.

Khalidi, Rashid. *Palestinian Identity: The Construction of Modern National Consciousness*. New York: Columbia University Press, 1997.

O'Malley, Padraig. *The Two-State Delusion: Israel and Palestine – A Tale of Two Narratives*. New York: Penguin Books, 2015.

Polk, William R. *Crusade and Jihad: The Thousand-Year War Between the Muslim World and the Global North*. Newhaven: Yale University Press, 2018.

Rabkin, Yakov M. *What is Modern Israel?* Translated by Fred A. Reed. London: Pluto Press, 2016.

Rogan, Eugene. *The Arabs: A History*. New York: Basic Books, 2009.

Ross, Andrew. *Stone Men: The Palestinians Who Built Israel*. London: Verso, 2019.

Roy, Sara. *The Gaza Strip: The Political Economy of De-Development*, expanded third edition. Washington, DC: Institute for Palestine Studies, 2016.

Roy, Sara. *Hamas and Civil Society in Gaza: Engaging the Islamist Social Sector*. Princeton: Princeton University Press, 2011.

Sfard, Michael. *The Wall And The Gate: Israel, Palestine and the Legal Battle for Human Rights*. Translated by Maya Johnston. New York: Metropolitan Books, 2018.

Stern-Weiner, Jamie, ed. *Moment of Truth: Tackling Israel-Palestine's Toughest Questions*. London: OR Books, 2018.

Thrall, Nathan. *The Only Language They Understand: Forcing Compromise in Israel and Palestine*. New York: Metropolitan Books, 2017.

Turner, Mandy and Shweiki, Omar, eds. *Decolonizing Palestinian Political Economy: De-Development and Beyond*. Hampshire: Palgrave Macmillan, 2014.

Weizman, Eyal. *Hollow Land: Israel's Architecture of Occupation*. New York: Verso, 2007.

Zurayk, Rami and Gough, Anne. *Control Food, Control People: The Struggle for Food Security in Gaza*. Washington, DC: Institute for Palestine Studies, 2013.